From Fidelity to History

Transatlantic Perspectives

Series Editors: Christoph Irmscher, Indiana University Bloomington, and Christof Mauch, Ludwig-Maximilians-Universität, München

While standard historical accounts are still structured around nation states, *Transatlantic Perspectives* provides a framework for the discussion of topics and issues such as knowledge transfer, migration, and mutual influence in politics, society, education, film, and literature. Committed to the presentation of European views on America as well as American views on Europe, *Transatlantic Perspectives* offers room for the publication of both primary texts and critical analyses. While the series puts the Atlantic World at center stage, it also aims to take global developments into account.

From Fidelity to History

*Film Adaptations as Cultural Events
in the Twentieth Century*

Anne-Marie Scholz

berghahn
NEW YORK · OXFORD
www.berghahnbooks.com

Published in 2013 by
Berghahn Books
www.berghahnbooks.com

© 2013, 2016 Anne-Marie Scholz
First paperback edition published in 2016

Library of Congress Cataloging-in-Publication Data

Scholz, Anne-Marie.
From fidelity to history : film adaptations as cultural events in the twentieth century /
  Anne-Marie Scholz.
     p. cm. — (Transatlantic perspectives ; 11)
  Includes bibliographical references and index.
  ISBN 978-0-85745-731-8 (hardback) ISBN 978-1-78533-034-6 (paperback)
  ISBN 978-0-85745-732-5 (ebook)
(ebook)
  1. Film adaptations—History and criticism. 2. Motion pictures and literature.
3. Motion pictures and history. I. Title.
  PN1997.85.S37 2012
  791.43'6—dc23

                                                            2012012574

British Library Cataloguing in Publication Data

A catalogue record for this book is available from the British Library.

ISBN 978-0-85745-731-8 (hardback)
ISBN 978-1-78533-034-6 (paperback)
ISBN 978-0-85745-732-5 (ebook)

Contents

Illustrations

Acknowledgments

I grew up a child of German immigrants living in Southern California. We visited my German relatives frequently, and I pretty much took my transnational life for granted. That changed when, after completing my PhD in U.S. history from the University of California, Irvine, I moved to Germany to teach American Studies at the University of Tübingen. Teaching American Studies in Germany made me very aware of what it meant to move between two very different cultures with two very different histories. While revising my dissertation, which considered the British author Jane Austen's reception on the other side of the Atlantic, I became fascinated by the process of translating literature into film, particularly because of the boom in Jane Austen movies. During these years, I also became intrigued by the ways that Anglo-American culture in postwar popular films, such as *The Third Man,* were understood and received by German audiences. At first, these interests appeared to be distinct, for one dealt with the movement from literature to film and the other with the reception from one nation to another. After all, what did Jane Austen adaptations and *The Third Man* have in common? "Apples and oranges," I was told by many. However, as I continued to explore questions of film adaptation over time and transnational reception across space, I realized that they were indeed related and that my interdisciplinary background in American Studies suggested the importance of connecting them.

The Department of American Studies at California State University, Fullerton and the History and Theory Program in the Department of History at the University of California, Irvine (UCI) gave me the scholarly foundations to be able to cross boundaries in more ways than one, as well as friendships and scholarly support that continue into the present. In particular, I would like to thank Leila Zenderland, professor of American Studies at Cal State Fullerton. Leila was one of my undergraduate teachers, and when she came to teach at the University of Bremen on a Fulbright, we became friends. Since then, her counsel, intellectual vitality, and unwavering faith in my work have influenced my research profoundly. Robert Moeller, professor of German History at UCI and also a former teacher of mine, graciously offered scholarly support for my "shift of focus" to postwar Germany and shared his own work on questions of popular film and postwar German nationalism with me at a crucial time.

The opportunity to teach American literary and cultural studies and to develop my research interests in unorthodox directions was encouraged and supported by Professor Bernd Engler during my years in the Program in American Studies at the University of Tübingen. I am grateful to him and to my former colleagues in Tübingen for making the transition from Southern California to Southern Germany so seamless and for making me feel so welcome in my new home.

In 2000, I moved to Northern Germany and to the University of Bremen to develop a longer work (a *Habilitationsschrift*) out of studies begun in Tübingen. I am grateful to Sabine Broeck, professor of American Studies and the chair of my Habilitation committee, for the opportunity to teach American Studies in Bremen and for her willingness to take my project on. I also wish to thank Professors Dirk Hoerder, Norbert Schaffeld, and Logie Barrow, and the late Christiane Harzig and Monica Unzeitig for good advice and for helping me to see the project through to completion. I am also especially thankful to Dr. Guowen Yang and Angela Schmidt-Küppers for their friendship, resolve, and expert encouragement.

During my years in Bremen, I had the opportunity to attend the Salzburg Seminar entitled "'Here, There, and Everywhere': The Foreign Politics of U.S. Popular Culture," co-chaired by Reinhold Wagnleitner, and to work with Lary May, professor of History and American Studies at the University of Minnesota. Lary offered generous scholarly support for my research as well as an intellectually rich approach to film history that has influenced this work.

During the years I worked on this book, I was fortunate to hold adjunct professorships in the American Studies Programs at the Universities of Hamburg and Bonn. I thank Professor Susanne Rohr for the chance to teach in Hamburg. I am also grateful to Professor Sabine Sielke at the University of Bonn. The opportunity to take over the chair of the North American Studies Program while she was on research leave and to teach a lecture course devoted to "Adaptation as Reception: Interdisciplinary Approaches to the Relationship between Literature and Hollywood Film" proved very helpful in my work.

The research for this study would not have been possible without the outstanding archival collections of the Deutsches Filminstitut, Frankfurt and the Deutsche Kinemathek and Film Museum in Berlin. Over the last decade, both institutions provided me with wonderful resources, quiet space, open access, and consistent support at every stage of this project. I am also very grateful to the anonymous peer reviewers for the excellent revision suggestions that helped turn this study into a book, and to the production, editing, and graphic design team at Berghahn, which included Ann DeVita, Melissa Spinelli, Elizabeth Berg, Adam Capitanio, Ben Parker, Lauren Weiss, as well as others. I appreciated their insights, craftsmanship, and, in particular, the sense of being actively integrated into the production process at all stages. To the best of my knowledge, I have located the copyright holders for the images in this book. For assistance in acquiring licenses for these images the following people were especially helpful: Massimo Moretti at Studiocanal in the United Kingdom, Howard Mandelbaum at Photofest in New York, and Margarita Diaz at Sony Pictures.

My friends Tanja Zimmer, Ingeborg Mehser, Diana Lim-Kemper, Dr. Jutta Person, and Carol Renner—citizens of the world one and all—have shared their strength, creativity, and expertise with me here in Germany over the last decade. The insights and emotional support supplied by my friends in the "Phoenix" group in Bremen have also proven invaluable. Dr. Belinda Peters, Tom Peters, and David Zalusky—dear friends across the Atlantic—provided affection and counsel and kept me in touch with my love for Jane Austen, long after it had gone into hibernation.

Finally, I would like to thank my parents, Christa and Heinz Scholz, for laying the foundations of my sometimes restless, but always challenging, transnational life.

Different versions of parts of this work have appeared in the following journals: *Amerikastudien/American Studies, The European Journal of American Studies, Film and History, German History,* and *The Journal of South Texas English Studies.* Translations of German texts are my own, as are any remaining errors of form or content.

Introduction

Adaptation as Reception

How Film Historians Can Contribute to the Literature to Film Debates

A certain popular self-consciousness and cynicism has developed about the many adaptations of both "classic" and bestselling novels that have been released on film and television over the last few decades. "So why another *Jane Eyre*," critic Charles McGrath complained in *The New York Times*, in response to the most recent adaptation of the Charlotte Brontë novel by the Japanese-American director Cary Fukunaga, "with so many perfectly serviceable ones already available on DVD and download?" Of course, the list could be extended: why another version of *Pride and Prejudice*? Of *Sense and Sensibility*? Why another *Harry Potter*? Indeed, why focus on a literary pretext at all when making a film? The various answers to the question—a desire for market share or even less compelling, the notion that "movies get remade all the time"—are less interesting than the question itself, as it calls attention to the importance of the cultural phenomenon of adaptation in the history of film and television. Since the invention of moving pictures, literary works have "proved to be an inexhaustible and almost foolproof resource" for filmmakers worldwide.[1] Novels such as Brontë's *Jane Eyre* have been adapted nearly thirty times since 1910.[2] Jane Austen's works experienced a resurgence of adaptation in the 1990s that has yet to be exhausted. Over the years, international filmmakers ranging from Orson Welles, David O. Selznick, and Alexander Korda to Ang Lee, Emma Thompson, and Jane Campion have relied on specific literary works by authors such as Austen, Henry James, Graham Greene, and Franz Kafka to produce adaptations for audiences and readers the world over. However, the question of the historical significance of adaptation—the ways filmmakers have relied on literary works and what the relationship between a specific work of literature and its adaptation has meant to filmmakers, audiences, authors, and readers in different times and in different national contexts—has suffered from scholarly neglect by film historians who have left this important area of inquiry to other disciplines.

Until relatively recently, the scholarly study of film adaptation was the exclusive province of literature departments and was characterized primarily by a series of case studies of adaptation that tended to reproduce conventional distinctions between high and popular culture and ignored the ideological aspects of the relationship between cinema and storytelling. In their exclusive focus upon questions of "fidelity to the original work," that is, that a filmic adaptation should attempt to reproduce the literary original as faithfully as possible, adaptation scholars often did not recognize the ways that "the basic interest of the field of film and literature in how stories travel from medium to medium might have allowed the field to anticipate contemporary theory's linked concerns with narrative, intertextuality, and ideology." Instead, they preferred to adhere to New Critical assumptions in their isolated adaptation studies in an effort "to shore up literature's crumbling walls."[3] Since the study of film adaptation did begin in literature departments rather than in the fields of film or media studies—which developed much later—the focus upon "fidelity" to an "original" reflected the prioritizing of the "high cultural" literary text over the "popular" film text. Though there have been adaptation studies that focused upon other aspects of the relationship between literature and film, the fidelity model continues to be the one most closely associated with this area of study.[4]

Approaches that have emerged since the "fidelity" model and that have sought to displace it shift quickly from the specifics of the adaptation of a certain work to the general frame of "intermediality" and "intertextual dialogism"—preferring to emphasize the multiple facets of adaptation theory without committing to any particular practice of "adaptation studies": "Adaptation theory by now has available a well-stocked archive of tropes and concepts to account for the mutation of forms across media: adaptation as reading, rewriting, critique, translation, transmutation, metamorphosis, recreation, transvocalization, signifier, performance, dialogization, cannibalization, reinvisioning, incarnation, or reaccentuation. Each term, however problematic as a definitive account of adaptation, sheds light on a different facet of adaptation."[5] While this model offers many options, it seems to "protest too much" against the traditional fidelity model by opposing it with a sheer impenetrable wall of alternative concepts. Other recent scholarship suggests that the intransigence of the fidelity model can only be undermined on the level of a metadiscourse that emphasizes the long entrenched opposition in Western culture between "word and image."[6]

Both the fidelity model and the model of "intertextual dialogism" ultimately privilege the "textual" or "literary" aspects of the literature/film relationship, either by prioritizing the former or by eliminating all notions of historical materialism in favor of a "free play of signification." Today's "texts," as opposed to yesterday's "literary works of art," circulate "freely" and are no longer beholden to historically defined oppositions, such as that between high and popular culture. The dialogue between and among them now suggests "the infinite and open-ended possibilities generated by all the discursive practices of a culture—the entire matrix of communicative utterances within which the artistic text is situated, which reach the text not only through recognizable influences, but also through a subtle process of dissemination."[7]

Film adaptation certainly qualifies as an example of "intertextual dialogism"; however, the idea of "infinite and open-ended possibilities" is misleading. Rather, concrete material interests, political and ideological differences, and power relations based upon such variables as gender, nationality, and class all mould the ways texts are transformed into other media and received by audiences in very concrete, materialistic ways. It is one of my goals to actively demonstrate the ways adaptation operates in cultural force fields that are tangible, confrontational, and that carry with them concrete material effects. Intertextual dynamics are material dynamics and are therefore subject to the controls and limits that cultures everywhere impose upon the texts that circulate within them.

For these reasons, I will analyze the significance of film adaptations as social and cultural events in history.[8] To do this, I will rely upon the methodology of reception study as proposed by Barbara Klinger and Janet Staiger in order to shed light upon the relationship between "narrative, intertextuality, and ideology."[9] Because I define film adaptation as a form of reception throughout the work—on the three-tiered level of, first, the relation between the literary work and the film director and production teams; second, between literary work, film, and historically specific audience reception; and, third, between the films and my own readings in what I will refer to as a "post–Cold War" and "post-feminist" context—I will pay close attention to the relationship between specific films and the ways they were received at particular times and in particular places. I wish to focus closely upon individual films in order to highlight how their relationship to their precursor texts, as well as to their transnational and sociocultural contexts, illuminates changing social and cultural circumstances and offers inroads into reading these films in a novel way.[10] In short, I wish to enlist the classic "case studies" approach to different ends: to demonstrate the ways in which film adaptation can function as a kind of cultural strategy for grappling with different types of social and cultural change.[11]

Since 2006, scholars interested in developing the field of adaptation study as an autonomous disciplinary endeavor have called increasing attention to the significance of material concerns in adaptation.[12] However, with the exception of Guerric DeBona's fine study *Film Adaptation in the Hollywood Studio Era*, which explores issues of the "cultural politics" of film adaptation by way of historical case studies of classic Hollywood studio films such as MGM's *David Copperfield* and John Ford's *The Long Voyage Home*, this newer work ends by remarginalizing history as a disciplinary center of adaptation studies, in that, it seeks to eliminate the framework of comparing a specific literary work with a specific adaptation of that work. Many seem to agree that this framework has been the major weakness—an Achilles' heel—of adaptation study, and the key challenge of the "new adaptation studies" will be to "wrestle with the undead spirits of "fidelity," first of which is "the defining context of literature."[13] Instead, "industrial" factors, that is, primarily economic factors, should be the key focus, concentrating upon structural developments in the publishing and film industries since 1980.[14]

Dispensing with the case study as a central component of adaptation study is premature for three reasons: first, it ignores the fundamentally chronological relationship between literature and film—one that offers inroads to historical analysis between two different media without implying the hierarchical relation between them of the fidelity model.[15] Second, the specific case of literature to film transformations can be effectively enlisted in the transnational reception study of adaptation, comparing the ways both film production teams and audiences around the world conceptualized the adaptations they saw in relationship to the literary works they read. As filmmakers of the past ranging from David O. Selznick to Orson Welles, as well as filmmakers and publishers of the present, know all too well, the connections between specific works of literature and specific films have market value and cultural value. All the more reason to continue to analyze this connection historically. Third, case studies of specific adaptations can continue to shed light on the relationship between auteurism and culture. Like their counterparts in the 1950s, present-day auteurs such as Emma Thompson, Jane Campion, and Agnieszka Holland continue to be interested in the ways adapting literature to film can address important contemporary cultural questions. Particularly in light of the increased number of female art directors in the contemporary period, it is important to pay attention to their specific works, rather than subsume them under general categories such as "heritage cinema" or "the adaptation industry."[16]

*   *   *

My study begins in 1950s West Germany and will explore the strategic function of three now classic "blockbuster" adaptations: Carol Reed's adaptation of Graham Greene's *The Third Man*, David Lean's adaptation of Pierre Boulle's *The Bridge on the River Kwai*, and Orson Welles's adaptation of Franz Kafka's *The Trial*. These Anglo-American adaptations played a significant role in postwar West Germany by generating debates about the cultural and political role of U.S. popular culture in the postwar context of both the Cold War and the legacy of National Socialism in West German society. In contrast to the "official" goal of the Anglo-American film industries, that is, to "entertain audiences worldwide" and appeal to an apolitical "international market," these adaptations' receptions reveal historically specific dynamics that demonstrate the ways the relationship between literature and film was perceived as profoundly political—both by film audiences and by filmmakers. Film adaptations would thus play a mediating role in addressing such significant historical and material concerns as the relationship between culture and politics in future relations between the U.S. and Europe and the legacies of militarism, racism, and genocide in German society. Adapting literary texts to films in Cold War Germany was never exclusively about issues of "fidelity" or "aesthetics" alone. Rather, the process could reveal West German efforts to establish a national identity that could both integrate itself within and be actively critical of the postwar Cold War NATO (North Atlantic Treaty Organization) alliance.[17]

Substantial interest in the cultural and ideological impact of the Cold War on societies world wide has emerged in the wake of the official Cold War—the political, economic, and ideological conflict between the "capitalist" United States and the "communist" Soviet Union, which began after World War II and came to a political end with the fall of the Berlin Wall in 1989.[18] Given my focus upon the specific historical and national context of Europe and West Germany during the first phase of the official Cold War, my own readings of these films will incorporate that context and rely upon a "post–Cold War" perspective, that is, a perspective that frames the Cold War's opposition between democracy and communism as an historical construct that affected the ways media such as literature and film could circulate and interact within a specific context.

In the second part of my study, I will move the focus to the United States in the 1990s and evaluate the renewed filmic interest in the literary works of Jane Austen and Henry James. Close attention to such Austen adaptations as Ang Lee's *Sense and Sensibility* (1995) and Roger Michell's *Persuasion* (1995) and to such James adaptations as Agnieszka Holland's *Washington Square* (1997), Jane Campion's *The Portrait of a Lady* (1997), and Iain Softley's *The Wings of the Dove* (1997), as well as to the ways these films were received, reveals a complex, intercultural, and intertextual dynamic that enlisted "classic" literary texts in filmic efforts preoccupied with questions of contemporary gender identity. How did this preoccupation manifest itself?

The last fourth of the twentieth century saw the emergence of what has been called postfeminism or third-wave feminism. In contrast to second-wave feminists' focus upon the importance of material conditions, postfeminists became increasingly preoccupied with the realm of media representation.[19] The answer to many of the unmet hopes of the second-wave women's movement for economic and political equality began to be sought more and more in the realm of consumption. The economic and political subject was also a desiring subject, and desire was the realm of media and popular culture. How could the women who had made real gains in the public sphere also fulfill their desires for sexual and familial relationships? This desire for a compatibility of private and public identities, rather than having to choose between the one or the other or consciously privileging one over the other, became a central aspect of the rather diffuse agenda of postfeminism.

However, if consumption-oriented "shopping" films set in the present, such as *Pretty Woman,* would focus upon the liberating potential of fashion, the agendas of the Austen and James adaptations went a step further.[20] Filmmakers in the 1990s used Austen's and James's texts to create an indirect cultural negotiation between feminism and postfeminism about the meaning of gender in a postfeminist political context. In particular, these adaptations sought to explore "both/and" solutions for women and men to the conflicts the novels analyze between love and money, autonomy and commitment, thus exploring new ways of thinking about relationships between public and private realms. They also encouraged their viewers to negotiate constructive relationships to consumer culture and to identify and avoid male narcissism. Classic nineteenth-century novels lend themselves to this type of adaptation task precisely because those works, with their focus upon the domestic realm, marriage, family, and individual identity, offer a basis of comparison to gauge changes in contemporary gender issues.

In turn, I will also read these films from a postfeminist perspective. This will involve taking into account the goals of the second-wave feminist movement that emerged in a number of Western countries in the 1960s and 1970s and comparing these with the more media-oriented feminisms that developed in the 1980s and 1990s.[21] If postfeminists emphasize the ways women can utilize the realm of media, communication, and consumption to create alternatives to conventional gender roles, their forebears concentrated more upon the alteration of material conditions in the realms of economics, politics, and law as a means of promoting equality between the sexes.[22] Many scholars, such as Tania Modleski, have defined these media-oriented postfeminist developments as opposed to the goals of second-wave feminism.[23]

In contrast, I wish to focus upon how cultural forms such as film adaptation, particularly in the 1990s, would try to mediate between these increasingly opposed realms of "material" and "celebrity" feminism in order to counter the polarized popular debate between "feminism" and "conservatism," what Susan Faludi defined as "backlash"—the media and politically generated conservative reaction to the political and social inroads made by activism on behalf of women's rights in the 1970s.[24] This campaign characterized "feminist" attitudes as those in opposition to traditional notions of "family values" and suggested women and men had to take sides "for" or "against" "feminism," rather than work to develop new ways of negotiating the relationship between the "public" sphere of work, career, and activism and the "private" sphere of personal and familial relationships.

Thus, the investigation of these two versions of the adaptation phenomenon reveals broader processes that demonstrate the ways historically specific intertextual dynamics between literature and film can become important sites of cultural negotiation and struggle.

* * *

In "Film History, Terminable and Interminable: Recovering the Past in Reception Studies," Barbara Klinger defines the field of reception studies in the following terms: "Those engaged in reception studies typically examine a network of relationships between a film or filmic element ... adjacent intertextual fields such as censorship, exhibition practices, star publicity and reviews, and the dominant or alternative ideologies of society at a particular time. Such contextual analysis hopes to reveal the intimate impact of discursive and social situations on cinematic meaning, while elaborating the particularities of cinema's existence under different historical regimes from the silent era to the present."[25] Klinger's definition is relevant to my study and is indebted in particular to the field of British cultural studies. Cultural studies encouraged an exploration of the wider cultural contexts mediated by specific film texts and focused more closely upon the ways "cultural values, meanings, and identities[were] made, negotiated, and remade in historically situated power relationships."[26] Klinger's definition of reception study has also been influenced by the Foucaultian idea of "discourse/practice," which takes issue with the opposition between ideas and practice and instead focuses upon the ways in which ideas shape practice for good or ill.[27] As Pierre Bourdieu has written: "...discourse about a work is not a mere accompaniment intended to assist in its perception and appreciation, but a stage in the production of the work—of its meaning and value."[28]

However, if film and literature scholars tended to fetishize the "original work" in their studies of film adaptation, reception studies scholars tend to overlook it completely. Klinger's definition mentions such "intertextual fields" as censorship and exhibition but does not include literature. There is a tendency to say too little about the historical and ideological significance of literature in relationship to film.[29] However, Klinger's model does provide a space for conceptualizing adaptation within the intertextual zones that exist in relationship to specific cinematic events and which make it part of the larger project of "recovering the past in reception studies."

Thus, my work will look at three levels of reception or "intertextual zones" in relation to film adaptation. First, the reception of the original literary work by the filmmaker(s) in the form of the production event of the film itself. Second, the reception of this "image object" by reviewers and critics who expressed their views in newspapers, letters to the editor, and periodical criticism—star publicity, film production publicity, censorship board recommendations, oral interviews, and for later material, internet databases will also be used.[30] Third, I will offer my own readings of these adaptations in light of their transnational receptions. I distinguish among these three levels, because I am interested in the ways they interact and play off each other: how they can engender different types of cultural conflict and in turn demonstrate their significance through the responses they elicit. Debates about "fidelity to an original," for example, may raise significant issues of the political function of a literary text in a particular culture, even as the filmic adaptation negotiates cultural debates that go far beyond the original work. My own approach to these films will also situate my study squarely within today's post–Cold War and postfeminist context. In this sense, my method differs considerably from that of Janet Staiger, who defines "historical materialist reception studies" as an exclusive focus upon interpretations of films or, as she terms it, "attempting an historical *explanation* of the event of interpreting a text" without also offering either an explanation or an interpretation of the films whose reception she analyzes.[31] Adaptation study allows one to see film production as a version of reception, revealing the interactive potential of production and reception without leveling the distinction completely.

Conceptualizing adaptation in relationship to reception studies and applying the three-tiered model outlined above will not necessarily be a parallel task. In most—but not all—of the cases, the discussion of the reception of a specific adaptation will precede analysis of the adaptation itself and attempt to show interconnections between them. Sometimes, the relationship between literary work and film adaptation will follow the conventional chronological model, as in my discussion of the adaptations of Austen's novels; in others, such as Greene's *The Third Man,* the relationship between film and source text will be more complex, continuing on even after the film's release. Focusing upon the reception of adaptations will sometimes reveal a clear interest among critics in questions of the meaning of film reception itself, as in the film *The Bridge On the River Kwai;* in other cases, such as Welles's *The Trial,* critical interest will focus upon the perceived differences between novel and film. Unlike the conventional academic "fidelity" model of adaptation, the critical historical reception will not always define the relationship between source text and film in the same way.[32] Finally, my own readings will take into account the dimensions of production and reception, thus attempting to engage in a dialogue with both the films and the responses to them in order to shed light upon contemporary issues. Attention to the ways adaptations create new discourses will demonstrate the ways intertextual dynamics between works of literature and films can have concrete material effects.

* * *

The French historian Marc Ferro has looked at how filmmakers transformed literary works in order to explore the ways films, as image objects, can have meanings "that are not solely cinematographic."[33] Analyzing the Soviet filmmaker Lev Kulashov's 1926 film *Dura Lex* as an adaptation of a short story by Jack London, "The Unexpected," Ferro demonstrates that plot alterations made by the filmmaker transformed the story into a filmic critique of the Soviet Union, though the action took place in Canada. Noting other changes and omissions, Ferro asks "can such additions, omissions, modifications, and reversals be attributed merely to the "genius" of the artist? Do they not have another meaning?"[34]

Ferro's interest is in establishing the historical relevance of specifically narrative films. In contrast to "documentary" and newsreel films that enjoy a more legitimate status as evidence among conventional historians, narrative film is often dismissed as subjective, because it is primarily imaginative in nature. Therefore, he offers a model for analyzing narrative films as cultural documents, one based upon a psychological model of manifest and latent content, where the latent content represents the social/ideological level of the narrative. His method for deducing this meaning, which he vaguely defines in a diagram as a "search for signs," derived from comparing the film with the story upon which it was based. In other words, Ferro was able to gauge differences between manifest and latent content based on changes Kulakov made to London's original story (see Appendix 1, Tables 1 and 2). This method is timely and important, because it suggests the significance of analyzing differences between narratives and their film adaptations for ideological import. It also suggests the fruitfulness of going beyond the "auteur theory" of filmic meaning, as such changes, combined with an analysis of a film's reception, reveal multiple layers that cannot be explained solely by reference to the conscious "aesthetic" intention of the individual film director.

Ferro's model also recalls such seminal works as Siegfried Kracauer's *From Caligari to Hitler* that attempted to find mechanisms for mediating between specific films and the society within which they circulate. Such models have been criticized by more quantitatively oriented historians distrustful of generalizations made based upon limited quantitative evidence. However, the issues between film and society raised by the model of "mediation" continue to be central. As Gomery and Allen have stated, "relating the social structure of a given time and place to the representations of that structure in film is one of the most tantalizing yet vexing tasks faced by the entire field of film historical study."[35]

Film adaptation can function as just such a form of mediation. When filmmakers and film production companies choose to transform pre-existing cultural texts into filmic texts, that transformation is informed by a variety of sociocultural processes that tap into existing cultural discourses about a given work, such as traditionally defined "classics" such as Jane Austen's *Sense and Sensibility* or Henry James's *The Portrait of a Lady*. Market identification is a critical element, but other factors play a role as well. The transformation is also defined by a cultural struggle between filmmakers and their relationship to an established work and author. Filmmakers such as Orson Welles, David Lean, Jane Campion, and Ang Lee seek to establish their own unique opinion or interpretation of a particular work. In this struggle to establish something "new" in relation to a "previous text" a certain history is created; a text in a new medium writes a new history. However, this history is not necessarily based upon the conscious intention of a specific filmmaker in classic auteur fashion. Rather, looking at a number of related film adaptations reveals the ways the struggle against the tradition of a text taps into ideological struggles going on at other levels in a specific time and place.[36]

The text-into-film dynamic takes place on both diachronic and synchronic levels. Texts adapted diachronically reveal ideological change over time, as in when the changes made to the original text are related to the different sociohistorical contexts into which the novel and the film emerge. This is particularly evident in the case of the adaptation of nineteenth-century fiction. Robert Stam defines this dynamic in terms of "the source novel as a situated utterance produced in one medium and in one historical context, then transformed into another equally situated utterance that is produced in a different context and in a different medium."[37] Even for contemporaneous works adapted to film, other types of changes and modifications can reveal ideological struggles indirectly through the progression from narrative to visual form. "Transmutations of plot and character," for example, often go beyond technical changes required to transform written into visual sources and reveal novel ideological dynamics at work.[38] The political dynamics are particularly significant when characters' nationalities are modified, as was the case in Carol Reed's *The Third Man,* in David Lean's *The Bridge on the River Kwai,* and in Orson Welles's *The Trial.* Alterations to the genre of the story also carry political implications, as in *Kwai* where a satire was transformed into a melodramatic narrative. In such cases, questions as to the meaning and significance of the changes arise.

In both instances, film adaptation is conceived in this study as a transnational phenomenon, which has implications for both the relationship between the literary work and its filmic adaptation, as well as the responses it generates. To begin, all of the films under discussion in this work were adapted cross-culturally: originally British, German/Czech, or French texts are transformed by Australian, Taiwanese, U.S. American, and European filmmakers into new works. In turn, the audiences intended for these films are multinational, as indeed, the Hollywood film industry has intended them to be since its inception.[39] However, conventionally this dynamic has not been understood as one emphasizing the differences in the ways audiences from different cultures view films; rather, films were "standardized" to "appeal to" or "not to offend" as large an audience as possible. In Part One of the study, European texts are adapted by Anglo-American production teams for international audiences. As these films entered the German context, their reception exemplifies the unique ways they were received across cultural borders. In Part Two, critics and audiences come largely from the United States, while the films, several of which have been recently classified as "British Heritage Retrovisions," were produced by cross-cultural teams for global audiences.

My readings of these films will also reflect my own position as a historian with a U.S. American and German cultural background.[40] Working in Germany as a U.S. cultural historian and moving between these worlds through language, psychology, and geography has made me aware of the ways cross-cultural phenomena, such as film, can be linked to the histories of the two cultures of which I am a part. It has made it possible for me to take advantage of excellent archival sources and to "see" the uniqueness of each cultural field that has shaped my own development. My own position also calls attention to the emphasis upon the "post-ness" that characterizes the points of view of each part of this study. The point of view of the early twenty-first century—the "post–Cold War" perspective that emerged following the end of the Cold War between the U.S. and the former Soviet Union in 1989, and the postfeminist perspective that was shaped by debates during the 1990s over the legacy and future of the feminist movement of the 1970s—shapes my cultural analysis and historicizes my project, calling attention to earlier movements and power relations. Overall, the different cultural and historical contexts explored in this study illustrate the fruitfulness of widening adaptation and reception study, so as to highlight the cultural and ideological complexity of the issues they raise.[41]

This study conceives of itself as "historical" in nature. It is conscious of theories of the "textualization of history" as propounded by scholars, such as Hayden White, and addresses the question of the ways the term "history" will be understood.[42] In a late 1980s forum discussion of the *American Historical Review,* White commented on the issue of representing history on film, what he called "historiophoty." He suggested that film was just as capable as historical narrative of offering plausible historical accounts because both were based on the same principles of narrative construction. Yet, oddly, in the same text he suggests that the analysis of visual images requires a manner of reading quite different from that developed for the study of written documents.[43] I would argue, in contrast, that reading a film historically requires skills similar to those necessary for reading written texts, that is, literary texts. Here, too, reception and adaptation study can offer options. Indeed, Ferro's model of manifest and latent content in relationship to the transformation from literary work to film, exemplified in his reading of *Dura Lex,* might be understood as such a method. Finally, combining reception and adaptation study might also serve the purpose of encouraging historians to rely upon literary and filmic evidence more frequently, and thus to further an appreciation among historians of the relationship between literature and film.

As a cultural historian who has spent many years teaching in literature departments, I have been confronted with the question of the epistemological status of historical discourse more frequently than have colleagues in history departments. As Wulf Kansteiner has argued, historians tend not to respond to White's assertions about history in the same way literary critics [and even film critics] have responded, primarily because they often adhere to the "myth" of historical objectivity and feel threatened by the blurring of distinctions between "fiction" and "non-fiction" that White's theory of historiography seems to imply.[44] However, the similarities between literary and historical texts need not necessarily lead to the collapse of all things historical into the realm of the literary. Indeed, scholarly developments, such as the New Historicism, in literary studies might even suggest that White's ideas have influenced scholars to pay more attention to the historical dimensions of the literary.[45] White has also stated that "it is absurd to suppose that because a historical discourse is cast in the mode of a narrative, it must be mythical, fictional, substantially imaginary, or otherwise "unrealistic" in what it tells us about the world."[46] What this seems to imply is that White's ideas have contributed to a recognition of the interrelationship of narrative forms such as literature, history, and film and so have expanded the ways scholars can legitimately construct arguments about the past and its relationship to the present.[47] White's argument has triggered a heightened theoretical awareness among many historians. This may not have led them to subscribe to White's theory, but it definitely influenced the ways they understood the constructedness of their own work and how this constructedness was related to their own theories of history.[48]

My notion of history is based upon my longstanding interest in questions about the interrelationship between cultural forms, such as literature and film, and the ways they have functioned as social and political phenomena. I have been especially influenced by women's history and feminist theory, as well as by Foucaultian notions of discourse/practice and the cultural Marxism of British cultural studies. My interest in the relationship between culture and society is governed by the conviction that an understanding of specific contemporary cultural phenomena can be illuminated by a study of its past forms. Current trends regarding the contemporary relations between culture and social power can often be critically illuminated by exploring these issues "historically," that is, over time—with an eye toward discontinuities rather than continuities and conflict rather than consensus. I also appreciate the heuristic value of close (qualitative) attention to specific cultural texts rather than a more general (quantitative) attention to many texts.

Most film viewers will have a strong sense of historical context in relationship to films, though they may not be conscious of it. When viewers look at their television programs in the evenings to select a film to view, they are usually confronted with three types of information about any specific film: its title, its country of origin, and its date of production. But if viewers were to find the following entries in their TV programs, how might they respond?:

Gone with the Wind (USA)
Spur der Steine (DDR)

Without the references to chronological origin, I would say that most viewers would feel deprived of a sense of orientation, even of important knowledge. They might tune in and try to "figure out" when the film was made based upon certain clues: fashion, car types, hair styles, furniture styles, actors; they might venture an educated guess based upon these clues. They might feel irritated, because they know the date but nonetheless miss seeing it printed. The dynamic that this sense will set off is profoundly "intertextual," for once the date of production is affixed to the film each viewer will construct for themselves an understanding of the context that specific date implies; it will be informed by more or less knowledge about the time period based upon personal experience, nostalgia, texts about the era, other films, film studies courses, or any number of other possibilities. Different viewers will construct different versions but all will engage in the process of attempting to link the filmic text with a context.[49] It is this sense of "lack" or absence that I would define as the necessary—though not sufficient—prerequisite for a sensibility defined as historical.

Notes

1. Charles McGrath, "Another Hike on the Moors for 'Jane Eyre.'" (4 March 2011): http://www.nytimes.com/2011/03/06/movies/06eyre.html; see also Monica Hesse, "'Jane Eyre' movie

rekindles Austen vs. Brontë, the battle of the bonnets." *The Washington Post* (17 March 2011): http://www.washingtonpost.com/lifestyle/style/jane-eyre-movie-rekindles.

2. "Jane Eyre - Do all good things come in threes? Fukunaga believes in thirties!" Weblog article (placed online 23 January 2011). See http://storybird70.wordpress.com/2011/01/23/jane-eyre-do-all-good-things-come-in-threes-fukunaga-believes-in-thirties/

3. Robert B. Ray, "The Field of Literature and Film," in James Naremore, ed., *Film Adaptation* (New Brunswick, New Jersey, 2000), 41–42; 46.

4. A characteristic example of such a volume that contains a number of interesting isolated studies is Constanza Del Rio-Alvaro & Luis Miguel Garcia-Mainar, eds., *Memory, Imagination and Desire in Contemporary Anglo-American Literature and Film* (Heidelberg, 2004). The volume edited by James Naremore, cited above, tends also in this direction. See also Wendell Aycock and Michael Schoenecke, eds. *Film and Literature: A Comparative Approach to Adaptation* (Lubbock, Texas, 1988).

5. Robert Stam, "Introduction: the Theory and Practice of Adaptation" in Robert Stam and Alessandra Raengo, eds. *Literature and Film: A Guide to the Theory and Practice of Film Adaptation* (MA, Oxford, Victoria, 2005), 25.

6. See Robert Stam, "Introduction: the Theory and Practice of Adaptation" in Stam and Raengo, eds. *Literature and Film* (MA, Oxford, Victoria, 2005), 1–52. See also Robert Stam, "Beyond Fidelity: the Dialogics of Adaptation," in James Naremore, ed. *Film Adaptation* (New Brunswick, NJ, 2000), 54–76; Kamilla Elliott, "Novels, Films, and the Word/Image Wars," in Robert Stam and Alessandra Raengo, eds., *A Companion to Literature and Film* (MA, Oxford, Victoria, 2004), 1–22. I would tend to see the stubborness of the fidelity model as more closely tied to concrete "material/disciplinary" interests, in line with Ray, cited above, than with a deep-seated cultural prejudice against images.

7. Robert Stam, "Beyond Fidelity: The Dialogics of Adaptation," in James Naremore, ed. *Film Adaptation*, 64.

8. Like literary studies, film studies has tended to be dominated by poststructuralist and especially psychoanalytic approaches, which, I believe, has played a role in downplaying the relationship between adaptation and historical issues more generally. Indeed, it has played a role in drawing attention away from the richness and diversity of the field of film history itself, to which this study ultimately wishes to contribute: combining reception studies and adaptation studies as a means to create new ways of addressing the relationship between history, literature, and film.

For an overview of the diverse ways film historians work, see especially Robert C. Allen and Douglas Gomery, *Film History: Theory and Practice* (New York, 1985). European film critics have tended toward a historical approach much longer than have their U.S. counterparts. See, in particular, Marc Ferro, *Cinema and History* (translated by Naomi Greene) (Detroit, 1988). For different frameworks for understanding the field of U.S. film history see David Bordwell, Janet Staiger, and Kristen Thompson, *The Classical Hollywood Cinema: Film Style and Mode of Production* (New York, 1985) and Lary May, *The Big Tomorrow: Hollywood and the Politics of the American Way* (Chicago, 2000).

On the concept of the "event," see Rick Altman, ed. *Sound Theory, Sound Practice* (New York 1992): 1–14, and Sabine Nessel, *Kino und Ereignis* (Berlin 2008).

9. Ray, 42; See especially Barbara Klinger, "Film history terminable and interminable: recovering the past in reception studies," *Screen* 38.2(Summer 1997): 107–128 and Janet Staiger, *Interpreting Films: Studies in the Historical Reception of American Cinema* (Princeton, New Jersey, 1992).

10. Timothy Corrigan emphasizes the importance of specific analysis: "the exchange between film and literature demands, especially now, rigorous historical and cultural distinctions." See

Timothy Corrigan. *Film and Literature: An Introduction and Reader.* (Upper Saddle River, NJ, 1999), 2.

11. Several of the chapters in this work have appeared in print, online, and on CD-ROM in modified form: Anne-Marie Scholz, "Adaptation as Reception: How a Transnational Analysis of Hollywood Films can Renew the Literature to Film Debate." *Amerikastudien/American Studies* 54.4(2009): 657–682; "Thelma and Louise and Sense and Sensibility: New Approaches to Challenging Dichotomies in Women's History Through Literature and Film." *Journal of South Texas English Studies* 1(2009): n.pag. Web. 10 December 2009. URL: http://southtexasenglish .blogspot.com; « "Josef K von 1963": Orson Welles' "Americanized" Version of *The Trial* and the changing functions of the Kafkaesque in Postwar West Germany », *European Journal of American Studies*, EJAS 2009-1, [Online], article 5, put online Jun. 17, 2009.URL:http://ejas.revues .org/document7608.html; "Jane-Mania: The Jane Austen Film Boom in the Nineties," in Peter C. Rollins, John E. O'Connor, and Deborah Carmichael, eds. 1999 *Film and History CD-ROM Annual* (Stillwater, OK, 1999); "Eine Revolution des Films": *The Third Man*, the Cold War, and Alternatives to Nationalism and Coca-Colonization in Europe." *Film and History: An Interdisciplinary Journal of Film and Television Studies* Vol. 31.1(2001): 44–53; "The *Bridge on the River Kwai* Revisited: Combat Cinema, American Culture and the German Past." *German History* (Oxford Journals) 26.2(2008): 219–250.

12. Guerric DeBona, *Film Adaptation in the Hollywood Studio Era.* (Urbana, 2010); Thomas Leitch, "Adaptation Studies at a Crossroads," *Adaptation* Vol. 1.1(2008): 63–77. (p. 65); *Film Adaptation and Its Discontents: From "Gone with the Wind" to "The Passion of Christ".* (Baltimore, Md., 2007); Simone Murray, "Materializing Adaptation Theory: The Adaptation Industry." *Literature/ Film Quarterly* 36.1(2008): 4–20; "Phantom Adaptations: *Eucalyptus*, the adaptation industry and the film that never was." *Adaptation*, Vol. 1, No. 1(2008): 5–23. Anne-Marie Scholz, "From Fidelity to History: Film Adaptations as Cultural Events in the Twentieth Century" Habilitationsschrift (Unpublished Postdoctoral Dissertation). Universität Bremen, Germany, 2006.

13. Leitch, "Adaptation Studies at a Crossroads," 65. However, as the many specific cases published in the recently founded journal *Adaptation* (2008) also show, it may be more pragmatic to address the continued perseverance of the case study than to call for its elimination.

14. See esp. Murray, "The Adaptation Industry" as well as Eckart Voigts-Virkow, ed. *Janespotting: British Heritage Retrovisions since the Mid-1990's* (Tübingen, 2004).

15. Here, I definitively part company with Robert Stam, who argues that the chronological relation between literary work and filmic adaptation is inherently hierarchical. See Stam and Raengo, eds., *Literature and Film: A Guide to the Theory and Practice of Film Adaptation*, 4.

16. Voigts-Virchow, ed. *Janespotting: British Heritage Retrovisions since the Mid-1990's*, and Simone Murray, "Phantom Adaptations," 5–23.

17. Heide Fehrenbach. *Cinema in Democratizing Germany: Reconstructing National Identity after Hitler.* (Chapel Hill, 1995).

18. Patrick Major and Rana Mitter, eds. *Across the Blocs: Cold War Cultural and Social History.* (London, 2004), 1–22.

19. Charlotte Brunsdon, "Post-Feminism and Shopping Films," in Joanne Hollows, Peter Hutchings and Mark Jancovich, eds., *The Film Studies Reader* (London & New York, 2000), 289–299; Yvonne Tasker and Diane Negra, eds. *Interrogating Post-Feminism* (Durham and London, 2007); Stacy Gillis, Gillian Howie, and Rebecca Munford, eds. *Third Wave Feminism: A Critical Exploration* (New York, 2004).

20. Brundson, 289–299.

21. Jennifer Wicke, "Celebrity Material: Materialist Feminism and the Culture of Celebrity." *South Atlantic Quarterley* 93.4(Fall 1994): 751–778.

22. Brundson, 289–291.

23. Tania Modleski, *Feminism without Women: Culture and Criticism in a "Postfeminist" Age.* (London, 1991).

24. Wicke, "Celebrity Material," 751–778; Susan Faludi, *Backlash: The Undeclared War Against American Women* (New York, 1991).

25. Klinger, 108.

26. Joanne Hollows, *et al. The Film Studies Reader* (London & New York, 2000), 265–66. See also Graeme Turner, *Film as Social Practice,* 2nd edition (London and New York, 1993).

27. See especially Mark Poster, *Foucault, Marxism and History: Mode of Production vs. Mode of Information* (Cambridge & New York, 1984), 9–16.

28. Pierre Bourdieu, *The Field of Cultural Production,* ed. Randal Johnson, (New York, 1993), 110. For the affinities between Bourdieu and Foucault, see the introduction to this volume.

29. For an important general discussion of the significant relationship literature has played in the history of the film industry as a whole, see Joachim Paech, *Literatur und Film,* Zweite Auflage, (Stuttgart und Weimar, 1997) and Corrigan, *Film and Literature: An Introduction and Reader.*

30. The concept of "image object" comes from Ferro, *Cinema and History,* (Detroit, 1988), 29.

31. Staiger, 81.

32. Corrigan, *Film and Literature: An Introduction and Reader,* 1–78.

33. Ferro, *Cinema and History,* 29–30.

34. Ibid, 33–34.

35. Siegfried Kracauer, *From Caligari to Hitler* (Princeton, New Jersey, 1947). Kracauer's study can be defined as a "founding text" of film/society mediation; Robert C. Allen and Douglas Gomery, *Film History: Theory and Practice* (New York, 1985), 158.

36. In *The Field of Cultural Production,* Pierre Bourdieu offers a compelling definition of "history" in his discussion of the production of belief within the field of cultural production. He writes: "It is not sufficient to say that the history of the field is the history of the struggle for the monopolistic power to impose the legitimate categories of perception and appreciation. The *struggle itself* creates the history of the field; through the struggle the field is given a temporal dimension. To introduce difference is to produce time." Pierre Bourdieu, *The Field of Cultural Production,* ed. Randal Johnson, (New York, 1993), 106.

37. Robert Stam, "Beyond Fidelity: The Dialogics of Adaptation," in James Naremore, ed. *Film Adaptation,* 68.

38. Ibid., 71.

39. See esp. Reinhold Wagnleitner, *Coca-Colonization and the Cold War: The Cultural Mission of the United States in Austria after the Second World War,* (Chapel Hill and London, 1994), 230–251.

40. E.H. Carr discusses the importance of the biographical background of the historian in relation to his (in this case, her) materials at length in *What is History?* (New York, 1961), 24–29.

41. Scholars of filmic reception study and adaptation study have been calling for this type of "widening" for some time. See Naremore, 12, Staiger, 93 as well as Klinger, 122.

42. Hayden White, *Metahistory: The Historical Imagination in Nineteenth Century Europe* (Baltimore and London, 1973).

43. Hayden White, "Historiography and Historiophoty," *AHR* Forum, *American Historical Review,* Vol. 93.4(1988): 1193–1199.

44. Wulf Kansteiner, "Hayden White's Critique of the Writing of History," *History and Theory,* Vol. 32, No. 3(Oct. 1993): 273–295; see also Peter Novick, *That Noble Dream: The "Objectivity Question" and the American Historical Profession* (London and New York, 1988), 599–607.

45. Hayden White, *Figural Realism: Studies in the Mimesis Effect* (Baltimore and London, 1999), 63–64.

46. Ibid., 22.

47. This more positive approach to White's challenges to historians is apparent, for example, in the work of Jörn Rüsen. See "Historical Narration: Foundation, Types, Reason," in *History and Theory*, Beiheft 26, No. 4(1987): 87–97.

48. The "History and Theory" program at the University of California, Irvine, as I experienced it in the late-1980s and early 1990s, was very much a systematic attempt made by a history program to offer a reformist middle to the likes of figures like White and traditional empirical historians.

49. While the culture of television viewing continues to promote the historical classification of film by affixing the date of production to the title (for example, in TV guides), increasingly, the marketing of the DVD relegates dates of production to very small print on the back of the packaging or else eliminates dates of production altogether, and this despite the high level of interest in marketing and restoring older "classics." The implications of this trend for viewers' perceptions of the historical situatedness of films require analysis. Many, I would argue, will search the small print until they find the historical marker, though increasingly (and frustratingly) they won't find what they are looking for.

PART I

Post-Cold War Readings of the Receptions of Blockbuster Adaptations in Cold War West Germany 1950–1963

Central to the politics of the three adaptations I will explore in the context of West Germany in the 1950s—Carol Reed's *The Third Man* (1949) based upon the story by Graham Greene, David Lean's *The Bridge on the River Kwai* (1957) based upon the best-selling novel by Pierre Boulle, and Orson Welles's *The Trial* (1962) based upon the novel of the same name by Franz Kafka—was the phenomenon of the Cold War following the military defeat of Germany and the end of World War II. As a political and ideological showdown between the state socialism of the former Soviet Union and the representative democracy of the United States, the Cold War was central to the political realignments that had shaped the European continent after the war. The division of Germany after 1945 into "East" and "West," communist and capitalist, the former aligned with the Soviet Union and the latter with the United States culminated with the building of the Berlin Wall in August of 1961. The intranational political division within Germany reflected the international division between Eastern and Western Europe in concentrated form and rendered Germany a central symbolic battlefield in this particular war.

However, the immense ideological differences between the contending Cold War parties were almost less problematic than the ways they chose to defend their respective differences. The Cold War got its bite through the military/ideological policy of "nuclear containment." The atomic bomb was in the possession of both the United States and the Soviet Union, and the threat of a global nuclear war in the event of an offensive military action taken by one or the other of the parties would spell the annihilation of whole societies. Consequently military alignments such as the North Atlantic Treaty Organi-

zation (NATO) headed by the United States and the Warsaw Pact headed by
the Soviet Union were formed in order to promote "strength in numbers" to
prevent the proverbial "first strike": the first offensive action against a nation-
state using a nuclear weapon.

The dynamics of the political Cold War and the threat of nuclear war had
important repercussions for West Germany. Its proximity to the Iron Curtain—the separation between the "free Western world" and the world of
"communist totalitarianism"—increased the likelihood of potential military
and nuclear conflict on German soil, making West Germany particularly vulnerable. Moreover, the legacy of military defeat in World War II made Germans sensitive to the impact of war on West German society, and the broader
question of German accountability for war crimes against humanity under
National Socialism made them conscious of their political and national reputation worldwide.

Between 1950, when *The Third Man* opened in German movie theaters,
and 1963, when Orson Welles's *The Trial* had its premiere, West Germany had
gone through a process of cultural and national reconstruction that involved
grappling with military defeat, integrating into the Western anti-communist
NATO military alliance, rebuilding a national economy, and reestablishing
an international reputation as a democratic nation state. The three transnational Hollywood film adaptations I will analyze played an important role
in the process of cultural reconstruction of German society after the war and
will illustrate the ways film and literature could interact to produce important
material effects. Both popular blockbusters, such as *The Third Man* and *Kwai*,
as well as more art house fare, like *The Trial*, occupied intertextual zones that
actively politicized the relationship between film and source texts in different
ways and that elicited responses that called attention to the close ties between
culture and politics in the postwar German context.

Scholars of U.S. popular culture have become increasingly interested in
the ways cultures outside the United States, especially in Europe and Latin
America, appropriate and confront U.S. cultural products, thus establishing
a cross-cultural and transcultural basis for their study of U.S. popular culture.[1] However, in most cases such works tend not to fit into preestablished
nationalistic categories for the study of culture and hence do not really shape
debates in their respective countries.[2] I would like to demonstrate the ways the
methodologies of reception study and a focus on the ideological dimensions
of the adaptation process can provide a useful basis for cross and intercultural
film studies.

Given the global nature of the Hollywood film industry and the efforts it
has devoted to making its products marketable across national boundaries,
the dimension of the cross and transcultural acquires a good deal of signifi-

cance. Furthermore, as Janet Staiger has suggested, "if reception studies can contribute to the understanding of how culture and politics interweave and affect each other, then this type of research will have important use values."[3] In exploring the reception of three, twentieth-century, Anglo-American "film classics" in Cold War Germany, my major interest is the ways in which German audiences created interconnections between cultural and political issues in their responses to these films and what role the relationship between literature and film played in making such interconnections. Two of the three films explored were major commercial successes and perceived as better than average products of the mass culture industry: *The Third Man* and *The Bridge on the River Kwai*. All three were associated with significant literary works or literary figures popular in their own right. In the exploration of the German reception, a consistent dimension is the question of the construction of a new form of postwar German nationalism and what types of cultural and national interactions between West Germany and the United States were possible in the context of NATO and the Cold War alliance against the Soviet Union. Additionally, questions of German attitudes toward their own history have a central place.

Thus, these studies also contribute to dialogues suggested by German historians such as Heide Fehrenbach, Uta Poiger, and Robert G. Moeller, all of whom are interested in the relationship between film and postwar German nationalism.[4] Moeller explores the ways West German films of the 1950s dwelt at length on the figure of the German soldier as victim of Stalingrad, disregarding other victims of Nazi Germany and thus "selectively remembering" elements of the Nazi past. Fehrenbach looks at how the postwar German film sought to "reconstruct [West German] national identity after Hitler." While both Moeller and Fehrenbach emphasize German films, Uta Poiger has analyzed how U.S. films influenced and were received in West and East Germany by cultural elites in the 1950s. Poiger's was the first study to comparatively evaluate the ways U.S. popular culture was received in West and East Germany. However, her major focus was less on film and more centered on music, especially jazz and rock and roll; when she did focus on film she tended to emphasize the extent to which U.S. cultural products were becoming increasingly depoliticized as a means of accommodating Cold War tensions between East and West Germany.

All of these historians have made important inroads in the task of using film as a cultural resource to analyze the reconstruction of German nationalism after World War II.[5] However, none have thus far focused upon the important connections between the films they've analyzed and the literary texts upon which they were frequently based. With the exception of Poiger, they have not systematically explored the ways U.S. produced films were received by German critics and audiences. Reinhold Wagnleitner has made a case for the hegemonic function of U.S. cultural products, including film, in postwar Austria. By emphasizing "U.S. cultural imperialism," Wagnleitner attempted to explain the nature of U.S. cultural influence. On the one hand, he showed that the U.S. was a dominant cultural force during the postwar years; on the other hand, he also showed that this culture was itself shaped, ironically, by classically European hierarchical conceptions of the relations between "high" and "popular" culture. German speaking commentators would utilize this tension to define their own role in relationship to the Cold War constellation between the U.S. and the Soviets. However, Wagnleitner's analysis of the impact of U.S. cultural products on postwar Austria does not focus systematically on the receptions of specific films, nor does he pay any sort of attention to film adaptation as a cultural phenomenon. Instead, he interprets the overall impact of U.S. popular culture on Austria as a positive, constructive force and tends to read his generation's positive response to postwar U.S. culture as representative of the entire nation.

Focusing upon film adaptation in West Germany in the 1950s demonstrates that while the U.S. film industry certainly had its imperialistic cultural designs on German audiences, it was also aware that in order to gain legitimacy and popularity among those audiences, a production had to take those audiences into some kind of account. Nowhere is this more evident than in changes made between the original literary works and the adaptations. In the case of *The Third Man*, the attempt to downplay the ideological tensions of the early Cold War and instead to focus upon the relationship between Western Europe and the U.S. was especially relevant to the German context, where the communist/capitalist divide was intrinsic to the nation itself. However, in the case of a "war film" like *The Bridge on the River Kwai*, U.S. film publicity in Germany would, for example, attempt to offer conciliatory readings of its own films in order to anticipate the criticism of German commentators, who in turn astutely took note of the publicity's hidden agendas. To put it in Wagnleitner's terms, while production publicity for a film would emphasize the United States' shared cultural and political priorities with Western Europe, European commentators would tend to focus on what made those productions different.

Relativizing the Cold War: *The Third Man*

The British/U.S. co-production *The Third Man* was one of the most popular films in Germany in 1950. However, unlike the original unpublished story upon which it was based, its relationship to the developing Cold War opposition between capitalism and communism was decidedly ambiguous,[6] and its reception reflected this ambiguity. The film's West German reception, as well as its publicity in the West, read *The Third Man* as an exercise in aesthetic unity, realism, and cultural internationalism—a model of sorts for Europe. East German critics, in turn, read it as anti-communist propaganda, while East German audiences attended the film in high numbers. The production of the film and the life of the story upon which it was based also reflected this ambiguous relationship to Cold War politics. In Greene's original unpublished story, the cast of villains and antiheroes were British and Canadian subjects; in the film they would be Americans. The original story also contained many more explicit references to the Cold War, which would go through a series of revisions the leitmotif of which seemed to have been to eliminate as many Cold War dualisms as possible. When the story was finally published after the film's release, two versions would go into circulation: one with more references to the Cold War and one with fewer, while the film itself occupied a niche in between.[7]

The Third Man, in its efforts to downplay Cold War associations that were more apparent in the original version of the story, shifted the politics elsewhere: from questions of East vs. West and communism vs. democracy to those of West vs. West, that is, the nature of the relationship between the United States and Western Europe and their apparently oppositional conceptions of culture that associated "high culture" with Europe and "popular culture" with the U.S. In its sophisticated dissection of the opposition between high and popular culture through the interaction of the lead characters Harry Lime, Holly Martins, and Anna Schmidt, *The Third Man* explores the implications of this opposition for the future of the relationship between the United States and Europe and suggests the possibility of an autonomous cultural space for Europe as an alternative to its political niche between the Cold War sides.

The place of Anglo-American popular culture was hotly contested in postwar Germany, and despite the prevalence of U.S. films on the German film market, the consistently popular productions of the period were by and large of local—German or Austrian—origin.[8] *The Third Man* and its German reception suggests that for an Anglo-American film to gain popularity in Germany, it had to address some of the tensions between the United States and Europe that characterized the postwar relationship; in short, it had to engage in some sort of cultural mediation that actively addressed the power differences within "the West." The adaptation process of Graham Greene's "treatment" turned published story reveals specific political positions engaged in by adaptors and recognized and commented upon by audiences, as well as the cultural assumptions behind a British text as representing "Europe" in its embattled relationship to "America" in the post–World War II world.

The Cold War Anti-War Film: *The Bridge on the River Kwai*

By 1958, when *The Bridge on the River Kwai* was released in West Germany, a number of important developments had taken place in the relationship between West Germany and the United States. In 1955, West Germany joined the NATO alliance and, against the protests of a significant number of Germans who never wanted to see another German in uniform, created a new model army, the Bundeswehr. West Germany's strategic location at the border of the Iron Curtain made it an important ally for the United States during the Cold War. At the same time, the legacy of World War II and the German past raised questions about the possibility of new forms of militarism and ideological extremism.

From the mid-1950s onward, Hollywood had been exporting films with war as a central theme, and many German critics and commentators were highly skeptical of this trend.[9] Officially, Germany was defined world-wide as a defeated nation with a powerful legacy of dangerous cultural militarism. What then, critics asked, were films with militaristic themes doing on the German market? Moreover, was there a way to enlist films about war in the cause of criticizing rather than promoting war? The result was the emergence of the "war vs. anti-war" film debate. *Kwai* stood at the center of this debate, because it too, like *The Third Man* eight years before, was an enormously popular Anglo-American film import.

A central means critics used to gauge the film's political and social import as a "war" or "anti-war" statement was to compare it to the novel upon which it was based, *The Bridge on the River Kwai* by the Frenchman Pierre Boulle. In contrast to the United States where few were even aware that *Kwai* was based on a best-selling French novel in Europe, the novel enjoyed a wide audience in Germany and was frequently discussed by critics in relation to the film.[10] Overall, German critics considered the book much more critical of war than the film, despite the U.S. producer's claims that they had turned a "satire" into a "tragic anti-war story." Indeed, German critics discussed the implications of this shift in genre for the pro-war politics of the film and suggested, for example, that the conclusion of the film, the exploding bridge, symbolized the legitimation of state supported warfare if the right side—in this case, the Western Allies—won the war. Several German critics argued that while *Kwai* certainly contained anti-war sentiments and rhetorical criticism of war, its ideological promotion of the values of military heroism and honor, as well as its insistence upon the triumph of the British over the Japanese—not a theme in the novel—were intended to promote and support NATO policies; hence, *Kwai* was ultimately ambiguous: a Cold War anti-war film.

In my reading of *Kwai* in the context of the war vs. anti-war film debates, I will compare the film with the well-known German produced anti-war film *Die Brücke* (1959) in order to demonstrate the ways U.S. popular culture could influence the postwar German film industry and encourage German filmmakers to produce a novel and potentially radical type of war film: one filmed from the perspective of the official losers of war.

Historicizing "the Kafkaesque": *The Trial*

By 1963, the Berlin Wall had destroyed all hopes of a possible reunification of the two German states and cemented West Germany's position as a central NATO ally. Paradoxically, this extreme political polarization of the country led to a fundamental political stability in the West that was supported by the booming West German economy. In this context, questions of the meaning of German nationalism and the significance of Germany's past as a Nazi dictatorship became more prominent in public discussion.[11]

The reception of the American auteur and actor Orson Welles's adaptation of Franz Kafka's *The Trial* in postwar West Germany in 1963 highlights the ways questions of the German past and the legacy of fascism began to take on greater significance. The film's ambivalent reception by German critics was closely tied to the process of "*Vergangenheitsbewältigung*" (coming to terms with the past) that had emerged in Germany in the mid-1950s with the widespread circulation and publication of visual images of Nazi war crimes and that was in the process of a more politicized transformation in the early 1960s. Through the figure of Welles, I will focus upon the ways U.S. popular culture and the Hollywood film industry could influence this process. Welles's reading of Kafka as a "prophet of fascism," whose Josef K. actively resists his oppressors even if to no apparent avail, set off a timely discussion among commentators about the meaning and function of Kafka's works in West Germany in the 1950s and what had changed since. In 1963, in the midst of spectacular court cases and "trials" that began to highlight the widespread complicity of Germans in National Socialist war crimes, the theme of "active resistance" to tyranny that Welles's version of *The Trial* offered did not fit the picture. It was, as one critic suggested, a distorted, "Americanized" fantasy. However, others appreciated the didactic value of Welles's internationally co-produced film, which coincided with the beginnings of the movement of the New German Cinema, a more confrontational effort to engage questions of the past through film.

*   *   *

Overall, close attention to these three adaptations, understood as cultural events through the prism of reception, reveals highly charged political and ideological investments and calls attention to the ways the strategic cultural functions of adaptations change in different cultural contexts, and rendered the cross cultural aspect explicit and highly political in the case of mid-century, Cold War West Germany. While these films were "international products" intended for "international audiences," situating them within specific frames of nationality sheds light upon political and cultural debates that tap into significant historical issues involving cultural memory and nation building and that contribute to the process of "diversifying" the selective memory of Germans after World War II.[12]

Notes

1. Wagnleitner, *Coca-Colonization and the Cold War* (Chapel Hill, 1994); Reinhold Wagnleitner and Elaine Tyler May, eds. *Here, There and Everywhere: The Foreign Politics of American Popular Culture.* (Hanover, New Hampshire, 2000); Richard F. Pells, *Not Like Us: How Europeans Loved, Hated and Transformed American Culture Since World War II.* (New York, 1997).

2. While Wagnleitner's work has been an important exception to this rule, much new work in the area of cross cultural popular culture studies is still difficult to classify in conventional disciplinary terms. A fine example of such a study is Kirsten Trocha, "Das Lachen gefriert im Hals: The Reception of *Dr. Strangelove* (1964) as cultural and literary document in comparative perspective: Germany and the United States," Magisterarbeit, University of Bremen, Germany, 2003.

3. Staiger 15.

4. Fehrenbach, *Cinema in Democratizing Germany* (Chapel Hill, 1995); Uta G. Poiger, *Jazz, Rock and Rebels: Cold War Politics and American Culture in a Divided Germany* (Berkeley, 2000): Robert G. Moeller, *War Stories: The Search for a Usable Past in the Federal Republic of Germany* (Berkeley, 2001). See also Erica Carter, *How German Is She?: Postwar West German Reconstruction and the Consuming Woman* (Ann Arbor, 1997).

5. See, for example, Robert G. Moeller, "Geschichten aus der "Stacheldraht-universität": Kriegsgefangene im Opferdiskurs der Bundesrepublik," *Werkstadtgeschichte* 26(2000): 23–46; "In a Thousand Years, Every German Will Speak of this Battle": Celluloid Memories of Stalingrad," in *Crimes of War: Guilt and Denial in the Twentieth Century*, ed. Omar Bartov, Atina Grossmann, Mary Nolan (New York, 2002), 161–190; "What did You Do in the War, Mutti? Courageous Women, Compassionate Commanders, and Stories of the Second World War," *German History*, 22(2004):563–594; "Victims in Uniform: West German Combat Movies from the 1950´s," in Bill Niven, ed. *Germans as Victims: Remembering the Nazi Past in Contemporary Germany* (Basingstoke, 2006), 43–61; Philipp von Hugo, "Kino und kollektives Gedächtnis' Überlegungen zum westdeutschen Kriegsfilm der fünfziger Jahre," in Bernhard Chiari, Matthias Rogg und Wolfgang Schmidt, ed. *Krieg und Militär im Film des 20. Jahrhunderts* (Munich 2003), 453–477.

6. Klaus Sigl places *The Third Man* as the most popular film in Germany in 1950, whereas Joseph Garncarz places the film at number five. See Klaus Sigl, et al, *Jede Menge Kohle: Kunst*

und Kommerz auf dem deutschen Filmmarkt der Nachkriegszeit, Filmpreise und Kassenerfolge, 1949– 1985. (Munich, 1986), 123–138; Joseph Garncarz, „Hollywood in Germany: Die Rolle des amerikanischen Films in Deutschland, 1925–1990." In Uli Jung (Hg.). *Der Deutsche Film: Aspekte seiner Geschichte von den Anfängen bis zur Gegenwart.* (Trier, 1997): 167–213.

7. Judy Adamson and Philip Stratford. "Looking for *The Third Man*: On the Trail in Texas, New York, Hollywood." *Encounter* Vol. L, No. 6 (June 1978): 39–46.

8. See Garncarz, „Hollywood in Germany," 167–213; Fehrenbach, *Cinema in Democratizing Germany* and Tim Bergfelder, *International Adventures: German Popular Cinema and European Co-Productions in the 1960s.* (New York, 2005), 1–16.

9. On the increase in violent films and war films during the Cold War in the United States, see Lary May, *The Big Tomorrow: Hollywood and the Politics of the American Way* (Chicago, 2000), 202–211.

10. In a recent conversation about *Kwai* here in Germany, the first response to the topic was "wasn't that a book?"

11. Philipp Gassert and Alan E. Steinweis, eds. *Coping with the Nazi Past: West German Debates on Nazism and the Generational Conflict, 1955–1975.* (New York and Oxford, 2006*).*

12. See esp. Moeller, *War Stories.*

Chapter One
"Eine Revolution des Films"
The Third Man, The Cold War, and Alternatives to Nationalism and Coca-Colonization in Europe

"Shelved and safe" as a twentieth-century film classic, it is probably difficult for most filmgoers today to imagine the hope and enthusiasm that greeted the 1949 release of Carol Reed's *The Third Man* in Europe. Based upon a short novel by Graham Greene, *The Third Man*—set in a postwar ally-occupied Vienna—tells the story of the naive American writer, Holly Martins (Joseph Cotten), who discovers the corrupt activities of his allegedly murdered American friend Harry Lime (Orson Welles), and reluctantly helps the British police officers, Calloway and Paine (Trevor Howard, Bernard Lee) apprehend him. A romantic subplot focuses upon his unrequited infatuation for his friend's former lover, Anna Schmidt (Alida Valli), a Czech woman with a forged Austrian passport. Reed added to the basic "melodrama" of the plot by filming on location in Vienna; casting a distinguished collection of American, Italian, British, German, Austrian, and Russian players; using a multi-lingual script (English, German, and some Russian); adding a striking score by the zither player Anton Karas; and employing exceptional camera work. The film won the Grand Prize at the Cannes Film Festival that year; the score became perhaps the best known tune in the world in the early 1950s, and thousands of filmgoers all over the world flocked into the theatres to see it (Figures 1.1 and 1.2).

The movie was of particular interest to German speaking audiences, because it was actually filmed on location in the city of Vienna and cast a number of respected and popular Austrian and German stage actors, such as Paul Hörbiger, Ernst Deutsch, Erich Ponto, and Hedwig Bleibtreu.[1] Special emphasis was placed in the press upon the fact that the film would open in Germany at the same time as in other West European countries, even before the opening in the U.S., suggesting a gesture of reconciliation toward German-speaking audiences.[2] When the dubbed version opened in Germany's major theatres in January 1950, the response was overwhelming. In Hamburg, in addition to

Figure 1.1. Alida Valli and Joseph Cotten as Anna Schmidt and Holly Martins in *The Third Man*. (Courtesy: Deutsche Kinemathek, Berlin/Studiocanal)

Figure 1.2. Orson Welles as Harry Lime in *The Third Man*. (Courtesy: Deutsche Kinemathek, Berlin/Studiocanal)

very large audiences, there were even public requests that the film be screened in the original, English-language version. The *Filmblätter, Berlin,* for example, reported that by 17 March 1950, "every tenth Berliner"—an audience of 350,000— had seen *The Third Man*. When the film opened in East Berlin, 22,000 advance tickets were sold in the first two days.[3]

During the shooting of the film in early 1949, entire sections of Vienna were closed to the Austrian public, as Isa Hohmann noted in the *Bühne und Film, Berlin,* but Austrians were excited rather than resentful; they were proud that their city had been chosen by Reed as the ideal setting for his next film and pleased that "the Austrian people in the film would be played by Austrians." As if to underline the diplomatic significance of the filming, Hohmann begins the article by giving the entire plot of Reed's suspense thriller away and focuses upon the cooperation between Austrians and English: "das dürfte heut am Hohen Markt sein, wo die Engländer drehen!" ("The British should be filming at the High Market today!") Reed's decision to shoot on location had significant meaning to Austrians, as the presence of the British was interpreted as a gesture of cultural exchange, even as Hohmann's article relied on metaphors of occupation, with Reed as a kind of military leader with an excellent command of his film "crew." From the outset, Carol Reed's *The Third Man* was understood to be more than just another movie[4] (Figures 1.3 and 1.4).

Figure 1.3. "A revolution in film,"
"future-oriented community produc-
tion"—such comments marked the
German reception of *The Third Man.*
(Courtesy: Deutsches Institut für
Filmkunde, Frankfurt/Studiocanal)

Figure 1.4. Director Carol Reed towers over his "script girl," as Peggy McClafferty was
referred to in the caption to this publicity photo, which accompanied the article by Isa
Hohmann. (Courtesy: Studiocanal)

Indeed, the image of postwar European cooperation marked German discussions of *The Third Man*. The *Filmblätter, Berlin* "recognized in the film the first work of an explicit European spirit." "This was a significant example of a European community production," noted the *Frankfurter Neue Presse*. The *Schwäbische Zeitung* referred to it as "a truly international film." Austrian press promoters for London Films gave producer Alexander Korda credit for being "the first foreigner who did not simply bring his films into the country, but who risked putting together a genuinely English-Austrian production." The *Telegraf am Abend-Berlin* discussed the possible significance of this "European" dimension of the film: "The German London Film Society shows the way to the European film. *The Third Man* ... is a beginning with a good deal of potential: that would be something to show the world that the old Europe still lives and that it can exemplify culture, even in the modern context of film. What could be attained if the best actors ... directors ... architects ... [and] ... technicians were assembled [for the purpose of creating] great films." The issue here was both the reintegration of Germany into the European community and more significantly the establishment of Europe as a single living culture, the film being an exemplar of that culture. *The Third Man* was a model of such a community production, a signal instance of an independent European production that exemplified the possibility of a European *Gemeinschaft* (community). Walter Lenning offered a theory of internationalism in a critical essay entitled "New Ways Toward Community Productions," which was distributed to newspapers through the German London Films affiliate. *The Third Man* was an example of a film that showed what a genuine internationalism could contribute to the quality of a film, particularly in comparison to contemporary examples of German and Austrian films, which remained anchored in nationalism.[5]

What were the most significant dimensions of this internationalism? One aspect was the cast of performers. Lenning noted that the German and Austrian actors in particular regained their stature as stage artists via their *Third Man* performances, as they did not function merely as nationalist stereotypes (Figure 1.5). Victor Ally praised the characteristic of the star ensemble, which, instead of relying upon "the industrialization of the star," used the ensemble conventions of the stage to exhibit international talent. Moreover, the shift from star to star ensemble also served the purpose of highlighting the realistic plight of postwar Vienna, as it drew attention to the situation of the characters rather than to a particular "star." "The casting of the major roles," wrote the *Freie Presse, Bielefeld*, "offers an impressive example of what European community production means."[6]

Another significant dimension of the film's internationalism had to do with its depiction of the city of Vienna. In contrast to most German and Austrian productions that "sweetened" and "*verkitscht*" (kitschified) the city in order to

Figure 1.5. "Whoever misses this film, misses more than just a film." *Der Abend, Berlin*'s review along with the photos of the cast highlights the cultural investment placed in the international dimensions of *The Third Man*. (Courtesy: Deutsches Institut für Filmkunde, Frankfurt/Studiocanal)

render it a good export article, *The Third Man* showed a very different city, presumably the "real" city: "meeting place and whirlpool of all the peoples of the European Southeast, today, an object of contention between the Super Powers, just like Berlin. This is the Vienna depicted in *The Third Man*."[7] The popularity of the film and its new spin on Vienna led another reviewer to point out that "the fear of the contemporary film was without foundation." Why was it that foreign producers had to tell German filmmakers about their own backyard?[8] The "fear" of the contemporary film had to do with German filmmakers' tendency to prefer the *Heimatfilm* genre that romanticized the German rural landscape and tended to avoid the chaotic milieu of the postwar cities.[9] The popularity of *The Third Man* in Germany suggested to contemporary critics that German audiences were capable of absorbing and being edified by more "realistic" fare, fare that showed "the authentic face of the defeated … [where] no quick reconstruction ethos insinuates itself. Here, the consequences of a war in the face of the people and their surroundings after the disintegration. The truth, finally. A grandiose film."[10]

Shortly after the war's end, "*Trümmerfilme*" (Rubble films), depicting the rubble of the German present and uncertainties about the future of Germany's reconstruction, enjoyed some success, such as Wolfgang Staudte's *Die Mörder sind unter uns* (The Murderers are among us), a film depicting a communist survivor of a concentration camp and an embittered medical doctor and former soldier coping with resignation, guilt, and defeat amidst the ruins of Berlin. However, by the early 1950s, the agenda of many German films, notably the genre of the *Heimatfilm*, became one of emphasizing a healing, romanticized image of "home" that blended out the rubble and conflicts of the present and instead focused upon the rural countryside as a source of ethical stability and community cooperation. *Heimatfilms* introduced an ideological basis for a reconstruction of German nationalism in the postwar period that sought to blend out the legacy and implications of World War II. *The Third Man* recalled the "rubble films" in its emphasis upon the troubled present, and its success suggested to a number of critics that German audiences might possibly be capable of confronting the challenges of reconstructing a new postwar German nation without necessarily escaping from the present and the past it implied (Figure 1.6). Yet, at the same time, *The Third Man* also appealed to German audiences' tendency to define themselves as primarily victims of war—"the

Figure 1.6. The rubble of postwar Vienna in undramatic broad daylight. (left to right) Joseph Cotten and Carol Reed on the set of *The Third Man*. (Courtesy: Deutsche Kinemathek, Berlin/Studiocanal)

defeated"—rather than as aggressors. Paradoxically, it tapped into the appeal of the *Heimatfilm* genre with its use of the folk zither soundtrack that became a huge hit worldwide in the early 1950s.[11]

In addition to its internationalism and its realism, the film was praised for its "unifying effect." The film managed to combine art and entertainment, high and popular culture. It was this combination that made the film special, the ability to fuse two normally opposed realms and thus offer a third alternative of sorts. If the Austrian film distributor newsletter offered theatre owners the rather cynical tip of dividing their advertising strategies to suit the "type" of theatre where the film would be playing: if "sensational" then to focus upon that aspect, and if "cultured" then to focus upon the film's "quality," film critics and film clubs were preoccupied with how Reed managed to bring the two together and whether this fusion in film might provide a model for social and cultural relations in general. The mark of a production that managed to combine these two normally opposed realms of art and entertainment was its "unifying effect," which unsurprisingly had a number of connotations. Different critics attributed different levels of importance to the script of Graham Greene, the direction of Carol Reed, the international cast, the camera work of Robert Krasker, the music of Anton Karas, and, finally, the unusual and wholly unexpected ending of the film. However, they all agreed that it added up to a "unified whole": "the unbelievable and unusually intensive effect ... is based upon the artistic cooperation of all the intellectual, technical, and organizational strengths that carry this unusual film."[12]

This film "unifies the highest art and one hundred percent entertainment"; that, despite its many details, had "an inner and outer closure, a density of atmosphere, captured only rarely in a few filmic masterpieces, such as those by a John Ford or a William Wyler." "People fight over the value or lack of value of German films but never seem to find a liberating way out of the labyrinth of the dream factory. *The Third Man* does." While the "dream factory" in Germany and Hollywood continued to offer unedifying escapism, *The Third Man* confronted the public with something else: like a Van Gogh or a Cezanne painting, it offered "a true microcosm of human manners, thoughts, and feelings," a merciless depiction of the nihilism of the postwar years. Greene's stories are "*menetekel,* branded upon our skin, yet they carry forgiveness in their wake." In *The Third Man,* "the normality of his people and their circumstances become more apparent, more tangible—verifiable—to us here, who can exchange experiences with the film's characters." What German films needed was not formalist literary experiments, another critic argued; rather, a new way was assured via "the visual richness that satisfies both the primitive need for narrative as well as the more refined tastes." As Karl Klaer noted, while Reed's apparently seamless narrative was composed of over 1400 cuts, "the most striking aspect of [Reed's] directorial technique is the compelling rhythm of the images, the precise shift of the camera's perspective within fractions of a second, and the dialogues, cut up in surrealistic sketches that, in spite of everything, flow into a seamless whole."[13]

This "aesthetic" complexity, which nonetheless amounted to a "seamless whole," was precisely what German movie-goers needed. Because the film offered a compelling story without resorting to the standard film formulas: stereotypical characters, romanticized rural settings, flashbacks, and bombastic music, it was a film that could be viewed several times, and therefore a "filmic film" that could educate the German public to think critically (again) about art, to remove the taint of Nazi propaganda.[14] Teachers assumed that *The Third Man* would educate viewers to distinguish good from bad films, that is, to see through the ruse of filmic conventions, to become more conscious of their affect on one's feelings. This accorded with the assumption that Germans, by way of a careful viewing of *The Third Man*, could learn to work with their heads rather than their hearts and so prevent themselves from being manipulated by propaganda (again). In this sense, art could serve a decidedly political function by reeducating German audiences.[15]

Reeducating them in the tradition of Western capitalism, of course. For Eastern bloc film critics in Berlin, another divided "international" venue, called attention to the potentially ideological function of the film's claims to "internationalism," "realism," and "unity." For example, the notion that the film portrayed the "real Vienna" was contested; Berlin film critics in the Eastern sector rejected the image as "real"; they saw it as surreal, because, as Hans Winge noted, no one seems to live in this Vienna except for the actors. Therefore, it was merely a negative version of the romanticized bell-jar image of the city. Moreover, the assumption that criminals could roam free and find protection in the East, was clearly anti-communist propaganda. Reed had not produced a work of art; rather, he had merely aestheticized (*"veredelt"*) a crime film in order to make a profit. What was important to Winge was to question the film's claims to artistic status, as such claims presupposed a neutral standpoint the film clearly did not have.[16]

Carol Reed took particular interest in the film's reception in Germany, and in an interview with a German newspaper noted that the tendency to criticize the film as anti-communist propaganda tended to come from Germany, that is, from Berlin, whereas the British and the French did not raise the issue. The possible reasons given included Germany's proximity to the Iron Curtain, not shared by the other European countries, which suggested that the criticism of the film's claims to neutrality was confined to limited geographic space and thus not applicable elsewhere; indeed, as one magazine noted, "probably just [communist] propaganda."[17]

Thus, one way the film's marketers framed *The Third Man* was as a neutral aesthetic product, exemplified by its internationalism, its realism, and its unity of effect. To some degree, these characteristics—in a German context—were perceived to have political implications, insofar as they might assist in the task of making German audiences more critical and hence less susceptible to ideological "control." However, this capability was contingent upon the film's status as a neutral aesthetic object, and publicity for the film did everything in its power to market the film as an object of art beyond the sordid politics of the postwar world, as exemplified in its reception. Insofar as Eastern and communist oriented critics attacked the film, they did so by attacking its claims to internationalism and neutrality; indeed, they rejected its status as art, because they perceived it as ideologically biased in favor of the West.

The Politics of Producing *The Third Man*: Cold War and Post–Cold War Perspectives

The seeming idealism of the film's reception contrasted sharply with the stunning politics that marked the production of both the film and the story. Released in Germany in the first years of a Cold War that emphasized the ideological opposition between Western and U.S. values of democracy and capitalism and Soviet values of state socialism and communism, *The Third Man* contained enough plot elements that typified this conflict, such as the effort to prevent the character Anna from being "claimed" by the Russians as a citizen of Czechoslovakia, to suggest an anti-communist impulse played a central role. The members of the film's production team—Alexander Korda, Graham Greene, David O. Selznick, and Carol Reed—were all agents of the Cold War in some manner, either literally or figuratively. Korda, Greene, and Reed had ties to British intelligence both during and after World War II, and the production of *The Third Man* involved "observing" the unstable political state of affairs between Eastern Europe and the Soviet Union.[18] On the other side of the Atlantic, David Selznick, the film's U.S. producer, was an avid Cold Warrior and wished to see an increased emphasis upon the U.S. role as an anti-communist force in the film (see Figure 1.7).

However, *The Third Man* went beyond the polarities of the Cold War, which certainly helps to explain the film's "transpolitical" entertainment value even in the East, where audiences likewise filled the movie theatres, despite the aspects of anti-communist bias noted by East German critics. Several dimensions ultimately shaped its politics: most importantly, tensions between the British and U.S. film industries. The Hungarian born, British national producer of the film, Alexander Korda, made an effort throughout his career to promote and

Figure 1.7. This publicity still—showing Joseph Cotten distributing CARE packages to Austrian children—links the production of *The Third Man* to U.S. Cold War politics. Interestingly, this still was not reproduced in any German newspapers or reviews of the film I read, nor was this theme—certainly one that would have interested Selznick—ever given a place in the film itself. (Courtesy: Studiocanal)

protect the British film industry from the incursions of Hollywood, favoring a stance of relative autonomy for his British film team. Ironically, in the case of *The Third Man*, his efforts led to a distinct downplaying of Cold War tensions in the film to counter the nationalistic bias of producer David O. Selznick.

This clash between Selznick, Korda, and Reed reflected the cultural imperialist dimension of the U.S./European, especially the U.S./British relationship, because the British film industry had been nursing its resentment toward the dominant American film industry for some time—with some justification.[19] For example, according to Orson Welles, Korda was more or less forced to give the U.S. production rights to Selznick in exchange for the use of the two lead actors under contract to him: Joseph Cotten and Alida Valli. In a later conversation described by Welles in an interview with Peter Bogdanovich, Korda is reported to have said to Selznick that he (Korda) hoped he would not die before Selznick so as to prevent Selznick from going to the cemetery to scratch Korda's name from his tombstone.[20] Selznick also tried to influence other aspects of the production. Yet, by and large, Selznick's extensive memos sent to sent to Reed and Greene during the production of the film were deliberately ignored, most notably, the suggestion to rename the film and to highlight the Cold War thematically by drawing more attention to the role of the Americans in Vienna.[21] Thus, the conflict between Selznick and the production team of *The Third Man* in many ways symbolized the hope for the possibility of an independent European (British) film industry.

On the level of the "authorship" of both the film and the screenplay, several types of cultural politics, revealed in the critical and debated reception of the film, may be discerned. First, the later effort to link the core creative impulse to Orson Welles instead of to Carol Reed by reference to the number of similarities between *The Third Man* and *Citizen Kane* once again gave the credit back to the Americans. To some degree, this was linked to Welles's status as an *enfant terrible* (a controversial figure) in America, a Europeanized American director at odds with the Hollywood glamour machine. However, Welles disputed this reading of his dominant role in the production and linked it instead to the nature of his absence as a character in the film; the object of fascination, interest, and discussion of all the main characters. His contribution to the film of its most famous "cuckoo clock" lines has tended to be read as the tip of the iceberg. Welles denied the theory that he took over the direction of *The Third Man*. He noted explicitly, it was "Carol's film and Korda's" (i.e. not Selznick's).[22]

It was, of course, also Graham Greene's film, and Greene's contribution of the screenplay, which he insisted had begun as a full-fledged story rather than a mere "treatment," reinforced the film's artistic ambitions as a European literary adaptation, particularly vis-à-vis Hollywood. However, Greene's authorship of the short novel and the multiple screenplays that followed it become slightly relativized when the dynamics of story creation are taken into account and a connection is revealed between the film's German reception and the cultural politics of the relationship between the story and the film. The reception and distribution of the published story after the film's release will complicate the "story" further. Overall, the colorful relationship between the story and film reflect the shifting priorities of postwar filmmakers away from the classical, canonical adaptation of the prewar years to a more dynamic and openended relationship between the two media. Indeed, David Selznick's irritating interventionism reflects the clash between the old model of classical, fidelity cinema competing with new, postwar forms of auteurism that prioritized experimentation over fidelity to an "original" text.[23]

Within the context of the ideological dynamics of the Cold War, the creation of the story of *The Third Man* and the fortunes of its major villain, Harry Lime, take on the cast of a subtextual espionage thriller involving a British intelligence officer and former superior of Greene's in the British Secret Intelligence Service (SIS), Kim Philby. Philby was a double agent for the Russians during his years at the SIS, and his long friendship with Greene raised questions about what Greene "knew" of Philby's actions, as well as his own ambiguous relationship to the cultural absolutes of the Cold War in relationship to his literary interest in "the grey zones" of human motivation.

According to Michael Shelden's biography of Greene, the screenplay of the film was considerably enhanced by stories related to Greene by a Viennese journalist named Peter Smolka, who told him about their mutual acquaintance Kim Philby's anti-fascist resistance in the Vienna uprisings against Nazi occupation in the 1930s and alerted Greene to the underground tunnel network in the city; apparently, Philby had smuggled a number of communist resistors out of the city via the sewage tunnels. When Philby returned to England, he became one of the most notorious moles in the history of the Cold War, having infiltrated into the highest ranks of British intelligence before defecting to the Soviet Union in the early 1960s.[24]

Smolka was asked to sign a release form during the making of the film waiving all rights of authorship, which he signed. The entire connection was kept as a "private joke" between Reed and Greene, according to Schelden, with the only overt reference being a cryptic mention of Smolka's name actually written into the film itself in an early scene when Major Calloway directs his driver to a military bar, apparently called "Smolka." Greene and Smolka's historical connection to Kim Philby, as well as the possibility that the "Third Man," Harry Lime, is an imaginative reworking of Greene's preoccupation with Philby's communist history, which included the courageous actions in Vienna and a Jewish communist intellectual spouse, but also, more problematically, a studied unwillingness during World War II of taking the German resistance to Hitler seriously, certainly deepens the film's connections to the moral tensions of the Cold War and its immediate history.

However, from a post–Cold War perspective, the Greene/Philby/Smolka connection assumes a different cast. Shorn of the moral absolutes of the Cold War opposition between democracy and communism that made it necessary to disguise the Smolka subtext, today, ironically, this connection highlights the internationalism of the film's production and authorship, in many ways reflecting and mirroring the German reception of the film and the central impulses of the film's aficionados—*Europäische Gemeinschaftsarbeit* (European community work). After all, Smolka rescinded his rights willingly, and the authenticity of the story and the clear knowledge of Vienna the film reflects are more readily accounted for by the inside knowledge of a Viennese journalist than by the nostalgic tales about the origin of the story related by Reed and Greene, which suggested that the decidedly British Greene stayed in Vienna for a few days and "absorbed the atmosphere" or that Reed and Greene happily collaborated over coffee at Maxim's without incident.[25] Hence, the "collaboration" that went into the creation and production of *The Third Man*, understood within both a Cold War and post–Cold War context, highlights the unseemly political dimensions, as well as the international dimensions, of the film's history.

The relationship between the published story of *The Third Man* and the film cannot be understood within the conventional chronological model of fidelity. Rather, the dynamics of the cultural Cold War created a three way dynamic that might be characterized as "story/film/published story." Not only did the story appear after the film, "oddly enough," as the *Rundschau Köln* noted, but the French translation appeared before the English original.[26] Moreover, the story was considerably modified for American audiences in order to bring it into line with the film, that is, to remove as many references as possible to the Cold War, which are much more explicit in the original British version. These two variations on the story, the Cold War version—which included critical and "off-color" references both to the U.S. and the Soviet Union—and the more "neutral" version—where these references had been removed—were published in different countries. The U.S. and France had translations of the neutral version, whereas the Cold War version circulated in Germany. The more explicit Cold War references in Greene's original British version had already been pretty much expurgated from the film, and Greene's own ambivalent relationship to the published work suggested that he ultimately preferred the toning down of the Cold War dimension in the film, opening his preface to the published story with the line, "*The Third Man* was never written to be read but only to be seen"[27] (see Figure 1.8).

Nonetheless, *The Third Man* as a published work is a significant—though small—part of Greene's literary oeuvre, and

Figure 1.8. Joseph Cotten and Alida Valli on the set of *The Third Man*. Cotten appears to be holding a book as well as script pages—the image indirectly references the film's themes of "high" and "popular" literature as well as its own literary precedent: Greene's as then unpublished story. (Courtesy: Studiocanal)

the existence of the two versions sheds light on the central role of Cold War politics in the three way dynamic of the adaptation.[28] As it turns out, the expurgated version was published in the U.S. not due to virulently anti-communist editing teams at Viking, as was originally thought, but coincidentally. Greene and Carol Reed had produced this version of the story to pass on to the American and Soviet officers in Vienna to attain their permission to film, and Greene sent this version to the U.S. publisher by mistake.[29] Ironically, it was David Selznick, a great advocate of linking the marketing of films to literary "originals," who encouraged Greene to publish the story to publicize the film.[30]

Of course, Selznick had originally wanted more on the Cold War, but both the film and later editions of the story would eliminate this dimension to achieve a balance among the contending forces. Thus, though both Greene and Reed repeatedly disputed any expressly political motivations, focusing instead upon their desire to entertain, their effort to sustain a balance between East and West can certainly be interpreted as a political act on two levels.[31] First, to distance the film and its makers from the Cold War politics (for example, the Philby connection) in which all were obviously involved, thus increasing the international appeal of the film as a "disinterested" work of film art. Second, it was also an effort to create a cultural document that sought to address the problem of bringing Europe back into the world community on terms different from those envisioned by the United States. In short, Reed and Greene were primarily interested in casting light upon the future relationship between the United States and Europe, rather than focusing on the politics of East vs. West.

Reading *The Third Man*: Alternative Connections Between Politics and Culture

On 11 March 1950, shortly after *The Third Man's* release in Austria and a month after its release in the U.S., a very brief, apparently descriptive, article on a Viennese review of the film appeared in the *New York Times:* "The Austrian Communist evening newspaper, *Der Abend,* today called the film, *The Third Man,* "a foul libel on Vienna and the Viennese." In the film, which had its premiere here last night, Vienna appeared as "a mouldy heap of ruins, half cemetery, half night club; a macabre robbers' den where child murderers, pencillin swindlers, ... idiots, and international police rush about," the newspaper said."[32] That the *New York Times* would label an Austrian newspaper "communist" and quote from a critical review of *The Third Man* suggested that it defined the paper's criticism primarily in terms of the Cold War opposition between Western democracy and Soviet Communism, implying that a pro-communist paper was suggesting—ostensibly inaccurately—the film was "anti-communist" and thus an ideological endorsement for Western capitalist values. Surely in the minds of many American readers, the Austrian newspaper's political leanings as sympathetic to communism would have discredited its evaluation of the film by definition. Indeed, it might also have provided *New York Times* readers with the reassurance that as long as films such as *The Third Man* were being rejected by "Communist propaganda organs" like *Der Abend,* they were serving their function as agents of democratic culture or as agents of anti-communism. In any event, for the recently opened film, the comment offered a certain domestic propaganda of its own, playing with the cultural ammunition of the Cold War to get a few more folks into the theatres. This impulse was vaguely at odds with those that wanted to make sure the film was marketed as politically neutral, not so much as an aesthetic object, as in Europe, but rather as simply light entertainment.[33]

Though *Der Abend* was indeed a "communist" newspaper, one of several circulating in Austria at the time,[34] it seems to have been critical of the film less as a result of any overt representations of Cold War politics than of the representation of the city of Vienna, which to any Austrian publication would have signified the representation of high culture. The city's affiliation with "high culture"—its music, history, art, and stage productions—were key aspects of its national identity, a source of international prestige as well as a point of contrast to the other major German-speaking city in Europe, Berlin, which was now associated with a history of militarism and defeat. Vienna's cultural heritage was often invoked as a force of resistance to Nazi occupation, a claim that would not hold up on close inspection after the war but that nonetheless did its part to dissociate Austria from discredited German cultural institutions.[35] By establishing a link between Vienna and Berlin as divided, war torn cities, *The Third Man* called into question this division of identities and suggested—through its linking of "high culture" with images of corruption—that high cultural institutions were complicitous in the nationalistic hysteria that promoted European destruction through war. The aesthetics of Reed's film, with its stark contrasts and off-center angles, reinforce an image of the city of Vienna as worn and decadent, a pawn of corruption and destruction, a metaphor both for the decay of the cultural foundations of a society and the unfortunate infiltration of a new type of culture: "a mouldy heep of ruins, half-cemetery, half nightclub"—a shadow of its former self.

Clearly, such a depiction might have reinforced the elements of the film that explicitly delve into the charged symbolism of the Cold War, as noted by East Berlin critics when the film was released: the harboring of the criminal Harry Lime in the Russian zone, the seedy figure of Baron Kurtz and his Russian affiliations, and the generally shifty nature of the Russian police. However, more apparent is the clear association of the "darkness" of Vienna with the idea of high culture, an association that is metaphorically reinforced throughout the film, especially in scenes showing the apartments of Harry and Anna or the mysterious "collection" in Dr. Winkel's parlor. These metaphorical affiliations between corruption and high culture are crystallized in Harry Lime's famous comment to Holly under the Ferris wheel associating the Renaissance with terror and bloodshed and the more peaceful "democratic culture" of Switzerland with the cuckoo clock: "You know what the fellow said—in Italy, for thirty years under the Borgias, they had warfare, terror, murder, and bloodshed, but they produced Michelangelo, Leonardo da Vinci, and the Renaissance. In Switzerland, they had brotherly love … five hundred years of democracy and peace—and what did that produce? The cuckoo clock."[36] Lime's sinister, ironic contrast and the dark images of Viennese high culture were nonetheless compelling to most viewers of the film, if not to *Der Abend*. Spoken as they were by a famous American actor, Orson Welles, playing a very corrupt American, Harry Lime, the contrast created a productive link between politics and culture in a film that called into question the oppositional logic of the political Cold War and focused attention on the political meaning of culture in the developing relationship between the United States and Europe (see Figure 1.9).

In the 1950s, English language reviewers critical of the film's reputation as little more than sophisticated "entertainment" tended to associate its "political" message with the figure of Major Calloway and his role as representative of the Western occupation of Vienna. Symbolizing law, order, and justice, Calloway embodies the conventional understanding of the West's role in bringing political and economic order back into the chaos of postwar Europe. Cool, detached, and objective, Calloway's dogged pursuit of Harry Lime and his apparent contempt for Martins reinforces his separate, remote function. His purpose is the task of imposing order from without by rea-

Figure 1.9. A rarely seen publicity shot for *The Third Man*: a smiling Orson Welles chats with a policeman—very likely a film extra—in front of the Vienna Parliament. (Courtesy: Deutsche Kinemathek, Berlin/Studiocanal).

sonably just means. His goal is clear and unambiguous; he never waivers in his insistence upon the priority of apprehending Lime. Significantly, he is profoundly emotionally detached from the intrigue involving the central three characters: Anna, Holly, and Harry. Of course, emotional detachment is a prerequisite for assuming the role of objective arbiter of political affairs. Calloway triumphs in the end, eliminating the criminal and presumably destroying the penicillin racket, saving lives in the process. His role is crucial to our sense of the moral center of the film; however, he is not a player in the cultural politics the film is most interested in.

Those politics have to do less with the "official political" Cold War between East and West than with the opposition between the concepts of "high" and "popular culture" and their *political* significance for the relationship between America and Europe during the Cold War. Far from simply operating as "taste categories" or as crude oppositional indicators of cultural hierarchy, the drama surrounding Holly, Harry, and Anna is best understood in relationship to Reinhold Wagnleitner's concept of "U.S. cultural imperialism," and the ways America's cultural politics in Europe during the Cold War reflected both a shared conception of high culture, as well as a decided ambivalence about the relationship of U.S. popular culture to the future of European culture.[37] Unlike the concept of "Americanization," which connotes a one-sided dynamic between U.S. cultural dominance and European victimization (this is a widespread notion in Europe), the idea of "cultural imperialism," Wagnleitner argues, "ran on the psychological track of *defending the Occident*," thus presupposing a fundamental interconnection between these generally opposed concepts of high and popular culture.[38] By deconstructing the opposition between high and popular culture by noting the ways both concepts were eminently political and offering a meditation on the cultural limits of America's role in Europe, the film undermines the Cold War politics that situated the major dilemma of the mid-twentieth century as that between East and West. There was, and indeed is, a *Third Man*.

Analysis of the aesthetic dynamics in the film, particularly apparent in the German language reception, has tended to overlook their socio-cultural implications. Critics dissatisfied with Graham Greene's definition of the film as primarily "entertainment" often noted that it was "more" than this, had somehow to be "more" than that, but were uncertain how to conceptualize this "more."[39] In light of recent history and the ever increasing autonomy of Europe as an economic, political, and cultural entity, I think that this "more" is linked to the ways in which the film offers—and offered—a meditation upon the autonomous, political function of culture independent of the "official" political scene. It does this through the metaphorical function of the three characters Holly Martins, Harry Lime, and Anna Schmidt, the dimensions of "culture" each represents, their interrelatedness in terms of the increasingly significant relationship between the United States and Europe, and finally, the significance of that relationship for the future.[40]

In a 1987 review of Joseph Cotten's autobiography in the *New York Times,* Benjamin Stein called Cotten's role in *The Third Man,* "the most subtle, thought-provoking metaphor for the American meddling in postwar Europe ever to appear on screen."[41] Stein's comment is relevant to the film's resonance with viewers in 1950s Germany. While many associate the film with Orson Welles's brief appearance, it is the character of Holly Martins who clearly dominates the proceedings.[42] Critics have interpreted Martins's "meddling" in terms of his function as a metaphor either for "Western values" or else for "American innocence," both very broad categories that do not really get to the heart of what makes Martins such an appealing, problematic figure.[43] Which "values" does Martins represent in Vienna? What are the contours of his character? Holly Martins arrives on the scene as a self-described writer, but we do not learn what sort of a writer until his conversation with Major Calloway in the bar. When Calloway remarks that Martins's description of his relationship to Lime "sounds like a cheap novellette," Martins responds: "I write cheap novellettes." We learn that Martins is a writer of popular, western fiction, but he is also a writer of "cheap novellettes." He identifies with both characterizations of his work, thus mirroring an important aspect of his function in the film: a writer who identifies and promotes the values of American popular culture in a foreign land, but who at the same time does not identify with those values; instead, Martins identifies with the European critique of that culture, the European contempt for "popular" things. He attempts to "appreciate" the values of European "high culture," such as when he praises Anna's performance in the Josefstadt theatre or remarks on Dr. Winkel's "collection," yet Martins is dismissed by those Europeans he attempts to impress as a "vulgar" American, someone, to quote the comedians Mull and Rucker, "who wouldn't know a great painting if it bit him on the inner thigh."[44] Martins's ignorance is most clearly depicted in his lecture on the "crisis of faith" in contemporary literature, where he finds himself speaking on matters he knows nothing about, reinforcing the European stereotype of the vulgar, uncouth American. However, he shares this concept of himself, which renders him profoundly vulnerable and metaphorically effeminate, as his name, "Holly," suggests.

Nonetheless, Martins attempts to present his masculine function by relying upon the values of his own fiction to find out the "truth" about his friend, Harry Lime. As several critics of the film have noted, his motives here are profoundly conflicted.[45] At times, he seeks the type of justice associated with the values of Western pulp fiction; at other times, he is most interested in ingratiating himself with Anna or preserving the good memories of his friendship with Lime, as it is this friendship that gives him a sense of identification with the values of "high culture." Throughout his journey, he literally leaves pillage in his wake, as his indiscrete investigations lead to, among other things, the needless death of the porter. However, this profoundly transgressive dimension of his presence in Vienna is not just destructive. In the character of Sergeant Paine, we recognize that element of European society that identifies with the values of American popular culture. Recognizing Martins's name and praising his work—"I like a good Western … you can pick them up and put them down any time"—Paine's forthright presence reinforces our sense that those values represented by popular culture can be understood beyond their apparent opposition to the values of "high culture." Thus, Martins's ambivalent relationship to the popular culture he represents—both as "lesser than" high culture and, at the same time, appealing and popular—mirrors the forceful role that culture will play in European society in the postwar decades.

Holly Martins's friendship with Harry Lime and the frequency with which the film plays on the similarity between the names, encouraging a "confusion of identity" of sorts, was noted by a number of critics, and the significance of this similarity is worth discussing.[46] Very much based upon a form of hero worship, for Martins, Harry Lime represented all those dimensions of culture he seemed to lack: wit, flare, a forceful presence, a worldliness that can be linked to Martins's admiration for European high culture. The clear masculine connotations of the name "Harry" and its simultaneously close relationship to the more feminine name "Holly" represents the interconnecting, as well as the oppositional aspects, of the high vs. popular culture dichotomy. Particularly intriguing in this subjective identification/confusion between the two characters are the ways in which the transgressive dimension of Harry Lime's presence is so clearly linked to the concept of high culture, a fact crystallized in his speech by the Prater wheel in which he associates the democratic culture of Switzerland with cultural mediocrity and the "violent" culture of the Renaissance with high culture. It seems to me that the fact that Harry Lime is an American, signifies those dimensions of high culture that American and European elites shared, and notably, the underside of that conception: the annihilation of the other, the association of the spread of the values of that culture with a forceful imperialism.[47] Particularly noteworthy is that the two—Harry and Holly—coexist and cannot be separated from one another. The dynamic between Harry and Holly represents the complex dynamic of U.S. cultural imperialism, the interrelationship between both conceptions of culture, American and European, interacting in a world where America now had definitive control over the future of Europe.

In this context, the "third man" turns out to be a woman, Anna Schmidt's definitive role as the cultural wild card, the figure who literally embodies the dilemma of the European continent. Having been twice defeated, she finds herself in the predicament of being uncompromisingly loyal to a man who betrays her and contemptuous of a man who loves her. Her slips of identification regarding Holly and Harry mark her latent awareness of the relationship between the two; moreover, as a Czech with a false Western passport she has already decided in favor of the West, though she is in danger of being "claimed" by the Russians. She is the European pawn between the East and the West: the third man (Figure 1.10). Critics in the 1950s noted the significance of Anna's role as it manifested itself in the "surprise ending" of the film. Though commentators like Andrew Sarris noted that Anna's repudiation of Martins was also the repudiation of the director and the writer as European authors, rather than noting the cultural and political significance of Anna's role, Sarris shifts instead to a gendered analysis, linking the "social commentary" of the film to "Major Calloway as the embodiment of political power at the crossroads of the Cold War," and leaving Anna to join "Reed's gallery of fatalistic heroines who ask nothing of life but that it shelter the men they love."[48] Sarris transforms the conclusion of the film, a conclusion that marks Anna as an independent political factor, into a form of subjective female irrationality. Never minding the fact that Harry is dead and can no longer be sheltered, Anna has already told Holly that she no longer "wants" Harry, though he remains a part

Figure 1.10. German publicity still that visually situates the character Anna (Alida Valli) as "the third man." Here, too, in the picture column on the left, the international cast is emphasized. (Courtesy: Deutsches Institut für Filmkunde, Frankfurt/Studiocanal)

of her.[49] She has already repudiated Harry Lime for his misdeeds. By repudiat-
ing Holly, she claims a certain territory for herself.

In their dispute over the ending to the film, Graham Greene recalled that
director Carol Reed's main argument against the generically conventional
ending was that "the *audience* (my emphasis), who had just seen Harry die,"
would find such a conclusion "unpleasantly cynical." Greene noted that he had
not been persuaded by this argument at the time; instead, he found its fore-
sight less in the audience's expectations than in Reed's "masterful direction"
and Karas's zither music. Indeed, audience expectation would have been over-
whelmingly shaped to favor Holly Martins's overtures toward Anna. With
his unusual aura of manliness and vulnerability that was noted by critics from
the outset ("Tatkraft und Verträumtsein"[50]—enterprising and day-dreamy)
and the striking camera work that placed Joseph Cotten's problematic motives
within a context less of weakness than of a sympathetic aesthetic ambivalence,
I could not believe that Anna was capable of resisting Holly. Moreover, Anna's
resistance, which is consistent throughout the film, is never used to undermine
Martins's dignity; rather, he becomes more sympathetic as a result. The final,
bittersweet notes of Karas's zither reinforce the aesthetic signals the film has
offered from the start: that, in the final analysis, America and Europe are
more different than they are similar and this in spite of the conception of
high culture and anti-communism the architects of postwar policies shared. If
Europe's high cultural pretensions had betrayed her in times of war, America's
popular culture would nonetheless have to justify its postwar presence in terms
more substantive than sentimental attachment (Figure 1.11).

What is the perspective of Europe as Anna represents it? Like the zither
music, she functions as a source of commentary upon the proceedings, in particular, on the interconnection between Harry and Holly. In her dialogues
with Martins, she consistently points out to him those elements of corruption
and moral ambiguity he seems to share with Harry. Like Harry, Holly is not
what he appears to be. When she discovers Holly in the cafe acting as decoy,
she holds forth: "honest, sensible, sober, harmless Holly Martins. Holly, what
a silly name." In other words, his betrayal of Lime is no different in its funda-
mentals from Harry's betrayal of her. When she discovers Martins loitering
around the train station as she is about to be transported outside the Russian
zone, she needles him to the point where he admits he swapped his services
to apprehend Lime for her passport. "Look at yourself, " she says to Martins
as she leaves, "they have a name for faces like that." The camera then hones in
on Martins's profile, his hat shadowing his eyes, while the rest of the face is
illuminated. One can only conclude that she means "Janus-faced," which the
Random House dictionary defines jointly as "deceitful and two-faced," but
also, more neutrally, as "having contrasting aspects." Anna's words, combined

Figure 1.11. Anna approaching the waiting Holly Martins in the final scene of *The Third Man*. She will not leave with "her hand ... through his arm" (119), as Greene had ended his story, but will walk past him without word or look. (Courtesy: Deutsche Kinemathek, Berlin/Studiocanal)

with the profile shot, offer us both possibilities and again mark a point of commentary, one might say, on the European conception of the presence of U.S. popular culture on its soil.

Anna's ambivalence vis-à-vis U.S. designs on Europe and the fundamental difference between the two societies is the basis of much of the "foreign" dialogue among the characters, dialogue that is translated by bilingual characters, but only in its barest outlines. For German speaking viewers, many of the extended dialogues, such as Anna's landlady (played by Hedwig Bleibtreu) ranting about the "invasion" of Anna's chambers by the foreigners to the porter's (Paul Hörbiger) regret at having told Holly so much ("das hat man davon, wenn man freundlich ist mit den Ausländern"—that's what one gets for being friendly to the foreigners), highlights the ambivalence the locals feel at the presence of the foreigner and the culture he brings with him. The porter puts it well when he threatens to "forget his Viennese charm" if Holly doesn't leave immediately. The complex character of cultural imperialism and the Europeans' ambivalent relationship to it is starkly and ironically represented in the crowd's suspicion that Holly may have killed the porter. Little Hansl (Herbert Halbik), having witnessed the argument between the porter and Holly, implicates him in the porter's death. The crowd outside the porter's apartments becomes restless and Anna translates for Holly: "They think you did it." As Holly flees, we know of his innocence at the same time that we know of his complicity. His dualistic approach to finding the truth has, after all, played a clear role in the porter's death.

Most critics of the film have noted the striking use of music to underscore the story. Anton Kara's zither accompaniment to *The Third Man* functions like a commentary upon both the characters and developments in the story, literally foreshadowing significant dimensions of the plot, most notably, the "surprise ending," where Anna walks past Holly, leaving him to light his ciga- rette and ponder his losses.[51] Like the complex interaction of the characters in relationship to the dichotomy between high and popular culture, the music is distinctive, because it cannot be situated squarely within that dichotomy. Containing elements of a wide range of music styles, this unique dance music stemming from the mountain regions of Austria and Bavaria functions as its own language, assuming the role of emotional commentator and, as critic Bosley Crowther wrote in 1950, "the spirit and voice of the locale."[52] Thus, against the Cold War dichotomies of East and West, high and popular, the film's music offers a variation on the theme of the local, the cultural form that cannot be classified and hence retains its creativity and expressiveness, which may account for its international popularity in the 1950s.

Though the point of view of *The Third Man* is best situated as that of the generation of World War II Europeans who still insisted upon the importance of "high culture" as a humanistic endeavor, its aesthetic open-endedness in an increasingly polarizing political climate and its critique of both European high culture and U.S. popular culture continue to be persuasive, particularly in view of the "triumph" of U.S. popular culture in Europe since 1949, when *The Third Man* was first released. Today, the question of the "coca-colonization of Europe," lacking as it does the transgressive connotation it had for many young Europeans in the 1950s,[53] raises the question of what a new united European identity will ultimately be based on, much as *The Third Man* raised exactly the same question. As a Catholic film journal put it at the time the film was released in Germany: "(Hopeless? The film does not offer an answer, just as it offers no "end." It continues in our reality. So it is up to us …) We don't want to interpret anything into the film. Yet, the unusual way in which the film shows the human being in his capacity for decision, it likewise calls us to decide."[54] With the intensification of the Cold War and increasing affluence in the 1950s, the question of European unity, and hence alternatives to "coca- colonization," were again postponed. However, in the early years of the Cold War, films such as *The Third Man* held out the hope for an internationalist alternative, even if that hope was largely confined to the realm of art.

* * *

By 1958, when the next film under discussion, *The Bridge on the River Kwai*, was released in West Germany, ideals of internationalism had given way to the realities of Cold War conflict, West German remilitarization, and the threat of nuclear war. At the same time, the increasing political stabilization and economic expansion of West Germany contributed to a greater consciousness of its own war history and the cultural implications of Germany's legacy of military defeat. Thus, an Anglo-American "war film" adaptation like *Kwai* could trigger both tremendous popular response and decided critical ambivalence about the relationship between U.S. popular culture in Germany and Germany's history of militarism.

Notes

1. All of the following references to German newspapers and London Films press releases are based upon the sources in the collections on *Der dritte Mann* at the Deutsches Filminstitut in Frankfurt, Germany and the Library of the Filmmuseum Berlin and Deutsche Kinemathek. To the extent that the names and dates of sources were not always clear, I have noted gaps or alternative possibilities. All references to the film from: *The Third Man*. Writer Graham Greene. Director Carol Reed. With Joseph Cotten, Orson Welles and Valli. London Films, 1949.

2. "*Der dritte Mann* bald auch in Deutschland," *Bühne und Film*, Berlin (24 October 1949); "*Der dritte Mann* kommt nach Deutschland, *Internationale Film Rundschau, Wien* -or- *Erste Internationale Filmzeitung, Berlin* (29 October 1949). The delay of the U.S. release was due to disputes between the U.S. producer David O. Selznick and the European producer Alexander Korda; this, however, would not have been mentioned in the publicity.

3. *Filmblätter Berlin* -or- *Film Blatt* (10 February 1950); *Filmblätter, Berlin* (17 March 1950); "Ansturm auf den Dritten Mann" *Die Welt* (31 August 1950).

4. Isa Hohmann, "Carol Reed dreht *The Third Man*", *Bühne und Film*, Berlin (28 February 1949). On the significance of Carol Reed as a film director in the late forties and early 1950s, see Robert F. Moss, *The Films of Carol Reed* (New York, 1987).

5. *Filmblätter, Berlin*, 2/1950; "*Der dritte Mann*," *Frankfurter Neue Presse* (7 January 1950); "Unsere Filmvorschau: *Der dritte Mann*," *Schwäbische Zeitung* (3 March 1950); "Ihre Leser warten auf Sascha Film Nachrichten," *Pressedienst der Sascha Film Verleih und Vertriebsges. m.b.H.* No.26 (25 January 1950); *Telegraf am Abend-Berlin* (7 January 1950); Walter Lenning, "Neue Wege Der Gemeinschaftsproduktion," *Das Neueste über ungewöhnliche Filme: Nachrichten aus Alexander Kordas Europäischer Spitzenproduktion*, No. IX(1950) (1 February 1950):6–7.

6. Victor Ally, "Vom Star zum Star-Ensemble," *Das Neueste über...*, 8; "*Der dritte Mann*," *Frankfurter Neue Presse* (7 January 1950); *Freie Presse, Bielefeld* (4 February 1950); "Sascha Erfolgs Rezepte: Reklame-Ratschlag für den österreichischen Kinobesitzer," *Sascha-Film Verleih und Vertriebs-Ges. m.b.H.*, Nr.19, *Der dritte Mann.*

7. "Menschen im Dickicht der Stadt," *Ruhr-Nachrichten* (18 March 1950).

8. HHK, "Der dritte Mann," *Der Neue Film* (23 January 1950).

9. Heide Fehrenbach, *Cinema in Democratizing Germany: Reconstructing National Identity after Hitler* (Chapel Hill and London, 1995), 148–168.

10. Ft., "Der perfekte Film." *Berliner Blatt/Die Neue Zeitung* (8 January 1950).

11. For discussions of the *Heimatfilm* genre see Fehrenbach, *Cinema in Democratizing Germany*, 148–168, and Tim Bergfelder, *International Adventures: German Popular Cinema and European Co-Productions in the 1960s* (New York, 2005), 40–44.

12. "Sascha Erfolgs Rezepte…," Nr. 19, *Der dritte Mann*; "*Der dritte Mann*," *Frankfurter Neue Presse* (7 January 1950).

13. "Der dritte Mann gesucht," 1949; "*Der dritte Mann*," *Film Dienst* (21 November 1949); "Ein Film—Ein Beispiel!" *Allgemeine Zeitung, Mainz* (12 January 1950). "Der dritte Mann wird gesucht." *Der Spiegel* (29 September 1949). "Das Neueste über ungewöhnliche Filme," *Nachrichten aus…*, No.IX. "Ein Film Ein Beispiel!," (12 January 1950); Klaer, "Ein Film Gegen Alle Theorien," *Das Neueste über…*, 4–5. Pl. "*Der dritte Mann*": Visitenkarte eines Könners," (UT) *Lüneburger Landeszeitung* (27 January 1950).

14. Klaer, 4–5; Fehrenbach, 169–210.

15. WP. "Bemerkungen zu einem Film," *Pädagogische Rundschau,* Ratzingen (July 1950); Fehrenbach, 178.

16. Hans Winge, [*Der dritte Mann*], *Neue Filmwelt* (March 1950); Horst Werning, "Der Rummel Um Den Dritten Mann," (March 1950); see also Fer. A "Verschwendeter Lorbeer," *National-Zeitung, Berlin* (8 January 1950).

17. WS. "Droht schon Gefahr der "Manier"? [source unknown] (28 January 1950); see also Wolf Schirrmacher, "Ihm glückte der große Wurf," *Weser Kurier,* Bremen (1 February 1950).

18. Michael Shelden, *Graham Greene: Eine Biographie.* Translated by Joachim Kolka. (Göttingen, 1995), 329.

19. Judy Adamson and Philip Stratford, "Looking for the Third Man: On the Trail in Texas, New York, and Hollywood," *Encounter* Vol. L, No. 6 (June 1978): 39–46; Rudy Behlmer, ed., *Memo from David O. Selznick* (New York, 1973), 444–447 ; Fehrenbach, 174–175.

20. Orson Welles/Peter Bogdanovich, *Hier Spricht Orson Welles* (Weinheim, Berlin, 1994), 354–358.

21. Adamson and Stratford, 44–45; Behlmer, ed. *Memo From: David O. Selznick,* 444–447. See also Patricia Medina Cotten, *Laid Back in Hollywood* (Los Angeles, 1998), 140 and Brigitte Timmermann and Frederick Baker, *Der Dritte Mann: Auf den Spuren eines Filmklassikers.* (Vienna, 2002), 268.

22. Welles/Bogdanovich, 354–358.

23. See especially Timothy Corrigan's persuasive reading of the shift between prewar and postwar adaptation in *Film and Literature: An Introduction and Reader.* (Upper Saddle River, New Jersey, 1999), 39–53.

24. Shelden, *Graham Greene: Eine Biographie,* 315–337.

25. Graham Greene, "Preface," in *The Third Man/The Fallen Idol* (Harmondsworth, 1976), 9. (see also the dedication). The text was originally published in 1950.

26. *Rundschau Köln* (5 April 1950).

27. Greene, *The Third Man,* 9.

28. Adamson and Stratford, 39–46.

29. Sheldon, *Graham Greene: Eine Biographie,* 337.

30. Adamson and Stratford, 41.

31. Ibid., 44.

32. *New York Times* (11 March 1950): 8.

33. Bosley Crowther, Rev. of *The Third Man, New York Times* (3 February 1950) in *The New York Times Film Reviews, A One Volume Selection: 1913–1970* (New York, 1971), 255–256.

34. Roland Graf, "Anachronism or Sting in the Flesh: The Remarkable Success of Austria's Regional Communist Newspapers, 1948-2000." URL: http://users.ox.ac.uk/~oaces/conference/papers/Roland_Graf.pdf.

35. Sigrid Löffler, *Kritiken, Portraits, Glossen.* (Vienna, 1995), 175–193 and 203–215.

36. Quoted from the URL: http://en.wikipedia.org/wiki/The_Third_Man.

37. Herbert J. Gans, *Popular Culture and High Culture* (New York, 1974); Reinhold Wagnleitner, *Coca-Colonization and the Cold War: The Cultural Mission of the United States in Austria after the Second World War* (Chapel Hill, 1994).

38. Wagnleitner, 3.

39. Graham Greene, *"The Third Man,"* *New York Times* II (19 March 1950):4:1; "Preface" 9–11.

40. For a different interpretation of the politics of the film, emphasizing the opposition between the political systems of "totalitarianism" and "democracy" see Lynette Carpenter, "'I Never Knew the Old Vienna': Cold War Politics and *The Third Man." Film Criticism* 11 (Fall-Winter 1987): 56–65. See also Lothar Schwab, "Der Identifikationsprozess im Kino-Film: Analyse des Films *Der dritte Mann,"* in K.Hickethier and J. Paech, eds. *Didaktik der Massenkommunikation 4: Modelle der Film und Fernsehanalyse* (Stuttgart, 1979), 24–62.

41. Benjamin Stein, "Citizen Kane and Hedda Hopper," *New York Times* (13 September 1987):7:1:47.

42. Carpenter, for example, bases most of her reading on Harry Lime as the central figure.

43. Carpenter, 60; James Palmer and Michael M. Riley, "The Lone Rider in Vienna: Myth and Meaning in *The Third Man," Literature/Film Quarterly* 8:1(1980):14–21.

44. Martin Mull & Allen Rucker, *The History of White People in America* (New York, 1985), 19.

45. Glenn K.S. Man, *"The Third Man*: Pulp Fiction and Art Film," *Literature/Film Quarterly* 21:3(1993): 171–177.

46. Palmer & Riley, 19; Man, 175; Morris Beja, *Film & Literature* (New York, 1979), 180.

47. See Wagnleitner, 3–4. Gertrude Koch argues that Lime's nihilism can also be linked to the fascist logic of Germany and Italy: "Das Riesenrad der Geschichte: *The Third Man* von Carol Reed," in R. Beckmann and C. Blueminger, eds. *Ohne Untertitel: Fragmente einer Geschichte des österreichischen Kinos* (Vienna, 1996), 366–375.

48. A. Sarris, "Carol Reed in the Context of His Time," *Film Culture* Vol. 3, No. 1(1957), 12,13.

49. Schwab, 42.

50. "Cannes sagt: Bester Film des Jahres," *Westfalenpost, Soest* (14 January 1950).

51. R. Manvell and J. Huntley, *The Technique of Film Music* (London, 1975), 109–10.

52. Bosley Crowther, "Music to the Fore," *New York Times* (5 February 1950): II:1:7.

53. Wagnleitner, xiii.

54. *"Der dritte Mann,"* *Katholischer Beobachter* [no date].

Chapter Two

The Bridge on the River Kwai Revisited

Combat Cinema, American Culture, and the German Past

Inundated with awards in 1958, including seven Academy Awards and three New York Film Critics Circle Awards, *The Bridge on the River Kwai,* produced by the noted Jewish/Austrian/American producer Sam Spiegel for Columbia pictures and directed by the British director David Lean, tells the story of the construction of the Singapor-Bangkok railway by British POWs (prisoners of war) for the Japanese during World War II. It is based upon the bestselling novel by the Frenchman Pierre Boulle. In the film, a captured British troop led by Colonel Nicholson (Alec Guinness) marches into a Japanese prisoner of war camp and is ordered to help construct a bridge over the river Kwai by the camp's commandant, Col. Saito (Sessue Hayakawa). A contest of wills ensues, as Nicholson objects to Saito's order, which violates the Geneva Conventions that officers are not to engage in physical labor along with their troops. Nicholson is tortured but wins the contest of wills, because Saito is under pressure to complete the bridge in a short time. Nicholson assumes command of his troops and the bridge project with great zest, motivated by a combination of British cultural arrogance, pride in British technical knowledge, and military norms that stress the importance of discipline and order in a POW situation. However, along the way, Nicholson's identification with the bridge project assumes a life of its own, and he forgets that the purpose of the bridge is to help the Japanese win the war. In the meantime, a secret British commando reluctantly led by the American Shears (William Holden), a cynical escapee of the River Kwai camp, has orders to move into the jungle and destroy the bridge. The bridge has been rigged and is ready to be destroyed when Nicholson discovers the hardware attached to the pillar of the bridge. He alerts the Japanese Colonel, but all are killed in the final skirmish that ensues. After being shot, Nicholson seems to realize his delusion and utters the line, "What have I done?" That said, his dying body collapses onto the detonator and the bridge is finally destroyed. The camp doctor, Clipton (James Donald), observing the debacle, speaks the final line: "Madness, madness"[1] (see Figures 2.1, 2.2, and 2.3).

Kwai is known in film historical annals primarily as one of the first great "on location" epic films dealing thoughtfully with the difficult theme of war and also as part of a trend toward existential "anti-war" pictures coming out of Hollywood in the late-1950s. In the U.S., the film was praised by critics, such as Bosley Crowther of the *New York Times*, as a multi-leveled picture with an anti-war message that offered action without battle scenes. U.S. critics discussed different aspects of the film, but this discussion did not lead to public controversy or political debates. Generally, the film is discussed primarily as a part of the epic oeuvre of director David Lean, which includes films such as *Lawrence of Arabia* and which succeeded in bringing the increasing numbers of television viewers back into the movie theaters.[2]

In contrast, the film launched a heated debate in Germany, when it was released in March of 1958. Prior to its release in West Germany, producer Sam Spiegel gave a press conference in Berlin. Spiegel described the film— tongue in cheek—as a "love story between a man and his bridge," a tragic anti-war picture that differed from the predominantly satirical tone of Pierre Boulle's novel. Spiegel's name held a number of important cultural and political associations for German journalists and audiences. He had produced the popular film *On the Waterfront* with Marlon Brando (German title: *Die Faust*

Figure 2.1. Colonel Nicholson (Alec Guinness) next to the wooden plaque commemorating the completion of "his" bridge in *The Bridge on the River Kwai*. Photo: Columbia. "BRIDGE ON THE RIVER KWAI," copyright 1957, renewed 1985 Columbia Pictures Industries, Inc. All Rights Reserved. (Courtesy of Columbia Pictures/Deutsche Kinemathek, Berlin)

Figure 2.2. Sessue Hayakawa as the Japanese Col. Saito and Alec Guinness as the British Col. Nicholson. Photo: Columbia. "BRIDGE ON THE RIVER KWAI," copyright 1957, renewed 1985 Columbia Pictures Industries, Inc. All Rights Reserved. (Courtesy of Columbia Pictures/Deutsche Kinemathek, Berlin)

im Nacken); he was a Jewish emigrant to the U.S.; and as Universal Pictures' representative in Berlin in the early thirties, he had been active in promoting the release of the film adaptation of Remarque's well-known anti-war novel, *All Quiet on the Western Front* in Germany to the likes of Hitler and Goebbels, "Vergeblich, wie man weiß," ("to no avail, as is known,")[3] as one critic commented. Spiegel's efforts to help remove the 1930 ban that had been placed on the film in Germany had been unsuccessful.[4]

Close attention to the reception of *The Bridge on the River Kwai* by critics, journalists, and, to some extent, the general public reveals the ways that *Kwai* became embedded in a wide-ranging cultural dialogue that touched on both contemporary debates about the German present, notably the remilitarization of West Germany and the nuclear arming of the Bundeswehr, as well as questions about the German past directly tied to the shaping of West German "memory culture" in the 1950s. To situate my study, I will begin with a brief overview of the ways scholars have dealt with the relationship between U.S. popular culture and German memory culture; I will then focus on several bodies of commentary about *Kwai*: promotional essays about the film released by Columbia Pictures' publicity division and German translations of British reviews after the film's London release, both of which reflected or explicitly stated the points of view of the U.S. and British producers of the film; German critics and commentators who linked *Kwai* to a "pro-war" point of view in the sense of a glorification of militaristic values; those who tied it to an "anti-war" point of view, thus occasionally reflecting or, more often, partially incorporating elements of the Columbia publicity; and those who classified the film as primarily "ambiguous," as seemingly promoting and criticizing war simultaneously. Some of the critics who classified the film as ambiguous sought different approaches to "pinning the film down," such as comparing the novel and the film, which in turn reflected a loosening of the still dominant "Filmwirkungs" model of filmic reception, since it opened the possibility of active interpretation. Several dimensions of what might be termed the "general public's" response to the film will also be discussed. Finally, I will look at Bernhard Wicki's popular "anti-war" film *Die Brücke* as a filmic response to *The Bridge on the River Kwai*.

THE BRIDGE ON THE RIVER KWAI - USA 1957 Regie: David Lean
Quelle: Deutsche Kinemathek

Figure 2.3. Kwai's scenic bridge explodes dramatically at the film's conclusion. Photo: Columbia. "BRIDGE ON THE RIVER KWAI," copyright 1957, renewed 1985 Columbia Pictures Industries, Inc. All Rights Reserved. (Courtesy of Columbia Pictures/ Deutsche Kinemathek, Berlin)

* * *

The relationship between U.S. popular culture and the politics of memory in 1950s West Germany has barely been studied. Those who have focused on U.S. popular culture in 1950s West Germany, such as Uta Poiger and Heide Fehrenbach, have not looked at questions of the politics of memory.[5] In turn, historians of memory culture and visual culture in West Germany have focused almost exclusively on the impact of its German forms.[6] Debates about the 1950s reflect questions of the extent to which German political and visual culture contributed to the task of active "*Vergangenheitsbewältigung*," that is, the process of acknowledging and confronting the legacy of the German war and German war crimes, or rather suppressed such issues. Concepts such as Peter Reichel's "*erfundene Erinnerung*," Robert Moeller's "selective memory," or Habbo Knoch's "*Erinnerungskultur*" or "memory culture" attempt to show the complexity of the ways questions of memory manifested themselves in visual form.[7] Many scholars now agree that memory was actively constituted in the 1950s rather than passively denied or repressed and that German political and visual culture, though dominated by the image of the German as victim, also displayed other kinds of memory politics that could manifest political opportunism as well as moral responsibility, democratic convictions as well as residual fascist thought patterns.[8] U.S. visual culture's contribution to these dynamics of memory, despite its strong presence in 1950s West Germany, is either downplayed or else associated exclusively with the Cold War period of the 1950s rather than with the period of National Socialist rule between 1933 and 1945.

U.S. made war films in 1950s West Germany offer a good opportunity to explore the link between German memory politics and U.S. popular culture. If contemporary historians, such as Peter Reichel, tend to collapse the distinction between German and U.S. war films, commentators in the 1950s insisted on the distinction, emphasized the specificity of "American war films," and wished to talk at length about the impact of U.S. war films on German society.[9] West German critics focused specifically on "American produced" war films, because they assumed such films would promote militaristic values such as "oaths of allegiance, manly pride, heroic death as duty, blind obedience, and battle fame," both directly and indirectly. This assumption allowed them to assume an ironic distance, since such values had been dubbed as unacceptable in West Germany by the Allies after World War II. What were Germans supposed to make of being inundated with ideological assumptions they were no longer allowed to share? Armed with this ironic distance, a number of German critics used it as an opportunity to discuss their own past. The fact that the majority of U.S. war films exported to West Germany in the 1950s were not about the German war but rather about the war in the Pacific or in Korea reinforced the distance from which German critics could speak from a more or less "neutral" perspective about war.[10]

War films, not especially popular in the months immediately following the end of hostilities, nonetheless gained popularity as the 1950s progressed, showing a fourfold increase between 1952 and 1958. One of the top grossing films of 1958, David Lean's *Bridge on the River Kwai* "had been a war film," Werner Jungeblodt, member of the German Catholic Film Commission, noted apprehensively, "or had it been an anti-war film?" As the debate continued, he noted ironically, fans of the popular film were whistling the Col. Bogey March in the streets of Germany "from north to south." Indeed, *Kwai* was the number two grossing film in Germany in 1958 and among the most controversially discussed films of that year. In his review of the film in *Der Abend, Berlin,* Karl-Heinz Krüger concisely defined the dimensions of this controversy: "In this country, the key issue will be: is this film for or against war?"[11]

In "Stories from the Barbed-Wire University: POWs in the West German Discourse of Victimization," Robert G. Moeller links *The Bridge on the River Kwai's* popularity in the late-1950s to the West German public's receptivity to films about World War II, particularly films that thematized the plight of the POW as a victim. Furthermore, he suggests that *Kwai's* critical reception was characterized primarily by a shared understanding that *Kwai* was an anti-war film, punctuated by a continuing strain of racial bias rooted in the stereotypical depictions of Russians ("the Mongel hourde") from films of the Goebbels era.[12]

Moeller's principal interest is in the relationship between public memory and the German POW in West German films, and *Kwai's* general theme of the plight of the POW certainly linked it to West German films of the same period that dealt with that theme.[13] However, the overall critical response was not primarily concerned with the theme of the POW as victim nor was it characterized primarily by racism toward "Asians" or agreement about the film's war politics. Rather, *Kwai* was situated in relationship to the meaning of U.S. war films for German society and the increase of war films produced in the United States and exported to Europe during the Cold War. Its widespread popularity triggered both important discussions of the meaning of the film and its popularity, as well as filmic responses that sought to provide alternative frameworks.

Furthermore, as U.S. films became more complex and ambiguous in their use of war themes, as we will see in the case of *Kwai*, West German critics and commentators became increasingly uneasy. West Germany's position in terms of its war legacy in the 1950s did not encourage "ambiguous" renditions of war. Germans were either victims in their own eyes or perpetrators in the eyes of the world. However, when U.S. films like *Kwai* brought in more complex issues in other national war contexts, West German critics did not change the subject. Rather, they engaged in thought-provoking debates that revealed a clear preoccupation with and desire for more complex discussions of their own past. In this way, *Kwai* and its intertextual reception would call attention to the relationship between U.S. popular culture, film reception in Germany, the National Socialist past, and the Cold War present.[14]

*   *   *

The press releases for *Die Brücke am Kwai* from Columbia pictures reveal an active awareness of the sensitivity of West Germans to the war theme, and *Kwai* was aggressively promoted primarily as an anti-war picture. Two separate packages of promotion materials were released by Columbia. One, a series of translations of excerpts from the initial British reviews after the film's premiere in London in October of 1957 was directed principally at theater owners. The second, a set of essays written by German members of Columbia's distribution headquarters in Munich, were made available to the German press in time for the film's German premiere. The rave reviews excerpted from the British press were intended to reassure German theater owners that they could anticipate a very successful box office run based upon the enthusiastic British response, that the prospects of success in Europe were generally very high.[15]

Anticipating criticism that the film could harbor pro-war tendencies, Columbia publicity attempted to define both what the film was and what it was not. What it was not was a "*Durchhalte*-Film," a "last stand" movie: "that especially unctuous genre of war film that coined politically counterfeit money, that appealed to heart and reason with sentimentalism and lies and declared death on the battlefield as youth's worthiest goal." *Kwai* was not a "hold out to the last man" picture, because Nicholson's triumph over the torture inflicted by the Japanese Colonel was not a result of a "heroism complex" on Nicholson's part. Rather, it demonstrated that Nicholson tolerated the torture as a human being who saw his enemy as a human being and who expected human law to prevail. Self-respect, not honor or prestige, were Nicholson's ultimate goals. "Holding out to the last man," as all Germans knew from painful experience, was something very different from "clinging tenaciously to the holy vested rights of human dignity." Importantly, "*Durchhalte* Films" had been a familiar part of the film landscape during the Nazi era, but there were also "*durchhalte*" style films being imported to Germany from U.S. distributors, emphasizing similar "*durchhalte*" themes from a U.S. perspective in the context of World War II, the Korean War, etc.[16]

What ultimately gave *The Bridge on the River Kwai* its anti-war credentials according to Columbia's film publicity? "In the face of the present and future threat of hydrogen bombs, sputniks, and interplanetary interconnections," the film offered two dimensions of particular interest to German audiences: a coming to terms with World War II and an "unambiguous declaration against war that exposed its empty pride, racialism, and false heroism." The film functioned as a memorial to recent German history, somewhat illogically, because all sides in the film, from Saito to Nicholson to Shears to Warden, recognized the insanity of war. Colonel Saito, described in the material as the "Prussian of the Far East," was of interest to German audiences because of the complex way he was depicted, not as a pure villain but as a human being with black and white dimensions. If Saito reminded of the past, Col. Nicholson offered a vision of the future in the form of the bridge he had built. Nicholson was able to build a bridge for the enemy, because his idealism made it possible for him to see into the future, into a time when the bridge might serve as a connection between the different cultures (and former adversaries) of the world. When "his" bridge is destroyed, German audiences would realize that that same bridge had to be rebuilt somehow, "that after the power of destruction must follow the powers of construction."[17]

Thus, I would argue, Columbia publicity constructed a reading of the film that seemed to trace a seamless path from German national defeat—the destruction of the bridge—to German integration into the NATO alliance—the rebuilding of the bridge. As far as Columbia was concerned, if German audiences were to be reminded of the past, then it was not to come to terms with past crimes, but rather to "think about war in order to prevent the catastrophe of WWIII," i.e., becoming a member of the Western alliance. The bridge was ultimately a symbol of "freedom and cross cultural understanding corrupted by war" that would "rattle the conscience of the economic wonder Germany" and would persuade "both men and women" of the futility of war.[18]

Biographical depictions of the stars and producers of the film—David Lean, Sam Spiegel, Alec Guinness, Sessue Hayakawa, and Geoffrey Horne—emphasized the authenticity and veracity of each member's humanistic, antiwar oriented contribution to the whole. Here, the most explicit mention of Spiegel's Jewishness was made: that a family member lived in Israel. Lean was depicted as inordinately modest and interested only in the authenticity of the production, as demonstrated by the fact that he spoke with "hundreds of men about the period of the construction of the Burmese railway." The actors were depicted as primarily devoted to their craft rather than star-oriented.[19]

The film premiered in Stuttgart and Frankfurt in early March and in Berlin a week later. In Frankfurt, William Holden was greeted by young women in traditional Hessian folk costumes; in Berlin, Jack Hawkins accompanied a British military band. Audiences were "*überrascht, verblüfft, und hingeschmettert*"—surprised, perplexed and overwhelmed. The film proved to be a tremendous popular success throughout Germany. In Munich, the *Filmpress* reported that 200,000 "Münchner" had seen *Bridge* at the Mathäser Film Palast, the high-est attendance record at a Munich premier theater since the end of the war.[20]

Critical ambivalence about the film was directly proportional to its wide-spread popularity. First and foremost, critics wanted to know what that popu-larity meant. If, as the Columbia publicity argued, the film was fundamentally anti-war in its tendencies, then its popularity could well be linked to German audiences' increasingly democratic orientation and separation from its Nazi past. And indeed, a number of critics went ahead and made this connection explicitly, reiterating aspects of the Columbia argument and then reflecting upon the enthusiastic audience response. If, however, the film was pro-war in its tendencies, audience response could potentially mean the opposite.[21]

Interestingly, what many critics agreed upon was that *Kwai* was an Ameri-can film, despite the predominantly British influence and theme. This em-phasis succeeded in linking *Kwai* to the contemporary politics of the Cold War rather than to its own more historical theme of British military action during World War II. In a number of West German discussions of the film, the specifically British component was downplayed in favor of locating the film in a broader context ideologically oriented toward the NATO that co-opted the British aspects under U.S. Cold War auspices. Columbia publicity had not emphasized the national origin of the film, though they did generate a separate publicity pamphlet of British reviews that had a decidedly nation-alistic bent. West German critics rejected the nationalistic tone of the British reviews and criticized the film when they did focus on the specifically Brit-ish aspect as an homage to British imperialism in the wake of the Suez crisis of 1956—triggered when Egypt nationalized ownership of the Suez canal, and Great Britain, eager to regain control of the canal for European interests, intervened militarily; later, U.S. influence contributed to undermining these British military actions and the canal remained in Egyptian hands. While critics who pointed out the Suez connection also tended to classify the film as pro-war, those critics who emphasized the anti-war aspects of the film paid less attention to specifically British themes and instead focused on its trans-national character as, for example, a U.S./British co-production based on a French text.

The majority of critics assumed the American influence meant the film would have pro-war tendencies, as exemplified by one critic's insistence that the film had not been "Americanized," as so many of his colleagues claimed, but that the "European" or anti-war animus dominated. Thus, the war vs. anti-war debate was closely tied to the foreign national origins of the film based, I would argue, on the perception that most war films were indeed coming from the United States and that they were ideologically inclined to promote war, because the United States had triumphed in World War II.[22]

Most film critics in Germany subscribed to the "cultural absorption" or the "Filmwirkung" model of audience response. A film of quality would have a positive influence, emphasizing democratic and humanistic values, while one of negative quality would tend to promote militarism, materialism, and undemocratic values. Particularly, Protestant and Catholic film critics were concerned with the impact of films such as *Kwai* upon young people. Consequently, gauging the pro- or anti-war tendencies of a film became a litmus test for assessing the status of democratization trends in Germany, as well as a guarantor for ensuring that militaristic tendencies would not arise among the next generation. For example, the *Evangelischer Film Beobachter* ultimately could not recommend *Kwai* for younger audiences, because it advocated occidental military traditions and the cultural and racial superiority of the British over the Japanese; it depicted an unproblematic, seamless unity between troops and commander without ever showing disorientation or confusion. Finally, and centrally, the destruction of the bridge signalled that ultimately the war proceedings were justified by Allied triumph. Because these were not explicit themes but rather ideological tendencies, the ultimately pro-war effect was not intended and would therefore be even more pronounced among the general public. As this debate continued it became clear that both sides could find "ammunition" for their respective arguments, which called into question the "cultural absorption" model, because it suggested that the film could be actively interpreted by both sides in order to suit their purposes. For a number of critics, this proved to be the most problematic and unique dimension of *Bridge*; it suggested that a new type of war film had been created to please all sides in the war vs. anti-war debate, thus destabilizing political binaries.[23]

West German critics, commentators, and readers who classified *Kwai* as a "pro-war" film did so because they read it as a filmic product of specific national interests: those of the United States and its role in the NATO as gatekeeper of the Cold War, or as a legacy of British imperialism. For these commentators, nationalism and militarism went hand in hand, especially if it appeared that such tendencies were disguised or indirect. By way of powerful cinematic effects, the film managed to "seduce even the most skeptical critics into standing at attention." The film's music encouraged militarism; it sought "to synchronize the march of the amputees of 1939 to 1945 and that should not be." Ultimately, the film was a "heroic epic through the back door."[24] The West German Protestant film magazine *Kirche und Film* even quoted critics from the GDR: "Madness, but necessary! That is the NATO moral code! That is the intention of this film ... the responsible organs in the German Democratic Republic are protecting the public from this type of *sugar coated poison* and likewise cannot tolerate its indirect promotion through a musical hit."[25] Thus, the politicization of *Kwai*—as an ideological endorsement of Cold War politics rather than, as Columbia publicity claimed, as a "neutral" anti-war film—was actively criticized by a number of West German critics and demonstrated that this type of criticism was certainly not limited to the communist East.

Other West German readers and viewers, like Dr. D.C. from Coburg, a veteran and former POW in Russia, experienced *Kwai* as above all a film to which he was expected to respond in a specific way, and he resented the pressure. Columbia publicity had made a point of aggressively marketing the film to German audiences as an anti-war picture so that an expectation of sorts had developed that Germans "should" go to see the film, that it was a political act or "a sign of good citizenship," as Dr. D.C. sarcastically suggested in his critique of the film. He disagreed with the film's publicity: "The last two words: "Madness, Madness" are too thin a veneer to cover the absurd and questionable content of this war history."[26]

Historical issues of class and race played a key role in Dr. D.C's critique of the film. Far from admiring Col. Nicholson's staunch adherence to the letter of the Geneva Conventions, he argues instead that, in his experience as a POW and as a veteran, "the morale of the companies during the war actually increased when officers did not receive special treatment and worked alongside their company and decreased when they did not." In the film, Col. Nicholson's adherence to the conventions is a clear ideological signal for his respect for international law, symbolizing his essential democratic humanism, in contrast to the Japanese Colonel's aggressive disdain for international law. By linking the Geneva Conventions to military and class hierarchies, this educated reader calls attention to the film's misrepresentation of the dynamics of actual military life. Moreover, by depicting the Japanese military as incapable of building the barest of bridges, the bridge as constructed by the British becomes a symbol, in the end, for the reconstruction of the tarnished reputation of the white race. "Such [ideological] tendencies seem to me to be of little use in the task of creating a conciliatory international climate."[27]

Dr. D.C.'s criticism suggested that certain German viewers were as little keen on being told to forget about their past as they had been keen on being told to remember. Thus an important dialectic was set in motion between what Columbia Pictures producers thought German audiences wanted to see and hear—that *Kwai* was unbiased, transnational, anti-war, and future-oriented—and what some members of the audience actually saw and heard.[28] Moreover, Dr. D.C.'s thoughtful critique of *Kwai* was not couched in a rhetoric of "injured citizenship" that signalled nostalgia for the past in either the form or content of the criticism. Nor does his response to *Kwai* imply a one-sided agenda on behalf of "the private good" alone. Rather, his critique articulated ways toward an expanded German memory culture that was willing to engage critically with the public history of World War II.[29]

Far from being anti-war, several critics also insisted that *Bridge* was actually an homage to British imperialism. In the wake of the Suez crisis, the British needed a filmic "Hermann's Denkmal" to remind them of their glorious past. Much of the positive British press response to *Kwai* sounded too nationalistic and jingoistic in the opinion of German critics, "unusual in the normally balanced British critical response."[30] To misunderstand *Kwai* as anti-war is to miss the fundamental meaning of the Arc de Triumph, a *"Denkmal"* (a memorial that commemorates and celebrates) rather than a *"Mahnmal"* (a memoral that warns). "If we [Germans] had made such a film," Gert Schulte noted in the *Frankfurter Allgemeine Zeitung*, "we'd have been accused of being ... Prussians," i.e., warmongers.[31]

Such 'warmongering' was especially problematic in a nuclear age, and German critics made mention of the atom bomb in the context of discussions of *Kwai* in provocative ways. As one reviewer in the *Deutsche Woche* put it: "In our nuclear era, shouldn't a film [like *Kwai*] have a message, a clear "no?"[32] Colonel Nicholson works on his bridge, as another reviewer in the *Süddeutsche Zeitung* added, "with the same blind work energy that wishes to produce something technically perfect merely for its own sake. The atom bomb probably was created this way, and the bridge over the river Kwai was created with similar motives ... yet the Colonel's "heroic aura" is never called into question."[33] Though, historically, the atom bomb was created with very clear motives in mind, the analogy between bomb and bridge called into question the ethic of work discipline without regard to political and historical context. Moreover, the analogy linked *Kwai's* plot to an important political subtext: the relationship between individual agency and the creation of military technologies, not, as the Columbia publicity argued, to a call for understanding between former enemies. Dr. D.C. took it one step further and suggested that ultimately it was the destruction rather than the construction of the bridge that was the central pro-war point: "In the meantime that "heroic deed" has been prepared, that will lead to the destruction of the bridge, several heroes, and all of our illusions. Had it been historically feasible, one might have brought in a very small H or A bomb as a final note—but it was only just 1942."[34] This provocative satiric reference to the bombing of Hiroshima and Nagasaki by the Allies in 1945 signalled the reader's association of Allied victory with the actual use of nuclear weapons rather than with contemporary "anti-war" NATO policies of "deterrence."

Overall, the critics who insisted that *Kwai* was a bona-fide war film did so because, in their eyes, the film sustained a romantic link between the state and the military they had come to reject based on their own historical experience[35]; this link seemed even more dangerous in the new context of the prospect of nuclear war. Furthermore, critical energies were fuelled on the perception that viewers were being told what to think and how to respond to the film through U.S. and British propaganda.[36]

The critical contingent who read *Kwai* as an "anti-war" film in turn praised its tendency to downplay national interests and to emphasize that in "war" everyone was a loser. They appreciated in particular what they interpreted as a nonpartisan critique of military formalism that did not distinguish between the British and the Japanese, the war's winners and losers.[37] In this, German advocates of *Kwai* as an anti-war film parted company with Columbia Pictures' implicitly racist and nationalist emphasis on the differing "styles" of the British and Japanese commanders: Nicholson as "officer and idealist," Saito as caught "between arrogant racial and caste pride and the constant fear to be seen by Europeans as a second class human."[38] The anti-war *Kwai* critics were not, on the whole, interested in racial insinuations about the Japanese. They were more impressed with the nonpartisan rejection of military formalism, because it did not blame particular parties. This was not a film about "sadists who incinerate their fellow human beings." Instead, it was a criticism of military order and honor codes as embodied in Colonel Nicholson's "absurd loyalty to paragraphs." In comparison to the various B war films ("*Heldenschnulzen*") that were currently flooding the market, *Kwai* "forced one to think."[39]

However, the German anti-war *Kwai* advocates were also very aware of the implications of eliding questions of national difference, even if they uniformly praised this tendency. In *Kwai*, war was defined as "specific rules created for the exact implementation of deadly operations that end by slapping themselves in the face; questions of guilt and who is at fault remained unresolved." "*Kwai* did not raise the question of who was guilty … with those who became collaborators in the process of confidently fulfilling their military duties or with those who believed in the cause and then were punished for it." Surely for many German critics and many viewers of *Kwai*, this aspect was especially appealing as it managed to bracket issues of war culpability and accountability, while simultaneously offering a critique of war. In this way, *Kwai* could potentially offer a model of how to be against war without asking specific questions about the past. At the same time, German critics clearly recognized that this was not a film about "coming to terms with the past" and World War II, as the Columbia publicity claimed, because it did not address questions of guilt, accountability, or complicity.[40]

Given these contradictory pro- and anti-war readings, it was hardly surprising that a third category of German criticism defined *Kwai* as essentially *ambiguous:* "Both the British press and U.S. propaganda claim the film is anti-war, but instead it seems to want to please everybody: militant and pacifist alike." *Kwai* "both glorifies and unmasks—its anti-war tendency is as if inscribed into an optical illusion." According to critic Walther Bitterman, *Kwai* was "an ambiguous jungle saga for every man ... uptight veterans and radical pacifists will be equally impressed."[41] Ultimately, it would be difficult for German viewers to find their way through "the thicket of tendencies."[42] Three dimensions of the film's perceived "ambiguity" preoccupied critics: the relationship between its presumed anti-war message and its music, its characterization of Colonel Nicholson, and the political implications of the differences between the novel and the film.

A central problematic dimension of ambiguity in the film was the relationship between the film's anti-war aspects and the soundtrack, the well-known "Colonel Bogey March." "Just when cries of 'madness, madness' signal an anti-war message, a catchy military march ensues, so that we fall right back into our collectivist sleep after having been briefly scared awake," wrote Gert Schulte. Indeed, another critic argued that the "decision" as to whether the film was pro- or anti-war depended largely upon whether a viewer "values the collectively mastered task over reason, collective song, and collective enthusiasm." If so, *Kwai* would encourage precisely the "dark grandeur and muffled arousal that psychologically savvy organizers try to create." The Colonel Bogey March was a musical hit in West Germany, selling more copies there than in any other country world-wide: 1 million copies in five months. As one critic in the *General Anzeiger* concluded: "What no march composer has been able to accomplish since 1945, namely to bring a Prussian, Bavarian, or Northrhine Westfalien synchronized rhythm under the people, an American composer [Mitch Miller] has managed to do."[43]

Others rejected the militaristic collective obsession thesis and argued instead that "we would rather be obsessed with a fresh melody than with rotted ideas and ideologies. That this happens to be a military march shouldn't worry us, given the musical optimism. It helps to deal with such peace-loving tasks as kitchen work." Here, the "obsession" with the music signalled that German democratization through American consumer culture was firmly underway and that political obsessions such as militarism had given way to the peaceful occupations of private life.[44] The fact that young people invented sensational texts to the tune of the Colonel Bogey March that had little to do with military issues, for example, about the divorce of the Shah of Iran, tended to support the "civilian" readings of the phenomenon in their emphasis on the private sphere of marriage and domestic life. During the divorce proceedings of The Shah and Queen Soraya, whose German background made her particularly interesting to the German public, rhymes about her presumed barrenness—the reason for the divorce—were circulating to the "militaristic" march: "Too bad, Soraya can't have a child, Too bad, the Shah has air in his Spind," or a less raunchy, and less nationalistic, version of the second line: "Too bad, we aren't with her now."[45]

Concrete memories of war experiences were also triggered by the "Colonel Bogey March." One Bonn journalist ironically noted that Konrad Adenauer had recently suggested to journalists that they should write about the theme of the military march, given that the "reconstructed" German Bundeswehr did not yet have a new, fitting melody. Perhaps the River Kwai theme would do, the journalist noted, tongue in cheek. The journalist recalled that twenty years before, a command—directed at exhausted troops—to whistle "a song" did not spawn the optimism of the River Kwai march. Instead, soldiers obeyed passively, but would have preferred to "*pfeiff ihm was,*" that is, to tell the commander off. Like the Coburg reader, Dr. D.C., who also insisted that soldiers on the front and in POW camps rarely felt like whistling defiant tunes, the Bonn journalist emphasized those dimensions of *Kwai*'s military music that glorified the experience of war and thus falsified the history of World War II.[46]

Ultimately, what made the ambiguity of the link between music and anti-war theme questionable for critics was the relationship between military music and the "divided memories" of postwar Germans. The music could potentially trigger positive memories of war or negative memories of war; it could tap into a cultural reservoir of the past that associated military music both with "collective enthusiasm" and "passive obedience." This "both/and" dimension had a wide-ranging appeal, because it reflected the dynamics of cultural memory more effectively than did the "either/or" residual militarism/incipient democratization model set up by critics.[47]

Another suspect dimension of the film's ambiguity had to do with the figure of Colonel Nicholson, the British officer played by Alec Guinness: the conflict between the desire to build the bridge and the bridge's essential function as an aid to the enemy. Columbia publicity suggested Nicholson was an "officer and idealist," who in the end realized that the building of the bridge was "wrong." Critic Walther Schmieding, writing in the *Ruhr Nachrichten,* saw something different; for him, Nicholson was a devout militarist who recognizes his delusion much too late: "Twenty-eight years of schematic thinking have crippled his judgement ... He's like a Foreign Legioner, a robot, who works precisely without regard to consequences; he's infected with the 'spirit of the army' or rather with the spirit of the armies, since British and Japanese here are similar. This bitter criticism must be decoded, however. For two and a half hours we are on the side of Colonel Nicholson, only in the final minutes is the horrible point revealed."[48] Despite his militarism, the audience is on Col. Nicholson's "side," although it "ought to be shocked."[49] The film insisted upon holding a "protective hand" over Col. Nicholson: He loved his bridge and we sympathize, wrote Karena Niehoff,[50] picking up on Sam Spiegel's suggestion that *Kwai* was a "love story between a man and his bridge." U.S. producers' gendering of the bridge as female was thus interpreted by Niehoff as one mechanism the film used to render Col. Nicholson sympathetic or human. On the one hand, Nicholson was an obsessive militarist, on the other, a "tragic figure" representing a blind, perhaps "Prussian" energy that sees a difficult task as a purpose in itself.[51] The response to Colonel Nicholson's character revealed a pattern of reluctant empathy—almost all praised Alec Guinness's performance for the way he managed to render believable both "the regulation oriented stiff military man and the dream obsessed perpetrator."[52] However, rendering this type believable and sympathetic was not just an aesthetic accomplishment but also a multi-leveled political one: "Such types [as Col. Nicholson] existed—those that stopped at nothing to realize their ambitious plans, who even forced sick men to work. These types have the lives of countless good men on their conscience. From this we might learn how to train our officers, today, differently, then things should become different now, right?"[53] The fact that Colonel Nicholson contained aspects of both a victim and a perpetrator ultimately resonated with German viewers struggling with a war legacy that divided them neatly between the one category or the other. As Bob Moeller has suggested, a key dimension of coming to terms with the German past is to begin to understand the ways Germans could have been both victims and perpetrators.[54] German responses to the character of Col. Nicholson suggest that the process of deconstructing the opposition between victim and perpetrator could manifest itself in the responses to popular culture, and that it was beginning by the late-1950s. Habbo Knoch offers a useful model for understanding this phenomenon. West German memory culture, he puts forth, was characterized by a divided, yet osmotic, set of memory pictures consisting of the primary experience of war on the one hand, and the NS crimes on the other. Rather than being oppositional, this double memory structure of war and crime was a constituting factor of West German memory culture.[55] Films like *Kwai* both tapped into and shaped that culture.

Further efforts to decode *Kwai* for its ambiguous political tendencies included comparing the film with the bestselling novel by Pierre Boulle, upon which it was based.[56] Several key changes had been made to the book which transformed it from primarily a satire to a melodramatic tragedy. The American character Shears was added to what had originally been an all British team, and he was given a brief love interest. Female partisans replaced male partisans during the commando unit's trek through the jungle. The tension between Colonel Nicholson and the Japanese Colonel Saito is mostly retained, but the conclusion is significantly modified. In the book, Colonel Nicholson defends his bridge to the end and never has an epiphany, and the bridge remains standing. In the film, Colonel Nicholson realizes his "error," is shot, and then "accidentally" falls on the detonator, thus destroying the bridge. The final scene shows the doctor, Clipton, commenting on the destruction with the statement, "madness, madness," which replaces Colonel Warden's justifying his final violent outbreak to his superiors after the incident.

The book was well known in Germany, and the book's sales increased after the release of the film.[57] The *Westfalenpost* reported that the novel had sold 35,000 copies in four years, and when the film was released in France, sales of the novel reached 80,000 after four weeks. Furthermore, sales were holding up, presumably in Germany as well as in France. Sam Spiegel directly addressed the relationship between novel and film during his Berlin press conference in January 1958: "we made [an anti-war] tragedy with ironic overtones out of a satire," and "Boulle liked the film version better than his own novel." The film credited Boulle with having written the screenplay, but in fact he'd had practically no hand in it, as Spiegel's remark indirectly revealed. However, for German—and European—audiences, the novel's, as well as the screenplay's, European origins were important to emphasize in Germany, given the German tendency to question the anti-war credentials of cultural products produced in the United States.[58]

The actual authors of the *Kwai* screenplay, as would later be revealed and confirmed, were Carl Foreman, author of the critically acclaimed screenplay *High Noon,* and Michael Wilson, best known for *Salt of the Earth,* two blacklisted U.S. screenwriters who had refused to testify before the House Un-American Activities Committee and who were expatriated to Europe in the late-1950s. Foreman had written an early draft, which—after conflicts with Sam Spiegel and David Lean—was given over to Michael Wilson to rewrite. Interestingly, Foreman's primary conflicts with Spiegel and Lean had to do with questions of whether to retain Boulle's satirical and ironical point of view at key points, particularly at the end of the film. Foreman wished to emphasize the irony of the similarities between the British Col. Nicholson and the Japanese Col. Saito, as well as the final irony of the bridge's remaining standing and Colonel Nicholson's never realizing his error. While the pattern of conflict between the two military men was retained, Lean, presumably out of "British pride," ultimately rejected Foreman's desire to stick to the novel with regard to Nicholson and insisted that Nicholson "realize" his error at the end and "do" something to expiate himself. Spiegel, in turn, wanted the destruction of the bridge presumably for dramatic and commercial purposes. At that point, Foreman abandoned the project, and Wilson was hired.[59]

For several German critics, this shift from satire to tragedy had political implications. Analogous to the conflicts between Foreman, Lean, and Spiegel, German critics drew attention to precisely those changes that had been made to Boulle's novel within the context of their own concerns about whether *Kwai* was primarily war or anti-war oriented. Those who were familiar with Boulle's novel, like Walter Talmon-Gros, criticized the altered ending:

In Pierre Boulle's novel, the bridge does not remain standing for nothing. So Lean must construct the embarrassing coincidence, that the dying Colonel, himself, causes the detonation through his final fall. The insanity of war would have been more clearly shown, however—as in the novel—if only the two British parties that are positively and negatively preoccupied with the bridge had destroyed each other, while the object of their military efforts remained untouched. Through the conclusion, the film becomes rather sensationalized, which compromises its status as a great humanitarian document.[60]

Though Talmon-Gros basically accepted *Kwai* as an anti-war film, from his perspective the new ending compromised its anti-war tendencies, because it demonstrated that "Lean had obviously fallen in love with the bridge as much as had Col. Nicholson and so had lost sight of the correct standards." Rather than risk a clear anti-war message, the film compromised by resurrecting the "heroic honor" of the British colonel.[61]

Hellmut Haffner, writing in the *Abendzeitung*, München, attributed the pro-war message of the film to the medium of film itself, in contrast to the anti-war message of the book: "In the novel the sole survivor (Col. Warden) reports: "I am an excellent marksman. What luck! They were both (Shears and Joyce, his commando comrades) torn to pieces!" Here the grotesque blindness that characterizes militaristic thinking becomes clear. One cannot show or visualize or depict this. In that the film does so, it accomplishes the opposite of what it intends: to give the heroes their haloes. This wouldn't be a problem if the film wasn't so well made."[62] Haffner implicitly compares the book's ending, in which Col. Warden narrates the reasoning behind his decision to kill his comrades, with that of the film, where Warden is visually shown shooting and then apologizing for his actions to the female partisans who had each fallen in love with one of the men. In the film's conclusion, it is the military physician, Clipton, who looks out upon the carnage and comments, "Madness, madness."

Enno Patalas, co-founder of the leftist German film journal, *Filmkritik,* offered a different reading of the relationship between novel and film. For him, the film continued the "compromised truth" that the novel began, because it insisted on a linear narrative rather than focusing upon the "discontinuities of war." Like the film, the novel contained its problematic elements: it suggested that all positive actions contradicted the imperatives of war, but it also respected the principles of discipline and hard work; it ridiculed the mentality of colonialism, while it also suggested that only the white race was superior: "emotional ties to past or dying norms and the rational recognition that these are obsolete seem to be competing for the soul of the former rubber planter and intelligence agent Boulle." However, like Talmon-Gross, Patalas agreed that the novel's ending suggested the absurdity of war, whereas *Kwai's* ending was "pseudo-tragical and sentimental." Moreover, the film was even more racist for Patalas than was the novel: "in the novel the sadistic, alcoholic Saito and the incompetent [Japanese] engineers are extremes, whereas the film suggests they are the norm," thus taking advantage of existing prejudices and stereotypes.[63]

Like everyone else, Patalas assumed that Boulle had written the screenplay, and he emphasized further differences between "the scriptwriter Boulle and the novelist Boulle" that for him had significant implications for the war vs. anti-war debate. Whereas the novel has the commando unit accompanied by local [male] partisans, the film offered "pretty women" tagging along through the jungle, the clear waters of which were "attractively dyed with Japanese blood." Along with the filmic addition of the music, this all added up to one basic effect: "to distract viewers from the horrors of war depicted." Rather than emphasizing commercial motivations for the changes, Patalas highlighted indirect political effects that made *Kwai* into a film that ultimately "celebrated questionable triumphs."[64]

Critics might well have zeroed in on marketing as the major motivation behind the film's ambiguity: the film industry's desire to reach as wide an audience as possible. Instead, those critics who were preoccupied with the ambiguities of the film focused upon possible political motivations. Several times the film was referred to as being "*raffiniert*," (cunning) suggesting political subterfuge. What made the film's ambiguity a political issue for German critics? There were several reasons, and they were all linked to the specifically German issue of the politics of memory. One reason, already touched upon, was the concern for German youth and the assumption that young German people should not be exposed to war propaganda of any kind, direct or indirect. One effect of this was the concrete guidelines for the evaluation of war films developed by members of the Freiwillige Selbstkontrolle der Filmwirtschaft (FSK) (German voluntary self-regulation of the film industry). Another, also focusing specifically upon the question of German nationalism, suggested that the film's ambiguity, its simultaneous emphasis upon the glory as well as upon the criticism of war, was not a formula that could be used by Germans, because if they produced films that emphasized heroic virtues in any way, they would be criticized by the world community for falling back into old, warmongering patterns. In this sense, the film's ambiguity called attention to Germany's key point of vulnerability within the NATO alliance, namely, its past. West Germany was integrated but, due to its history, always under surveillance: an essentially unfree "partner." Additionally, critics assumed that exposure to war oriented propaganda could "fester" and encourage residual patterns left over from the Nazi era, thus jeopardizing efforts to democratize and mainstream

German culture. Finally, ambiguous messages about questions of war in film raised unique and problematic questions about exactly how Germany should orient itself toward the threat of nuclear annihilation, where it was clear that a different approach to the problem of war was necessary.

In many ways the war vs. anti-war debate in West Germany was a response to American produced and exported war films, to U.S. mass culture, and to those dimensions of what Reinhold Wagnleitner has called "U.S. cultural imperialism" that sought to direct German opinion about their own past through film production publicity/propaganda.[65] If American producers claimed to be producing anti-war films for the European public, and later film historians would see the late-1950s as an era of "thinking man's war films" that tried to grapple with the difficult theme of war, German critics saw here a new film formula that attempted to justify warfare in an anti-war guise.[66] Discussing such U.S. films as *The Caine Mutiny* and *From Here to Eternity*, as well as *Kwai*, critic Walther Schmieding made the following observation in 1958:

> The institutions of the army and the marines, of war in general, have become taboo for American films in a certain respect. In order to break through these taboos, the U.S. film must make cunning detours, to write between the lines, in other words. But this is only partially successful. The force of the criticism is reduced. Typical for *Kwai* is that a British Colonel has all our sympathies. He is an irreproachable officer. His counterpart, the civilian oriented American, for whom the others "reek of heroism," is a questionable character, a ne'r do well and confidence man.[67]

Certainly for many members of the German critical establishment, as well as for some members of the German public, war films like *Kwai* directly raised issues of the relationship between politics, memory, and culture that could not be cordoned off into non-political arenas, as, for example, the Columbia publicity attempted to do in its effort to promote an ostensibly non-political, "universal" anti-war message. Moreover, though *Kwai* was considered unique, it was clearly perceived as part of a trend of war pictures that increasingly sought to accommodate ambivalent public sentiments toward war: "An American distributor and American producer (from Vienna), the English director David Lean, the English actor Alec Guinness as the Colonel—well, that is a mixture that does the NATO justice. Politically, therefore, nothing can go wrong. Artistically, one can only express admiration. The problematic of the theme, however, that sways between love of peace, humanity, and the promotion of war remains unresolved."[68] Clearly, something had gone "wrong" politically, as Germany's membership in the NATO rendered Schulte's critique a political one, whether he liked it or not.

Kwai's ambiguity about war as a theme was also closely tied to its indirect ideological endorsement of NATO and the policy of nuclear deterrence. The logic of deterrence stipulated that only membership in the NATO could prevent the catastrophe of all out nuclear war, which theoretically rendered warfare a transnational phenomenon. By linking the concept of war to the idea of the potential destruction of all humanity, Columbia publicity for *Kwai* attempted to universalize and depoliticize war as a phenomenon. In the film, this is accomplished by way of the "existential" problem of the characters engaging in the project of conventional warfare of the past that appears to transcend national differences: the structural similarities between the main characters Nicholson and Saito, for example, or the multiple meanings of the bridge project. However, the threat of nuclear warfare, itself, is tied to the Cold War dynamic of nuclear deterrence as a policy between two world military alliances: the United States and the Soviet Union. Therefore, the anti-war message had to be rechanneled into a conclusion that was "NATO *gerecht*" (NATO just), one that ideologically justified Allied victory and legitimated future Allied actions. Colonel Nicholson's late "conversion" accomplishes this shift, as does the destruction of the bridge. National differences are reestablished, British military culture proves itself in the end, and NATO and its deterrence policies are vindicated insofar as the U.S./British alliance in the film reflected the Cold War politics of the film's production team.

Surely this was one of the major reasons Carl Foreman referred to the ending that was ultimately given to the film by Spiegel and Lean as a "cop out."[69] And indeed, much of the film's "ambiguity" can be traced back to the differences between Foreman, Wilson, Spiegel, and Lean as to the direction the film should go. As blacklisted writers, both Foreman and Wilson tended to frame their comments upon these differences in aesthetic terms. However, it was clear that the respective nationalistic sympathies of both Lean and Spiegel gave *Kwai* its ultimately pro-war framework, which was offset in different ways by the influence of Foreman and Wilson. Foreman emphasized the critique of military formalism that characterized both Nicholson and Saito, while Wilson contributed the character of Shears and the mirrored parallel tension between Shears and Warden. These tensions were not emphasized by German critics, probably because they tended not to link possible anti-war points of view with the U.S.. Had Foreman and Wilson been given credit for their contributions, the "ambiguous" patterns so many German critics discerned could have been more definitively linked to specific Cold War tensions that had emerged out of such postwar developments as the McCarthy "red scare" and the Hollywood blacklist, developments that added credence to Foreman's later assertion that "we had won the war, but we had lost the peace."[70]

For the German viewers who accepted Lean and Spiegel's cultural formula, there were certain perks, the most evident of which was the offer to forget about the past, and *Kwai*'s popularity signalled that the formula was effective. However, the war vs. anti-war debates, which the film triggered in West Germany, kept questions about war alive that the NATO alliance—with its emphasis on the Cold War in the present and "deterrence" in the future— could not resolve, namely, the legacy of war and militarism on German society, and demonstrated the conflicted ways U.S. popular culture shaped the ways Germans sought to grapple with that legacy. Especially in discussions of the "ambiguity" of the film, critics touched on issues most relevant to questions of the German past: the relationship between culture and ideology during the Third Reich, as in discussions of the "Colonel Bogey March;" the larger implicit questions of the "Clean Wehrmacht" and the relationship between agency and complicity in the responses to the character of Colonel Nicholson; and especially the critique of the link between nationalism and militarism that informed the comparison of Boulle's novel and Lean's film. Overall, the ambiguity actively encouraged critical speculation rather than passive acceptance and thus contributed to expanding and liberalizing German memory culture by calling into question the "victim/perpetrator" model associated with the German past.

In the wake of the *Kwai* debates, questions as to the filmic representations of war became increasingly controversial and came to a head when public discussion of the future of the German Bundeswehr and whether or not it should be armed with nuclear weapons were at their height.[71] Werner Hess, film commissioner for the Protestant Church in Germany, announced that "as demonstrations against the threat of nuclear death attract tens of thousands, the film industry, both foreign and domestic, sees fit to produce and circulate an overabundance of war films." Hess assumed that such films encouraged militarism and should be avoided by all those Germans who did not want to contribute to "sawing off our own weak democratic branch upon which we have laboriously built our nest." In the July 1958 issue of *Kirche und Film*, Hess called his fellow clergymen to encourage their congregations to "just say no" to military films, given that the criteria for determining "militaristic tendencies" in films as established and revised by the FSK in late March 1958 simply could not sort out such slippery features as *Kwai* and other films like it.[72]

Yet if conservative churchmen like Hess still assumed that "militaristic" films such as *Kwai* could rekindle nascent anti-democratic tendencies in the German public, some members of the public at least were marching to a different drummer. When a representative from Columbia Pictures came to the town of Schwabach for a discussion of *Kwai*, he encountered a group of sev-

enty—two thirds of which were young people, including young soldiers and
school kids, as well as older folks—who were very eager to discuss the film
and its social and cultural implications. Interestingly, whereas the older group
reacted to *Kwai* on an emotional level, the younger group asked questions
"cooly and logically," raising such matters as why the state triumphs in the end
of the film. What good was Albert Schweitzer, one participant noted, if state
power ultimately triumphed, to which another young person responded that
there could never be enough Schweitzers. Albert Schweitzer's criticism of the
dangers of nuclear fallout and his status as an apolitical humanitarian made
him a prominent figure in the movement to prevent the nuclear arming of the
Bundeswehr. This response pleased the journalist present at the discussion,
as the overall tone of the article attempts to downplay the political implications of the questions raised by the young people, preferring instead to classify
their analytical stance toward the film as "youth's right, that doesn't yet know
the right way and doesn't have enough people who can lead them." That the
representative from Columbia pictures took "half a notebook's worth of notes,
many more than the journalist," suggested how interested American film distributors were in the public responses to their films overseas.[73]

Increasingly, German cultural elites also wished to garner more systematic
information about the social and cultural effects of the genre of war films
on the German public. To this end, the Catholic Church sponsored a study
of the increase in war films in West Germany during the 1950s, written by
Werner Jungeblodt, an *Amtsgerichtsrat* (county court judge) and member of
the Catholic Film Commission, published by the Diocese of Rottenburg in
1960. Rejecting the Protestant Church's call to "just say no" as insufficient,
this erudite study presented an overview of the types of war films that had
been screened in Germany, offered a thesis about their origins and significance, and looked to recent German films as possible models for a genuinely
"anti-war" film. Because the study was grounded in conservative assumptions
about 'Filmwirkung' traditionally found in denominational film criticism and
concerned primarily with the effects of film on young people, it took seriously
another study done by the journalist Walther Schmieding on why the public
watched war films. Schmieding found that most viewers watched war films for
either "personal/psychological" or "historical/psychological" reasons. The former stressed reasons such as the desire for excitement and adventure, the identification with the hero, and working out hidden wishes. The latter stressed the
more problematic "encouragement of nationalistic feeling" through romantic
depictions of war. Significantly, these reasons were more widespread than artistic motivations or political/pedagogical motivations, which included coming
to terms with German history, though the meeting in Schwabach suggested
that "political/pedagogical" motivations" were definitely there.[74] Nonetheless,

Schmieding discerned that different models of film reception were at work spanning the gamut from instinctive response to active interpretation.

Jungeblodt's main thesis was that the majority of war films were coming from the United States and that most of these films had a tendency to promote militaristic values among a public inclined to spend money to see war films for "personal/psychological" or "personal/historical" reasons, that is, for the wrong reasons.[75] The success of such films encouraged and supported West German war film production with problematic war film formulas that offered largely distorted versions of the history of World War II. For example, successful U.S. films such as *Rommel der Wüstenfuchs*, (*The Desert Fox*, dir: Henry Hathaway, 1952) had developed formulas that influenced German productions such as the adaptation of Carl Zuckmeyer's *Des Teufels General* (The Devil's General): "famous, audacious soldier, deeply unpolitical and in the service of Hitler while simultaneously rejecting Hitler." What was positive about these films was that they criticized the thesis of collective guilt and tried to show how difficult the situation was for Germans during the Hitler dictatorship. However, it was problematic that all the responsibility for war was placed in the hands of a small clique and hence only half truths were told. In the meantime, the SS has assumed the role of the predictable evil-doer.[76] Other German films, equally troubling, offered a distorted picture of war as a "Betriebsunfall der Geschichte" (an industrial accident of history) and "fateful natural force." Here the study was quoting the decidedly left wing film critic Enno Patalas, which suggested that left of center arguments about German films were beginning to infiltrate the conservative churches.[77]

Significantly, Jungeblodt introduced his study with the example of *Kwai* as a problematic, ambiguous, U.S. war film that had taken West Germany by storm and provocatively juxtaposed it with the recent German film *Die Brücke*. Rather than making a direct comparison of the two films, Jungeblodt left it at the apparently unpolitical assertion that Bernhard Wicki's, *The Bridge*, which was nominated for an Academy Award and won the Golden Globe Award as Best Foreign Film in 1960, demonstrated that there was still such a thing as "German film art."[78] In light of the war vs. anti-war debate, comparing *Bridge on the River Kwai* with Wicki's *Die Brücke* might very well reveal that *Kwai* leaned toward the former and *Bridge* toward the latter. However, what is more interesting is to look at Wicki's film as a response to *Kwai* as an American 'anti-war' film, in other words, as a response to U.S. popular culture. This filmic response reveals what was at stake for many Germans in terms of their future role as a democratic nation: creating cultural forms that allowed for greater leeway in the construction of their memories of World War II within a Cold War context.[79] Scholars of German visual culture, such as Bob Moeller and Peter Reichel, have analyzed Wicki's *Die Brücke* in relationship to other West

German and East German films, respectively, emphasizing the ways it either parted company with or reinforced the prevailing tendency in German war films to idealize German victimization.[80] I would like to offer an alternative reading of *Die Brücke* by going beyond the German war film scene and comparing the film to the U.S. blockbuster, *Kwai*.

Wicki's *Die Brücke* tells the story of a group of adolescent German boys who are inducted into the German army shortly before the end of the war in the spring of 1945. Filled with patriotic spirit and eager to escape the adolescent frustrations of their limited rural environment, the boys are ready to join the more experienced soldiers at the front, as American tanks approach. The boys' teacher, exempted from service due to health problems, is appalled that his pupils have been inducted so late in the war and tries to intervene for them with the commanding officer. The officer rejects the teacher's arguments, but later issues the command that the boys should be "protected" by stationing them at a bridge already destined to be blown up by German forces to prevent American tanks from entering the town. This bridge turns out to be the boys' local town bridge, a far cry from the adventure on the front lines they had hoped for and none of them know of the bridge's fate. When their commanding NCO (noncommissioned officer) goes for coffee and is killed by a fellow military man who suspects him of desertion, the boys are left on their own. When one of their own is killed by a passing fighter plane, they are psychologically overcome and thrown into a frenzied disorientation that leads them to fight the oncoming tanks single handed. In the skirmish that ensues, there are scenes of agonizing violence and dying. Later, the commando unit originally sent to blow up the bridge shows up, and the boys are so shocked to discover that their "protecting" of the bridge has been a complete sham that they kill the leader of the unit. By the end of the film, all but one of the boys has been killed. In the final scene, the camera hones in on the object of all the dead boys' patriotic zest, the local bridge, and the film fades out, leaving the bridge demonstrably standing (see Figures 2.4, 2.5, and 2.6).

Die Brücke was based upon a novel of the same name by Manfred Gregor, published in 1958. When Wicki was asked to direct the film he made significant alterations to the original novel, based upon his desire, as he said, to make an "anti-war" film. The book, he argued, tended to emphasize the boys' heroic ardour unironically, and the bridge they were protecting had strategic significance in the novel which it would not have in the film. Wicki also altered the novel's complex flashback structure into a straight narrative, emphasizing the adolescent struggles and troubled family lives of the boys in the first part and then devoting most of the second half of the film to devastating battle scenes that emphasized the boys' fear and disorientation as opposed to any heroism.[81]

Figure 2.4. The young soldiers conscripted in the final days of World War II in *Die Brücke*. From left to right: Karl (Karl Michael Balzer), Klaus (Volker Lechtenbrink), Sigi (Günther Hoffmann), Hans (Folker Bohnet), and Albert (Fritz Wepper). Kirch Media GmbH. Used with permission. (Source: Deutsche Kinemathek, Berlin)

Though in interviews with Wicki and in secondary materials on *The Bridge* there is no explicit mention made of the film *The Bridge on the River Kwai*, there are significant clues to suggest that *Kwai* and the debate about what constituted a war or an anti-war film were on Wicki's mind. The first has to do with Wicki's clear intention to make an anti-war film. As most discussions of war films had to do with defining why films that claimed to be anti-war were actually not anti-war, the desire to make an anti-war film would have to be a dialogue of sorts with predecessors that tried but failed, so to speak, to get a genuinely anti-war message across. Second, aspects of the films' sound effects and plot suggested that *Kwai* had influenced the production. When the American tanks approach the small German town, the sound of their approach precedes their arrival by several moments, as do the sounds of the approaching train in *Kwai* just before the bridge is destroyed. Whereas in adventure-oriented *Kwai,* men find explosives attached to bridge pillars in the receding waters of the river, in the more mundane *Bridge,* the boys find smuggled bottles of alcohol hidden by the shore of the river and, dreaming of the glamour of war, fight amongst themselves over who can claim the bounty. Finally, in the conclusion of the film, producers requested that Wicki end the

Figure 2.5. The unspectacular and strategically insignificant bridge from *Die Brücke*. Kirch Media GmbH. Used with permission. (Source: Deutsche Kinemathek, Berlin)

film with a final shot of the bridge, not with the scene Wicki had originally intended of the surviving boy stumbling through the streets of his town as American tanks pass indifferently and white "surrender" sheets hang out the windows of the local houses. Wicki agreed to this change of his plans, where he had rejected other suggestions by the producers. The final scene of the dark, foreboding, little, German bridge surely must have conjured up images of *Kwai*'s bridge and the final scenes of its destruction. And indeed, the debate over *Kwai*'s anti-war status often hinged upon the meaning of the destruction of the bridge at the end with a number of critics suggesting that the final spectacular destruction was both a justification of war through a glorification of Allied victory and a commercial concession to the film industry. Wicki's bridge, on a symbolic level, might ostensibly avoid this trap.

Despite the lack of direct evidence, a close comparison of *Kwai* and *Bridge* is highly suggestive. On the level of both form and content, Wicki's *Bridge* offers stark contrasting dimensions to *Kwai* that reveal an important dialectic with *Kwai* through the prism of the war vs. anti-war film debates and suggests that creating a German anti-war film could mean offering a counterpoint to U.S. produced so called anti-war films of the late-1950s as much as it could represent either a "realistic" depiction of World War II in Germany or a com-

Figure 2.6. Screaming for assistance, Walter (Michael Hinz) is overcome by the sudden death of Sigi (Günther Hoffmann). Kirch Media GmbH. Used with permission. (Source: Deutsche Kinemathek, Berlin)

ing to terms with the question of the German past. In this way, *The Bridge* would offer a critique of war that took into account different factors than U.S. produced films and so widen the framework within which memories of World War II were being constructed. At the same time, it would adhere to *Kwai's* formula of rendering war a "transnational" phenomenon and thus fit into the NATO agenda.

On the level of form, *Bridge* couldn't have presented a more striking counterpoint to *Kwai*. Wicki's film offered the stark contrasts of black and white over *Kwai's* Cinemascope color and replaced dramatic music and catchy military tunes with highly abstract, modernist sound effects, electronically simulating the sounds of approaching tanks, for example, or inserting foreboding, sudden tones into scenes that seemed mundane and ordinary. If *Kwai* had taken place in the exotic jungles of Bangkok and Ceylon, as well as emphasized adventure and drama with a spectacular bridge as its center, *Bridge* was set locally and realistically in the grey "Alltag" of a dreary, little, German town.[82] Though several scenes borrow from the dramatic lighting of classic black and white films like Carol Reed's *The Third Man*, overall, Wicki consciously chose bare, unattractive settings, which couldn't have been easy, given the genuine beauty of the German rural landscape. A colleague of Wicki's remembers that he and his assistants had to "drive all over Germany" in search of a bridge with just the right qualities of unspectacularness.[83] Importantly, Wicki chooses to adopt a straight narrative story, significantly altering the more complex flashback point of view the novel offered. Here, of course, there is a similarity with *Kwai* that offered viewers a chance to compare narratives.

On the level of content, Wicki's *Bridge* dramatically altered precisely those dimensions of the story that had been criticized as pro-war commercialism in *Kwai*. Rather than depicting attractive, heroic male soldiers, he offers the viewers gawky, sexually self-conscious boys (compare Figures 2.1, 2.2, and 2.4). If *Kwai* had drawn from the sex and war format by inserting female figures as romantic interests or sexual objects, *Bridge* integrates women into the story in a more complex way, emphasizing that German mothers could represent both an anti-war and a pro-war point of view. There were lots of women in *Bridge*, none of whom were represented as sex objects, even as the boys saw women as a major source of sexual frustration and anxiety. In one fade out, a young civilian in the throes of a typical adolescent identity crisis is suddenly transformed into an awkward soldier in basic training. The short scene emphasizes the continuity of adolescent self destructiveness and frustration with military aggression. Wicki was clearly influenced by Freudian notions of adolescent identity crisis that defined adult attitudes toward youth in the late-1950s. In *Bridge*, he projects the notion of the adolescent who has to figure out who he is as an adult, the psychological model for postwar German youth onto the earlier more militaristic generation.[84] While the scenario of sending children to war clearly functioned as a critique of the heroic militarism in *Kwai*, it also bracketed questions of culpability for the war by suggesting that the German soldier was little more than a crisis ridden adolescent son of more or less cynical, self-serving fathers, who therefore could not fairly or responsibly be understood as an agent.[85]

Perhaps the most remarkable parallel between the two films is in the meaning and function of the bridge itself. Wicki's film opens without credits of any kind, only a shot of the dark, heavy bridge with the text "Die Brücke" superimposed over it. While in Gregor's novel the bridge did have strategic significance, Wicki altered the meaning of the bridge in the film in a way that gave it a function very similar to the bridge in *Kwai*—as a military object that ultimately sets countrymen against each other. If in *Kwai* this dynamic is a source of ideological and dramatic tension, then in *Bridge*, it is a foregone conclusion. The bridge is meaningless strategically, and the boys' efforts in its behalf are wasted. Though it was intended to be destroyed, the bridge remains standing, because the young soldiers chose to defend it. If in *Kwai*, the viewer is given opportunities to empathise with Col. Nicholson's desire to build the bridge and is impressed with the bridge's formidable scenic beauty, its destruction sends a clear signal that the right side of the conflict ultimately won the skirmish. In Wicki's film, the bridge serves no such ideological function. It is aesthetically unspectacular and militarily insignificant. However, when compared to *Kwai*, the bridge clearly serves an ideological function, namely, to demonstrate how the symbolism of the bridge in commercial films might promote a more anti-war message in a Cold War context than films like *Kwai* were doing (compare Figures 2.3 and 2.5).

Other themes raised in *Kwai* reappear in *Bridge*. The word "Wahnsinn", or madness, is repeated at several points, emphasizing the absurdity of sending boys to war or of war in general. Likewise, the theme of idealism is thematized in Wicki's film as well. If in *Kwai*, Colonel Nicholson is intended to be and defined by the Columbia publicity as an "idealist figure" whose idealism is corrupted by the external forces of war, in *Bridge*, the boys are defined as "idealist" by the commanding officer in dialogue with the teacher, who in turn questions the values of military idealism in his plea to spare the boys from the final throes of a lost war.

Many German critics in the late-1950s thought that Wicki had been successful in his efforts to create a genuinely anti-war film as he had managed to avoid even the typical "unconscious" promotion of military values.[86] In particular, Wicki's graphic and decidedly unglamorous use of violence in the battle scenes was seen as creating an uncompromising image of the horrors of war. And indeed, in comparison to other German war films, Wicki's film was the exception that proved the rule.[87]

However, though it sought to set itself apart from the ideological imperatives of such films as *Kwai* in so many dimensions of form and content, Wicki's *Die Brücke* shared with *Kwai* one central characteristic which, despite its clear deromanticization of the heroic soldier and the war film plot, nonetheless compromised its status as an anti-war statement: its unwillingness to understand war as a direct result of conflicts between specific historical nation-states. In his 1959 review of *Die Brücke* in *Filmkritik*, Enno Patalas argued that the film "respected the taboos of West German film production, that it managed to courageously break through at other levels," namely, the taboo of raising questions of agency and accountability for Nazism and fascism: "with one exception all of the adults in the film appear as innocent victims of History or Fate." Patalas continues: "though the film does show the motives that influence the boys' suicidal actions, they nonetheless remain private and coincidental. The general causes for the fanaticism of a part of German youth in 1945 are not discussed. Even the mechanism of the military is vindicated in that the superiors do ultimately wish to protect the boys from harm ... Hence, war ultimately once again wins the character of an unavoidable Fate, that was no one's fault and that no one could prevent."[88] However, what Patalas neglected to discuss was the influence of U.S. popular culture on this particular "Cold War anti-war" film formula, a formula that rendered issues of national accountability taboo that was manifested in films such as *Kwai*, and that would influence productions such as *Die Brücke*: the studied avoidance of questions of national accountability in favor of a transnational anti-war message that ultimately supported the Cold War policies of NATO and its allies.[89] As communist East Germany would increasingly lay ideological claim to issues of anti-fascism and link fascism to such contemporary issues as the nuclear threat,[90] or indeed, "the militarization of the West German film" to "imperialist Bonn,"[91] linking war to national accountability was potentially suspect politically and not the war film formula officially advocated by the largest producer of war films and exporter of war films to Europe, namely, Hollywood.

The kinds of dilemmas this formula could pose were suggested by the decidedly enthusiastic responses to the vicious battle scenes in *Die Brücke* by some German youths and children in the film theaters of Bremen and Hannover of the late-1950s: "That is our film. One should fight for one's fatherland just like these young guys. They are patriots! Where are such patriots today? Now I know what role models are!"[92] Whereas adults tended to respond to *Die Brücke* as an anti-war statement, some youths clearly read it as a war film.[93] One concerned journalist, Klaus Norbert Scheffler, wrote an open letter to Wicki suggesting the major reasons why he thought the youths had "misunderstood" the film: the film did not address the historical and social causes of war; it had failed to take an ethical stand on the question of the boys' induction and ultimate deaths, ultimately defining it as "meaningless" rather than "wrong;" and finally, that the problem of war could not be solved through aesthetic means alone, a point which Enno Patalas also supported.[94]

In 1961, Walther Schmieding responded to these ostensibly pro-war responses to *Die Brücke* by explicitly linking them to the ambiguity themes of *Kwai*. Such responses suggested that perhaps all anti-war films could ultimately be transformed into their opposites. A "textbook example" of this could also be seen in the American film *Kwai*: the final words of "madness" were drowned in the melody of a military march. Yet, what made Wicki's film different from *Kwai*, according to Schmieding, was that general critical agreement had dubbed *Kwai* a war film disguised as an anti-war film, whereas in *Bridge*, Wicki's "earnestness and absolute sense of responsibility could not be doubted."[95]

Schmieding's evaluation both linked the two films by way of the ambiguity theme and distinguished their respective political motivations. Certainly, *Die Brücke* shared with *Kwai* a basically ahistorical "anti-war" agenda that lent itself to the general imperative of the cultural politics of the NATO alliance—

condemning all conventional warfare, based upon the assumption that nuclear warfare was the new order of the day and that it was nuclear warfare that had to be prevented. And like *Kwai, Die Brücke* could be interpreted differently by different groups with different agendas. In West Germany, not raising the question of the origins of World War II also linked *Die Brücke* to other German war films, as Patalas noted. However, Wicki broke with the Cold War anti-war film formula even as he adhered to it, for he did not redeem the Allies as the ultimate victors, as did *Kwai* with the destruction of the bridge at the film´s conclusion. Thus, in its "dialogue" with *Kwai*, Wicki's *Die Brücke* manages both to separate war from German national accountability—a move that fits the NATO agenda—and to criticize the Cold War imperative in *Kwai* that ultimately justified war through Allied victory. In *Die Brücke*, the state does not triumph in the end, and in this sense, of course, it was very much about the German past.

In the conclusion of his chapter on war films, "Des Teufels Generäle," in the study, *Kunst oder Kasse: Der Ärger mit dem Deutschen Film* (1961) (Art or Profit: The Trouble with the German Film), Schmieding took German filmmakers to task for their unwillingness to confront questions of the historical origins of World War II: "Instead of offering concrete historical analysis, (German) directors yielded to general accusations against war that demonstrated a vaguely defined desire for peace. The goal they ought to have pursued [to address the historical origins of World War II] they did not see or did not want to see. Instead, they kept pursuing the goal of creating the ultimate perfect anti-war film. They did not recognize this as an illusion in a world that to this day sees its only hope of preserving peace in arming itself to the teeth."[96] What the reception of *Kwai* reveals is that the war vs. anti-war film debates and the films they addressed were key means of bringing this problem of choice, memory, and the relationship between history, culture, and politics to public light; that they revealed the symbiotic relationship between the United States and West Germany with regard to raising key questions (or not) about the transition from a fascist to a Cold War based democratic order. As we have seen and as Schmieding suggested, this general "Cold War anti-war" formula was tied to the new Cold War order which implicated the United States and West Germany and the representations of war that both produced. Yet if Wicki´s *Die Brücke*, the last of West Germany´s combat films of the 1950s, refrained from raising questions about the origins of World War II, when situated in relationship to the American produced *Kwai*, it nonetheless offered a German critique of the irony of preserving peace through both U.S. and German produced Cold War anti-war films. It was unintended but unmistakeable that in this process—engaging in dialogue with US blockbusters such as *Kwai*—German critics and commentators, film-makers such as Wicki, and surely also some members of the general public expanded the forms German memory culture could assume by calling attention to those dimensions of popular culture that encouraged forgetting rather than remembering.

*   *   *

When Orson Welles's internationally co-produced adaptation of Franz Kafka's *The Trial* was released in West Germany five years later, the question of what aspects of the German past ought to be remembered had undergone significant expansion. Whereas *Kwai* could trigger discussion of the legacy of militarism and defeat, Welles's adaptation of Kafka would tap into another dimension of German memory politics: the war crimes of National Socialism and the Holocaust. This in turn would raise questions about the ways U.S. popular culture sought to approach issues of German history.

Notes

1. *The Bridge on the River Kwai* (German title: *Die Brücke am Kwai*) dir: David Lean, producer: Sam Spiegel, with Alec Guinness, William Holden, Sessue Hayakawa, Columbia Pictures, 1957.

2. See esp. Steven Jay Rubin, *Combat Films-American Realism: 1945-1970* (Jefferson, North Carolina, 1981), 143-171; Michael Anderegg, *David Lean* (Boston, 1984), 91-102; Bosley Crowther, *New York Times* (22 December 1957, Sec. II): 3. See also Richard A. Kallan, "*The Bridge on the River Kwai*: The Collision of Duty and Pride," in Marilyn J. Matelski and Nancy Lynch Street, *War and Film in America: Historical and Critical Essays*. (Jefferson, North Carolina, 2003), 13-24. Kallan, somewhat belatedly, comes to the conclusion that *Kwai* "does not present an opposing framework to war." (23)

3. Horst Windelboth, "Der Oberst der die Brücke liebte," *Berliner Morgenpost*, (24 January 1958); Rolf Thoel, "Ein Filmerfolg-wie lange nicht," *Welt am Sonntag*, (26 January 1958).

4. Andrew Kelley, *All Quiet on the Western Front: the Story of a Film*. (London, 2002), 124-127.

5. Uta G. Poiger, *Jazz, Rock and Rebels: Cold War Politics and American Culture in a Divided Germany* (Berkeley, 2000); Heide Fehrenbach and Uta Poiger, eds. *Transactions, Transgressions, Transformations: American Culture in Western Europe and Japan* (New York, 2000).

6. Wolfgang Becker und Norbert Schöll, *In Jenen Tagen...Wie der deutsche Nachkriegsfilm die Vergangenheit bewältigte* (Opladen, 1995); Christoph Classen, *Bilder der Vergangenheit: Die Zeit des Nationalsozialismus im Fernsehen der Bundesrepublik Deutschland, 1955-1965* (Cologne, Weimar, Vienna, 1999); Helmut Dubiel, *Niemand ist frei von der Geschichte: Die nationalsozialistische Herrschaft in den Debatten des Deutschen Bundestages* (Munich, 1999); Norbert Frei, *1945 und Wir: Das Dritte Reich im Bewußtsein der Deutschen* (Munich, 2005); Michael Geyer, "Cold War Angst: The Case of West German Opposition to Rearmament and Nuclear Weapons" in Hanna Schissler, ed. *The Miracle Years: A Cultural History of West Germany, 1949-1968* (Princeton University Press, 2001), 376-408; Michael Th. Greven und Oliver von Wrochem (hrg.) *Der Krieg in der Nachkriegszeit: Der Zweite Weltkrieg in Politik und Gesellschaft der Bundesrepublik* (Opladen, 2000); Jeffrey Herf, *Divided Memory: The Nazi Past in the Two Germanys* (Cambridge, Mas-

sachusetts, 1997); Knut Hickethier, "Der Zweite Weltkrieg und der Holocaust im Fernsehen der Bundesrepublik der fünfziger und frühen sechziger Jahre," in Greven/Wrochem, *Der Krieg in der Nachkriegszeit,* 93–112; Herbert Marcuse, *Feindanalysen: Über die Deutschen* (hrg. Peter-Erwin Jansen), (Lüneburg, 1998); Hanna Schissler, "Writing about 1950s West Germany," in Schissler, *The Miracle Years,* 3–15; Frank Stern, "Film in the 1950s: Passing Images of Guilt and Responsibility," in Hanna Schissler, ed., 266–280; Frank Stern, "Gegenerinnerungen seit 1945: Filmbilder, die Millionen sahen," in Greven/Wrochem, 79–91; Edgar Wolfrum (Hrsg.), *Die Deutschen im 20. Jahrhundert* (Darmstadt, 2004).

7. See, for example, Peter Reichel, *Erfundene Erinnerung: Weltkrieg und Judenmord in Film und Theater* (Munich, Vienna, 2004); Robert G. Moeller, *War Stories: The Search for a Usable Past in the Federal Republic of Germany.* (Berkeley, 2001), 123–170, and, more recently, "What Did You Do in the War, *Mutti*? Courageous Women, Compassionate Commanders, and Stories of the Second World War," *German History,* 22(2004): 563–594; Habbo Knoch, *Die Tat als Bild: Fotografien des Holocaust in der deutschen Erinnerungskultur* (Hamburger Edition, 2001); Philipp von Hugo, "Kino und kollektives Gedächtnis? Überlegungen zum westdeutschen Kriegsfilm der fünfziger Jahre," in Bernhard Chiari, Matthias Rogg und Wolfgang Schmidt, ed. *Krieg und Militär im Film des 20. Jahrhunderts* (Munich, 2003), 453–477.

8. German historians and social scientists working in Germany and writing on the 1950s, such as Helmut Dubiel and Norbert Frei, tend to emphasize the role of political opportunism or the impact of external forces on the relationship between "*Vergangenheitsbewältigung*" and 1950s West Germany, whereas U.S. historians of Germany, such as Jeffrey Herf, pay more attention to the impact of indigenous traditions and questions of moral agency. In the area of visual culture, scholars such as Frank Stern and Habbo Knoch even locate the origins of progressive "Vergangenheitsbewältigung" in the culture and society of the 1950s, in contrast to other scholars who continue to locate those origins in the 1960s.

9. Peter Reichel in *Erfundene Erinnerung,* p. 115, for example, collapses the distinction between German and U.S. war films in the 1950s, even as he cites commentators who emphasize the distinction such as Werner Jungeblodt and Walther Schmieding.

10. Werner Jungeblodt, "Kriegsfilme-noch und noch," *Beiträge zur Begegnung von Kirche und Welt,* Nr. 47, hrg. von der Akademie der Diözese Rottenburg, 1960, 2–16 (pp. 4 & 94).

11. 7. Ibid., p. 2; Klaus Sigl, et al, *Jede Menge Kohle: Kunst und Kommerz auf dem deutschen Filmmarkt der Nachkriegszeit, Filmpreise und Kassenerfolge, 1949–1985.* (Munich, 1986), 123–138; Filmpress 12(20 March 1958):12–15; Karl-Heinz Krüger, "Tragödie-Satire-Reisser," *Der Abend, Berlin,* 15. March 1958.

12. Moeller, "Geschichten aus der "Stacheldraht-universität": Kriegsgefangene im Opferdiskurs der Bundesrepublik," *Werkstattgeschichte* 26(2000), pp. 23–46, esp. pp. 23–27.

13. Moeller, *War Stories,* pp. 123–170; Moeller, "'In a Thousand Years, Every German Will Speak of this Battle': Celluloid Memories of Stalingrad," in *Crimes of War: Guilt and Denial in the Twentieth Century,* ed. Omar Bartov, Atina Grossmann, Mary Nolan (New York, 2002), 161–90.

14. All primary source materials are taken from the archival collections of the Deutsches Filminstitut, Frankfurt am Main, the press archives and library of the Film Museum Berlin, and the Deutsche Kinemathek, Berlin.

15. "Die Brücke am Kwai," collection/summaries of British reviews, hrg von der Zentral-Presse- und Werbeabteilung der Columbia-Filmgesellschaft, MBH; Erich Müller, Columbia Pictures publicity pamphlet; "*Die Brücke am Kwai,* Columbia Pictures Publicity Pamphlet, collection of articles, 1–21.(Hellmut Gattinger, responsible for contents).

16. "*Die Brücke am Kwai* ein Durchhalte-Film?" Columbia Pictures Publicity Pamphlet, 9; Jungeblodt, "Kriegsfilme noch und noch", 7.

17. "Über die Menschenwürde," Columbia Publicity, 7; "Nicht nur die Frauen sind gegen den Krieg," Columbia Publicity, 4; "Götzendämmerung im Fernen Osten," Columbia Publicity, 5; "Die Brücke am Kwai-Brücke zum Frieden," Columbia Publicity, 8.

18. "Die Brücke am Kwai," Columbia Publicity, 3; Columbia Publicity, 8.

19. "Mut und Heisses Eisen," Columbia Publicity, 10a; "Auf der Mitte zwischen Europa und Asien," Columbia Publicity, 10; "Offizier und Idealist Dazu," Columbia Publicity, 12; "Angeekelt vom Krieg und dennoch Soldat, Jack Hawkins," Columbia Publicity, 13; "Soldat in Gewissens-not: Geoffrey Horne," Columbia Publicity, 15.

20. "Die Brücke am Kwai mit William Holden in Stuttgart und Frankfurt," *Film-Echo* 21(12 March 1958): 333; Karl-Heinz Krüger, "Tragödie-Satire-Reisser," *Der Abend, Berlin,* (15 March 1958); "200,000 Münchner sahen die B am K" *Filmpress* Jahrg. 10 (26 June 1958).

21. Werner Fiedler, "Die Brücke am Kwai," *Der Tag,* Berlin Westsektor, (16 March 1958); *Deutsche Woche* (26 March 1958).

22. On "U.S. produced" emphasis, see, for example, Gunter Groll, "Die Brücke am Kwai," *Süddeutsche Zeitung,* Munich (15 March 1958) and Walther Schmieding, "Das Heldentum wird Sinnlos," *Ruhrnachrichten,* Dortmund (8 March 1958) and countless others; E. Quadflieg, "Der Wahnsinn der kriegerischen Aktion," *Aachener Nachrichten,* (12 March 1958); Jungeblodt, 3–5. See also May, *The Big Tomorrow,* 202–211. May demonstrates that the increase in U.S. war films in the 1950s was part of a general film trend that saw "an unprecedented increase in films where violence provided the means to resolve the central problems presented by the plot" (206).

23. On "Filmwirkung" see Heide Fehrenbach, *Cinema in Democratizing Germany,* 119–120; Jungeblodt, 14; cK, "Die B am K" *Evangelischer Film Beobachter* 10 (13 March 1958): 125–26; Georg Ramseger, "Wider oder für den Krieg?" *Die Welt,* Essen (8 March 1958).

24. Hans Hellmut Kirst, "Nicholson baut keine Brücke für die Amerikaner," *Münchner Merkur* (15/16 March 1958), p. 13; Letter to the Editor, *Star Revue,* Hamburg, quoted in "B a K-Heldenepos durch die Hintertür" *Kirche und Film* (evang.) Jg. 11, Nr. 7 (July 1958), 16.

25. quoted in *Kirche und Film,* Jg. 11, Nr. 7 (July 1958), 18.

26. Dr. D.C., "Ein Leser schreibt zu DBaK" *Neue Presse,* Coburg, (26 April 1958).

27. Ibid. In "Geschichten aus der "Stacheldraht-universität," Bob Moeller quotes a reviewer with a clearly racist attitude toward the Japanese. (23) This dimension was indeed there, but the majority of critics emphasized that the film itself contained racist images of the Japanese, rather than expressing such sentiments themselves.

28. Norbert Frei locates the beginnings of West German "*Vergangenheitsbewältingung*" in the late 1950s and draws attention to how counterforces could be mobilized against the general consensus of "German victimization." He focuses upon East Germany as a source of counterforce. But U.S. popular culture could also mobilize counterforces, as some responses to Kwai reveal. Additionally, the dynamic of "Nötigung" Helmut Dubiel discusses in *Niemand ist Frei von der Geschichte,* that the West German government was "forced" to consider its past based on external pressures and its own national self understanding, is a dynamic in popular culture as well and I also see it in the *Kwai* reception. See, Norbert Frei, *1945 und Wir: Das Dritte Reich im Bewußtsein der Deutschen* (Munich, 2005), 26; 34–37; Helmut Dubiel, *Niemand ist frei von der Geschichte* (Munich, 1999), 76–77.

29. Michael Geyer, "Cold War Angst: The Case of West German Opposition to Rearmament and Nuclear Weapons," in Hanna Schissler, ed., *The Miracle Years,* 376–408.

30. A.F. Teschemacher, "Zeitzünder aus dem Dschungel" hp [Hannover Zeitung], 14 March 1958. Germans could speak on this subject with authority: "uns Deutschen sind diese Vokabeln gefährlich vertraut. Angefangen bei den Fredericusfilmen, endigend mit Harlans *Kolberg,* haben wir immer wieder dieses geschickte streicheln nationalistischer Gefühle erlebt und sind inzwi-

schen, abgesehen von den professionel Unbelehrbaren, immun gegen Phrasen geworden, die mit so viel Blut honoriert wurden." (Gert Schulte, "Grossbritannien-mal auf Preussisch, FAZ, 14 March 1958).

31. E.S. *Deutsche Zeitung,* (22 March 1958); Georg Ramseger, *Die Welt, Essen,* (8 March 1958); A.F. Teschemacher, "Zeitzünder aus dem Dschungel" hp [Hannover Zeitung], (14 March 1958); Gert Schulte, "Grossbritannien-mal auf Preussisch," *Frankfurter Allgemeine Zeitung,* 14 March 1958).

32. *Deutsche Woche,* (26 March 1958).

33. Gunter Groll, *"Die Brücke am Kwai,"* *Süddeutsche Zeitung* (15 March 1958).

34. Dr. D.C., "Ein Leser schreibt zu DbaK," *Neue Presse,* Coburg, (26 April 1958).

35. Geyer, "Cold War Angst," 399–400.

36. Here again Dubiel's notion of "Nötigung" is significant.

37. See, for example, *Karlsruher Filmschau,* "Demaskierung des Krieges, BNN (3 April 1958); Georg Hensel, "Der Krieg baut keine Brücken, *Darmstädter Echo* (14 March 1958); Helmut Stolp, "Die Brücke am Kwai, *Die Filmwoche—Karlsruhe* (15 March 1958); E. Quadflieg, "Der Wahnsinn der kriegerischen Aktion," *Aachener Nachrichten* (12 March 1958); N-n, "Wahnsinn," *Sonntagsblatt Hamburg,* (30 March 1958).

38. B.m. "Oberst Nicholson-der Held und der Verräter," *Düsseldorfer Nachrichten* (8 March 1958); Mogge, *Kölnische Rundschau,* (12 March 1958); H. Kübler, "Lodernder Protest gegen Krieg und Willkür," *Mannheimer Morgen* (7 March 1958); "Offizier und Idealist Dazu, Alec Guinness" Columbia Publicity, 12; "Vor den Befehlen kommt der Mensch, Sessue Hayakawa, Columbia Publicity, 14; "Götzendämmerung im Fernen Osten," CP, 5; Schulte, "Grossbritanien- mal auf Preussisch, *FAZ* (14 March 1958).

39. Karl-Heinz Krüger, "Tragödie-Satire-Reisser," *Der Abend, Berlin,* (15 March 1958); We, "Vollendete Filmkunst: DieBaK" *Kasseler Post* (8 March 1958); Martin Ruppert, "Wahnsinn kennt keine Grenzen," *FAZ,* (6 March 1958).

40. Karl-Heinz Krüger, "Tragödie-Satire-Reisser", *Der Abend, Berlin,* (15 March 1958); We, "Vollendete Filmkunst: DieBaK" *Kasseler Post* (8 March 1958); Martin Ruppert, "Wahnsinn kennt keine Grenzen," *FAZ,* (6 March 1958).

41. Gert Schulte, "Grossbritanien-mal auf Preussisch," (14 March 1958); Walther Bitterman, "Der Holzweg über den Kwai," *Rheinischer Merkur,* Köln-Koblenz (11 April 1958).

42. Anferäte, "Die Brücke am Kwai," No. 5, (15 May 1958).

43. Gert Schulte, *FAZ,* (14 March 1958); G. Ramseger, *Die Welt,* Essen, (8 March 1958); "River Kwai Millionär" *Abendzeitung* (15 July 1958); "Eine Million mal "River Kwai Marsch," *Tagesspiegel,* (16 July 1958); hck-"Die BaK" *General Anzeiger,* Bonn, (10 April 1958).

44. Fs, "River Kwai" BNN(9 June 1958); "Der Pfeifschlager," *Hamburger Abendblatt,* (11 May 1958); Poiger, *Jazz, Rock and Rebels,* 206–228.

45. Discussion with Ulla Antoni, Anne-Marie Kühne, Hannelore Lüking and Christa Scholz in Rheine, 28 August 2004.

46. Hck-"Die Brücke am Kwai," *General Anzeiger,* Bonn (10 April 1958) ; Dr. D.C., "Ein Leser schreibt zu "Die Brücke am Kwai," *Neue Presse, Coburg,* (26 April 1958).

47. Jeffrey Herf, *Divided Memory: the Nazi Past in the Two Germanys* (Cambridge, MA, 1997); Habbo Knoch, *Die Tat als Bild: Fotografien des Holocaust in der deutschen Erinnerungskultur* (Hamburger Edition, 2001).

48. Walther Schmieding, *Ruhrnachrichten,* Dortmund, (8 March 1958).

49. G. Groll, *SZ,* (13 March 1958).

50. Karena Niehoff, "Die Brücke am Kwai," *Tagesspiegel Berlin,* (18 March 1958).

51. G.H. "DbaK" (6728) Filmdienst 10 (6 March 1958), 87.

52. Erwin Gölz, "Ein ungewöhnlicher Film," *Stuttgarter Zeitung.* (6 March 1958).

53. Dr. D.C., "Ein Leser schreibt zu DBaK" *Neue Presse,* Coburg, (26 April 1958).

54. Moeller, "Geschichten aus der "Stacheldraht-universität," 45–46.

55. Habbo Knoch, *Die Tat als Bild,* 27.

56. The following discussion illustrates how the war vs. anti-war debate politicized the relationship between novel and film adaptation, rendering questions of "fidelity to the original work," usually understood as a purely artistic questions, into political ones. A further example is Walther Schmieding's brief analysis of the book/film *From Here to Eternity* in his review of *Kwai:* "Who failed to notice that the film *From Here to Eternity,* in contrast to the novel, attempted a rehabilitation of the army?" (W. Schmieding, "Der Heldentum wirkt Sinnlos," *Ruhrnachrichten,* Dortmund, 8 March 1958.)

57. The German edition of Boulle's novel was published by *ro ro ro* Taschenbuch in September of 1956. My copy of the German edition, published by Bertelsman around 1958, contains an inscription by a German military officer, Kapitänleutnant and Kompaniechef Gottmeyer to a colleague which reads: "lieber Smolka als Dank für treue Dienste"—Dear Smolka, in gratitude for loyal service—suggesting that the novel's satirical/ironical point of view on the military was circulating among members of the German military. Based upon the blurb in the back of the book for another work published by Bertelsman, Jessamyn West's *Lockende Versuchung,* made into the film *Friendly Persuasion,* starring Gary Cooper, Dorothy Maguire and Anthony Perkins, it's possible to say that Bertelsman was interested in publishing works that advocated at least modest criticism of war and the military, as the work was about a Quaker's conscientious objection to military service in the U.S. Civil War.

58. "Auch ein Bucherfolg," *Westfalenpost,* (21 May 1958); 'chen' "Tragik, Ironie und Wenig Worte," *Telegraf,* (17 Jan. 1958); Horst Windelboth, "Der Oberst der die Brücke liebte," *Berliner Morgenpost,* (24. Jan. 1958).

59. Steven Jay Rubin, *Combat Films: American Realism, 1945-1970,* (Jefferson, North Carolina, 1981), 143–171.

60. Walther Talmon-Gros, "Die Brücke am Kwai," Wiesbaden[source unclear] (8 March 1958).

61. Ibid., see also, b.m. "Oberst Nicholson-der Held und der Verräter," *Düsseldorfer Nachrichten,* (8 March 1958).

62. Hellmut Haffner, *Abendzeitung* Munich, quoted in "Neue Filme-im Spiegel der Kritik," *Filmpress* 12 (20 March 1958): 13.

63. Enno Patalas, "Die Brücke am Kwai," *Filmkritik* (April 1958): 82–83.

64. Ibid.

65. For Wagnleiter, "U.S. cultural imperialism" was not a one-sided affair. Rather he focuses upon the ways in which U.S. political elites shared with Europeans a fundamentally European conception of high culture. Thus certain U.S. cultural indoctrination efforts could actually be attempts to prove to Europeans that Americans, too, had "high culture," which they were now exporting to Europe in exchange for markets. Columbia Publicity's efforts to demonstrate the "anti-war" character of *Kwai* could be interpreted in light of this thesis, ironically. See Reinhold Wagnleitner, *Coca-Colonization and the Cold War* (Chapel Hill and London, 1994) and A.M. Scholz, Review of Reinhold Wagnleitner, *Coca-Colonization and the Cold War, Amerikastudien,* 42.1(1997): 126–129.

66. For an extended discussion of the ways in which Hollywood attempted to shape its films with the European (export) market in mind, see Wagnleitner, *Coca-Colonization and the Cold War,* 230–251.

67. Walther Schmieding, *Ruhrnachrichten,* Dortmund, (8 March 1958).

68. Gert Schulte, "Grossbritannien-mal auf Preussisch," *FAZ,* (14 March 1958).

69. Cited in Michael Anderegg, *David Lean* (Boston, 1984), 160.

70. "Dialogue in Film: Carl Foreman," *American Film* Vol IV, nr. 6 (April 1979), pp. 35–46. (p. 44)

71. On the social and cultural dimensions of the atomic weapons debates in West Germany in the late-1950s, see Ilona Stölken-Fitschen, *Atombombe und Geistesgeschichte*, (Baden-Baden, 1995).

72. Pfarrer Werner Hess, "Filmgeschäft mit dem Krieg," *Kirche und Film* 7(Juli 1958): 2–5.

73. "Bei "Columbia" spricht man von Schwabach…" *Schwabacher Tagblatt* (6 Oct. 1958).

74. Werner Jungeblodt, "Kriegsfilme-noch und noch," *Beiträge zur Begegnung von Kirche und Welt*, Nr. 47, hrg. von der Akademie der Diözese Rottenburg, 1960, 2–16.

75. Peter Reichel in *Erfundene Erinnerung* calls Jungeblodt's study "aufmerksam und besorgt" (115) (attentive and concerned), yet rather than focusing on Jungeblodt's thesis, he prefers to concentrate on the general problem of the "war film as anti-war film" to demonstrate that even seemingly "anti-war" films made in West and East Germany were compromised due to their avoidance of the question of the historical origins of war. "Faszination und Abwehr" (fascination and resistance) characterized all war films of the era. With this thesis Reichel in effect dehistoricizes the phenomenon of the war vs. anti-war film debate. By focusing strictly on the German context, Reichel downplays the historical function of this ambiguity in the Cold War context of the time. See esp. pp. 115–126.

76. Jungeblodt, 10. See also Walther Schmieding, *Kunst oder Kasse: Der Ärger mit dem deutschen Film* (Hamburg, 1961), esp. pp. 35–55). Jungeblodt's study is a modest example of what Habbo Knoch has referred to as "a portion of the population that used the wave of war entertainment as a pretext for demanding "other memories/recollections of NS crimes." (Knoch, *Die Tat als Bild*, 429)

77. Jungeblodt, 10.

78. Jungeblodt, 2.

79. *Die Brücke*, (BRD 1959), Director: Bernhard Wicki.

80. For a discussion emphasizing how Wicki's film significantly parted company with the German war films of the 1950s, see Robert G. Moeller, "Victims in Uniform: West German Combat Movies from the 1950s," in Bill Niven, ed. *Germans as Victims: Remembering the Nazi Past in Contemporary Germany* (Basingstoke, 2006): 43–61; Peter Reichel emphasizes Wicki's continued reliance on the theme of German victimization, and compares *Die Brücke* with the East German film *Die Abendteuer des Werner Holt* in *Erfundene Erinnerung*, 123–126. See especially the chapter, "Der Kriegsfilm als Antikriegsfilm," 115–126.

81. Interview mit Robert Fischer, in Robert Fischer, *Bernhard Wicki: Regisseur und Schauspieler.* (Munich, 1994, und Autor), 33–40; Richard Blank, *Jenseits der Brücke, Bernhard Wicki: Ein Leben für den Film.* (Munich, 1999), 101–116. See also Peter Zander, *Bernhard Wicki* (Berlin, 1995. [1994] 2., überar. Aufl.), 17–23.

82. While the settings of both films couldn't have been more different, they both share the significant dimension of on-location shooting.

83. Blank, 108.

84. See, for example, Uta G. Poiger, *Jazz, Rock and Rebels*, ch. 3.

85. The controversy surrounding Günther Grass' late revelation that he joined the Waffen SS as a teenager was exacerbated by Grass' tendency to rely on this line of argument, for which he had criticized others in the past.

86. Enno Patalas, "Die Brücke," *Filmkritik* 3(December 1959), 315. Patalas, however, ends by criticizing the films ahistorical conception of war. For reviews that defined *Die Brücke* as an "anti-war" film, see Von Hugo, 468.

87. Ibid., Moeller, "Victims in Uniform."

88. E. P. (Enno Patalas), "Die Brücke," *Filmkritik* 3 (December 1959): 316–317.

89. Reichel reads this dimension within a German historical context alone: "Der Film wurde weithin als ein Stück erfundener Erinnerung an ein großes politisches Verbrechen verstanden, das mit den Deutschen und nicht durch sie geschehen war." (124)

90. Television documentary footage, opening a holocaust memorial in Ettersberg, DDR 1958, Jüdisches Museum Berlin, Dauerausstellung. In this film, a West German politician links fascism to the threat of nuclear destruction at the dedication of a Holocaust memorial in East Germany.

91. See Erhard Kranz, *Filmkunst in der Agonie* (Berlin, 1964), 176.

92. *Weser Kurier*, (9 December 1959), quoted in Von Hugo, "Kino und Kollektives Gedächtnis?", 469.

93. Von Hugo, 469. Von Hugo suggests that this response by the youths calls into question the anti-war status of *Die Brücke* and the viability of classifying films as war or anti-war in general.

94. Primary sources quoted in Von Hugo, 470–71.

95. Schmieding, *Kunst oder Kasse: Der Ärger mit dem deutschen Film* (Hamburg, 1961), 51–52.

96. Schmieding, 54–55.

Chapter Three

"Josef K. von 1963"

Orson Welles's Americanized Version of The Trial *and the Changing Functions of the Kafkaesque in Postwar West Germany*

The American auteur and actor Orson Welles's lifelong interest in a critique of fascism was evident in his 1962 adaptation of Franz Kafka's *The Trial* as well as in the ways he modified the story for his purposes. Welles's reading of Kafka as a "prophet of fascism," whose Josef K. actively resists his oppressors—even if to no apparent avail—sought to shift the story's focus from Josef K.'s anonymous, personal torment to the larger institutional and political structures of the post-war period, totalitarianism, fascism, state communism, and Cold War angst. Within these structures, Welles suggests that Josef K.'s irrational and absurd trial paradoxically made a strange kind of sense and called attention to the protagonist's status as a human agent capable of resisting authoritarianism.

When Welles's adaptation of Franz Kafka's *The Trial* was released in West Germany in 1963, many critics were preoccupied with the changes Welles had made to the original work, perhaps unsurprising at first glance, given the assumption that film adaptations are meant to abide by the literary work. However, the key issue here is the meaning of fidelity. What makes specific texts meaningful within a particular culture, so that issues of "textual fidelity" become significant?[1] Since the end of World War II and the Third Reich, during which time Kafka's works were banned in Germany, those same works had reentered the Federal Republic—they continued to be banned in East Germany—essentially transformed in their original meanings. They had become symbolic of what is still known as "the Kafkaesque," an atmosphere of "angst," resignation, and powerlessness linked with the anxieties of postwar life. Promoted primarily through the editorial efforts of Kafka's friend and literary executor, Max Brod, who encouraged a reading of Kafka's works as allegories with a universal philosophical dispensation and an understanding of their author as a type of spiritual figure outside all historical and literary context[2], the "Kafkaesque" would nonetheless find itself circulating in very real historical and national contexts where the idea of "postwar anxiety" meant different things to different people, including fear of nuclear annihilation, communist takeover, and in the case of West Germany, fear and unease over the legacy of the Third Reich and its effects on German society as well as on its international standing as a nation.

By the early 1960s, West Germany had been definitively integrated into the Cold War alliance with the United States, which tended to encourage a focus upon the "immediate" threat of communism and to discourage an open confrontation with and working through of the fascist past. Until recently, many scholars of German history have argued that an active effort to confront the legacy of the National Socialist past did not begin until the late-1960s. However, revisionist historians have recently put forth that the issue of how to remember World War II and what conclusions to draw from it were already on the agenda by the mid-1950s.[3] Habbo Knoch conceptualizes this process of active memory construction in terms of what he calls "the long 1960s": "the "modernization" of memory took place between 1955 and 1965 when Nazi crimes attracted public attention and when they were reinvented as a visual, emotional, but virtual and limited, experience. In the long 1960s that began in the second half of the 1950s, West German society continued its long process of "coming to terms with the past." It produced its images of Nazi crimes to serve not as a mirror but as a movie of something that took place far away and remote from everyday life.[4] This chapter seeks to explore a small corner of this process by focusing upon the ways in which a German speaking author banned by the Nazis was appropriated by an American film auteur and how postwar German commentators responded to his attempt to combine "mirror" and "movie."

Certainly one of the founding texts of "the Kafkaesque," *The Trial* was written by Kafka as a fragment during World War I and organized and published as a novel by Brod after Kafka's death in 1924.[5] In the original story, the protagonist Josef K. is arrested in his apartment without being informed of charges, accusers, and without being imprisoned. Instead, his ensuing trial becomes an extension of the hierarchy and regimentation he experiences at his job as a bank administrator, where he attempts to save face and keep the proceedings a secret to protect his reputation. Though he is never informed of the charges, Josef K. is progressively integrated into the legal formalities of constructing a defense within a system that offers him no basis upon which to act. Throughout his trial, Josef K. comes into contact with a number of figures who aid and abet him within this absurd scenario: Miss Burstner, his boarding house neighbor, Hassler, his attorney, and Leni, Hassler's nurse. Throughout *The Trial*, a series of erotic scenarios involving Josef K. and a variety of female figures tend to link sexuality to the other corrupt dimensions of the court. As

Josef K. becomes increasingly frustrated and disoriented, searching for help that only seems to involve him more deeply in the unjust proceedings, he is eventually found guilty and executed by knife at the hands of two "wardens" of the court.

In his internationally co-produced and "co-acted" film, which starred Anthony Perkins as Josef K., Welles as the attorney Hassler, Romy Schneider as the nurse Leni, and a number of other internationally prominent stars, Orson Welles altered the story in a number of telling ways.[6] Most significant for the German reception, he linked Kafka almost directly to the issue of German fascism in his adaptation of *The Trial*. Welles tapped into one of the then prevailing interpretations of Kafka as a "prophet of fascism," a writer whose works had anticipated the dehumanization and tyranny of the concentration camps in their focus upon how the rational, bureaucratic mechanisms of the state can lead to the annihilation of the individual. However, rather than linking the figure of Josef K. to the idea of victimization under that system, he instead focused upon the protagonist as a figure of ambivalent resistance. In an interview with the French film journal *Cahiers du Cinema,* Welles explained why he refused to take over the ending of *The Trial* where Josef K. is executed without resistance: "To me it's a 'ballet' written by a Jewish intellectual before the advent of Hitler. Kafka wouldn't have put that after the death of six million Jews. It all seems very Pre-Auschwitz to me."[7] Welles's sense of *The Trial* as being narrated by a Jewish man in pre-fascist Europe ultimately motivated him to alter it in such a way for his film so as to emphasize the themes of agency and resistance. Josef K. is executed at the end, but he resists his oppressors, and the theme of resistance plays a far greater role in the film than it does in the novel. In the novel, Josef K. offers a certain amount of resistance at the outset, which gradually breaks down, whereas in the film his level of resistance actually increases.

Welles reinforces his emphasis on agency through his modification of the "Parable of the Law," which appears quite late in the novel, as a frame for understanding the proceedings of his film. In the parable, a guard stands before the door of the Law, controlling entry. A "man from the country" comes requesting admittance, but is not allowed to enter. The man decides to wait by the door, in the hope of some day gaining admittance. In old age, still waiting, he asks the guard why in all the years of waiting no one else has ever come by to request admittance to the law, to which the Guard replies: no one else could gain admittance at this door, as it was intended only for him, and now he (the guard) would close the door. This parable, presented on pin screens in the film created by Russian artists, begins the film, thus framing the subsequent plot, whereas in the novel the parable is told towards the end. However, in the film, the parable reappears briefly towards the end as well, emphasizing the contrast

between "the man from the country" and the figure of Josef K. Indeed, Josef
K. interrupts the figure played by Welles as he attempts to tell the story again,
thus disrupting its function as parable (i.e. having universal, humanistic significance). Welles's reframing of the "Parable of the Law" highlights Josef K.'s
resistance to its message of chaos and arbitrary power.

As Josef K. prepares his case, he moves through a series of modernist and
baroque spatial environments—not specifically located anywhere—that tend
to dwarf and overwhelm him from the perspective of the viewer and that make
his efforts to take charge of the situation appear quite ludicrous. He becomes
progressively more active and resistant as his case becomes more involved and
tends to put up a front of resistance whenever he is confronted with court
officials. When he is finally executed, it is not with a knife but rather with dynamite that sends up a cloud of smoke, reminiscent of an atomic explosion for
a number of critics, though Welles denied the connection. In the film, the two
court wardens appear to be uncomfortable with the prospect of stabbing the
condemned man and prefer to dispense with him "at a distance" by throwing
sticks of dynamite into the pit where he had been lying.

One very telling change was noted only by a few critics. In Kafka, as Josef
K. is being carried to the execution sight, he spots a figure raising a hand toward him in a window. He then speculates who this person might be, a foe, or
even possibly a friend? No such figure appears in the film, and several critics
noted this as a point of even greater unremitting pessimism in the film than in
the novel. At least Kafka offered the hope of some kind of human connection
in the midst of the tyranny of arbitrary power. In contrast, Welles offered only
the nervous resistance of a completely isolated individual.[8]

Throughout the proceedings, Josef K. has a series of erotic encounters, most
of which find their precedent in the novel. However, unlike the novel's protagonist, Welles's Josef K. is active in the legal sphere but generally passive
in the erotic sphere. Consistently, he is reluctantly seduced by the women he
meets. For example, during the first "realistic" scene, Josef K.'s arrest, Welles
links Josef K.'s sense of "guilt" to his sexual feelings for his neighbor, Miss
Burstner, who has been transformed from a stenographer in Kafka to a nightclub dancer. Thus, sexuality in the film is a source of guilt and anxiety for Josef
K., rather than a means of resistance to the system that entraps him.

Josef K. moves among a group of other "accused persons" who take on the
contours of concentration camp victims/survivors, and throughout the film,
there are explicit references to the cruelties of the concentration camps, such
as a row of meat hooks Josef K. walks past as he moves through the building
where his trial is taking place.[9] Welles works symbolic references and associations to modern forms of state run totalitarianism and tyranny into the plot,
including the legacy of concentration camps under German fascism, the threat

of nuclear annihilation as a result of the Cold War, and the subordination of the individual to a technocratic mass society. By integrating these references to different forms of state tyranny as a series of surreal confrontations that Josef K. has with his environment as he prepares his trial, Welles, in effect, links all of these totalitarian forms into one "modern order," suggesting cultural connections between them that transcend national boundaries. As we will see, German fascism in a film for German viewers functions both as a specific historical referent and as a part of a larger transnational tendency toward totalitarianism that ideologically linked "the brown and the red" worlds.[10] This tension between the historically specific and the metaphysical general would prove to be a central aspect of the identity of "Josef K. of 1963" and marked a development in Kafka's German reception away from philosophy and toward history, meaning German history (see Figure 3.1).

Figure 3.1. Anthony Perkins as Josef K. in Orson Welles's adaptation of Franz Kafka's *The Trial.* The row of meat hooks in this still makes the visual connection to Nazi war crimes explicit. (Courtesy: Deutsche Kinemathek, Berlin/Studiocanal)

*   *   *

When Welles's version of *The Trial* was released in the United States, the issue of textual fidelity played only a minor role in critics' responses to the film,
both negative and positive. Those critics who didn't like *The Trial* tended to
blame the ego of Orson Welles and his inability to discipline it in such a way
as to produce a second world class film. Since *Citizen Kane*, several argued that
Welles had not made a similar masterpiece, and the *The Trial* was no exception.
Living up to *Citizen Kane* was more important to U.S. critics than whether or
not *The Trial* was an adequate adaptation of Kafka.[11] While critics who didn't
like the film tended to argue that the film was not true to Kafka, those who
liked the film didn't necessarily make fidelity the major issue. The film had of it
"more Welles than Kafka," to be sure, but then again it was so much better than
other films, "even when they are well made."[12] The film had humor; American
critics appreciated the humor in the film. However, this was associated with
Welles rather than Kafka. American audiences won't catch the humor, critics
argued, because they will see the name Kafka and automatically think of "polite
despair."[13] That Welles actually derives much of this humor from Kafka was not
at issue. U.S. critics also frequently mentioned the portrayal of sexuality in the
film. Here, too, they assumed this was a Wellesian addition; it wasn't. When
Peter Bogdanovich asked Welles where he got the concept of the "dirty pictures
in the judge's textbook," Welles responded, "From Kafka. And I got all the dirty
eroticism of the rest of the movie out of that one thing." Later in the interview,
Welles told Bogdanovich to "read the book sometime. It's short."[14]

*   *   *

Few critics who reviewed Welles's film in West Germany in 1963 were unfamiliar with Kafka, and most based their observations on the comparison
between novel and film. Yet here, too, this was not an inevitable approach. As
in the U.S., there were critics in Germany who linked the film to Welles's oeuvre, especially to *Citizen Kane*, primarily because *Citizen Kane* was not even
screened in Germany until twenty years after its release. This gave viewers the
chance to make comparisons, and one Berlin critic wryly noted that Welles
hadn't developed his film technique much since that time.[15] Indeed, a number
of critics titled their reviews "Citizen K," suggesting that the themes of *The
Trial* had more in common with Welles's earlier film than they did with Kafka,
that it was, in essence, more American than German.[16] Another critic linked
The Trial to the era of German expressionism and referred to it as in its essence
a silent film, "even if Orson Welles lets his actors talk too fast."[17]

When Welles's film was released in West Germany, the indigenous film
industry was under fire on a number of fronts. As elsewhere, television was
making major incursions into formerly movie-going audiences. But more sig-

nificantly, the German film industry was subject to major criticism for not managing to keep up with the quality productions issuing from other European countries, such as France and Italy. The German film was in a moribund state and needed revivifying. Film clubs in West Germany that came into existence after the war to promote international films as a source of recultivating and recivilizing German society were generally appalled by the escapist *Heimatfilm* fantasies and other film fair that was popular with German audiences, but not, in their eyes, of great aesthetic or didactic value. In 1962, young German filmmakers issued the "Oberhausen Manifesto," a moment that has been linked to the beginnings of the New German cinema. However, as Heide Fehrenbach has argued, the Oberhauseners were not part of a new generational trend, but had emerged out of the critical film club scene and film festival scene of the 1950s. It was not until the mid-1960s that New German cinema began to come into its own.[18] In the meantime, art cinema in Germany was coming from elsewhere and looked to as potential models for a new German cinema. Orson Welles was a respected American auteur and popular actor with international credentials; Kafka was an internationally respected German speaking author who had been banned by the Nazis. This combination promised something novel and sought after: greater political and artistic diversity for German audiences in need of reeducation and aesthetic quality for German filmmakers in need of inspiration.

Publicity for the film in West Germany was managed by the Schorcht Film Verleih. The Schorcht Verleih had distributed some of the most successful films of the 1950s, such as *Kinder, Mütter und ein General* (Children, Mothers and a General) (1955), *Das Bad auf der Tenne* (The Bath on the Threshing Floor) (1956), and *Ein Stück vom Himmel* (A Piece of Heaven) (1958). However, after the death of its founder, Kurt Schorcht, in 1959, it "lost direction," despite increased investment and went out of business in 1965.[19] The publicity Schorcht generated for Welles's *The Trial* reflected a film industry in a time of transition in its effort to market the film as politically aware cinema, an elite art cinema product and a potentially popular blockbuster. Its overarching goal seems to have been to reclaim Kafka as a German author of international renown. Kafka "could not conquer the walls of German dictatorship" of the past and was rejected as decadent by communist East Germany. Nonetheless, his work triumphed in France, England, and the United States.[20] Now an American auteur of the highest caliber had decided to adapt a famous Kafka text, and expectations for the film were very high. The Schorcht publicity quoted Welles's emphasis upon the "prophet of fascism" model at several points,[21] and now, at a time of a "*Kino tief,*" a "cinema slump," Welles had taken a great risk with controversial material that had arrived late on the German scene due to its place on the "*rassische Verbotsliste,*" the list of racially banned authors.[22]

Furthermore, the publicity emphasized that the film was true to Kafka, despite one invented love scene by Welles involving Anthony Perkins and Romy Schneider. With this pronouncement, Schorcht seemed to be attempting to appeal both to elitist Kafka aficionados as well as "average filmgoers" interested in love and romance between attractive and popular actors.[23]

Most German critics of the film—as well as some French critics whose work was published in German periodicals—relied on a number of aspects from the Schorcht publicity as a jumping off point, but then went in decidedly different directions. The majority of German critics did not agree that the film was true to Kafka and sought to understand the film within the framework of "Welles vs. Kafka," two auteurs with decidedly different agendas. Yet, interestingly, this was not primarily a question of a demand for textual fidelity. Rather, setting up this opposition was a means of understanding the meaning and function of Kafka's work in German society since the end of the "*rassische Verbotsliste*," as well as understanding the meaning that the "Kafkaesque" held for elite members of German society since the end of the war and, crucially, what had changed since.

Schorcht's publicity, as well as several critics, pointed to a recently published (1961) Kafka bibliography that contained over five thousand entries, testifying both to the literary significance of Kafka, as well as to the many possible ways Kafka might be understood.[24] The socialist-oriented critic, Rolf Traube wrote in the *Deutsche Volkszeitung*, Düsseldorf, that Kafka had been a very fashionable author after World War II: "The awareness that one has barely escaped a terrible catastrophe and is most likely moving toward an even greater one gave a snobbishly cultivated 'Kafkaesque' a popularity that soon irritated professional literary observers, so that in 1955 the young people in the Group 47 resolved the following: whoever pronounces the name Kafka one more time today, will be fined one German Mark."[25] The "Group 47," whose membership included such figures as Hans Magnus Enzensberger, Ingeborg Bachmann, and Günther Grass, had been founded to create a more innovative, politically aware space for literature as a counter voice to the Adenauer era's social, political, and cultural conservatism, and their satiric criticism clearly called attention to the more conservative function of the "Kafkaesque" that was often associated with what Andreas Huyssen referred to in 1986 as a "depoliticized version of modernism that had come to provide a much needed cultural legitimation for the Adenauer restoration. During the 1950s, the myth[s] of … universal existentialist Angst … helped block out and suppress the realities of the fascist past. From the depths of barbarism and the rubble of its cities, West Germany was trying to reclaim a civilized modernity and to find a cultural identity tuned to international modernism, which would make others forget Germany's past as predator and pariah of the modern world."[26]

Traube's review demonstrated that criticism of this depoliticized version of Kafka was already circulating in the 1950s.[27] By 1963, Traube continued, the "Kafkaesque" could no longer function exclusively as an elitist form of intellectual contempt. Welles's production would be subject to objective scrutiny rather than to fashionable acceptance. Critical reflection upon Welles's film was one means of coming to terms with the different possible meanings attached to the "Kafkaesque" in the postwar period.

Confronted with Orson Welles's reading of Kafka, German critics often felt compelled to put into words what it was that Kafka meant to them. Few did this by dismissing the film; indeed, the film was praised by most critics as a fascinating attempt to come to terms with Kafka. However, by and large, German critics were profoundly ambivalent about Welles's version of *The Trial*. Within the framework of the "Kafka vs. Welles" debate two principle definitions of the "Kafkaesque" emerged from the critical discourse. The first was the "prophet of fascism" model, the notion that Kafka's works had "anticipated" the concentration camps in their emphasis upon arbitrary tyranny and violence, which was understood as at odds with the second notion of Kafka as a metaphysician whose stories raised general questions of the meaning of existence. This tension between a "historical" Kafka and a "metaphysical" Kafka governed the discussion of the ways Welles had updated or modernized Kafka to make him relevant to the early 1960s. Even if critics "preferred" an ahistorical, metaphysical version, the debate nonetheless created a space for a historical Kafka that Welles, in his film, had inextricably linked to the German past.

*　*　*

The first definition, the "anticipation of fascism," was one that was quite familiar to most German critics, though it did not go uncontested. Welles offered this version in the Schorcht film publicity, reprinted in the *Welt am Sonntag*: "Why Kafka? Because of his up-to-dateness. This story of a person, who winds up underneath the wheels of the organized society, the wheels of the police, the army, the justice system … and then there is this premonition of the times of concentration camps, that still exist today. And will always exist."[28] Overall, in contrast to his early films, which focused upon the U.S. plutocracy, Welles understood his later work as an attempt to analyze abuses of state power: "because today [1958] the state is more powerful than money."[29] *The Trial* was in keeping with the former. The motif of "abuse of state power" allowed Welles to incorporate references to different tyrannical political systems into his film, but his specific reference to "concentration camps" was an unmistakable reference to German fascism.

There were a number of German critics who also associated the name of Kafka with a "premonition" of "things to come": "Franz Kafka predicted what—in the decades following his death—happened to so many people: the state of absolute lawlessness"[30]; K.H. Krüger noted that "this premonition [of Kafka's] of the concentration camps is nonetheless made palpable by Welles."[31] A critic in the *Westfälische Rundschau,* following the Schorcht publicity, wrote: "That is the story, that is a dream, filled with dream logic. "Do not try to solve puzzles!" Orson Welles warns. Despite this reality shimmers through everywhere. The reality of the concentration camps and the Gestapo, that Kafka anticipated. The reality of today, where the individual is lost in the whirlpool of the masses. A film that finally demonstrates what film is and should be."[32] In his analysis of *The Trial,* Reinold Thiel, film critic for the German film journal *Filmkritik* and SPD activist, linked the "anticipation of fascism" model to Hannah Arendt's reading of Kafka as a critique of the bureaucratic government form of the antebellum (pre–World War I) administration of Austria and suggested that Welles had taken over Arendt's perspective in his film and transferred it to the bureaucratic state of modern times.[33] Like Arendt, Thiel argued, Welles ignored Kafka's "metaphysical aspect," his interest in "the meaning of existence," and instead focused solely upon historical dimensions. Ultimately, Thiel did not think Kafka's *Trial* was an appropriate vehicle through which to critique the totalitarian state and that Welles's version left the viewer "with the baroque violence of isolated ideas."[34] Others disagreed, Volker Baer wrote in the *Tagesspiegel Berlin*: "over these pathetic creatures, who are being intimidated to death by a totalitarian system, hang coldly threatening meat hooks that recall terrible associations with concentration camps. Welles has extended and concretized Kafka's vision."[35] Baer thought that the most authentic dimensions of Kafka had been captured by Welles in the visual images of the film and less in the dialogue and performances.

Enno Patalas, founder of the journal *Filmkritik,* suggested that the interpretation of Kafka as a "prophet of fascism" had had a critical function in the immediate postwar years. Particularly, such works as "*In der Strafkolonie*" (In the Penal Colony) began to be taught at German universities just as the first eyewitness accounts of concentration camps were published after the war.[36] By the early 1960s, many critics were ambivalent about this model and tended to reject it by referring to it as a "fashion" or "trend" that had long since passed and that, moreover, had been imported from outside. According to critic Walter Kaul, foreigners had essentially made Kafka into "a world fashion, in whose train concepts such as Angst, mechanization, and bureaucratization cavorted with one another."[37] Orson Welles had picked up on this model in his adaptation. Critic Karena Niehoff also passionately rejected this interpretation: "Welles would like to persuade Kafka, as have others before him, that he had prophesied Hitler, all terror dictatorships, concentration camps, and other anonymous tortures: a visionary contemporary critic … Welles misunderstanding is "horribly banal"; he views Josef K. as a classical hero, who goes to his death with the courage of a Russian anarchist, the Scholl siblings, or the Warsaw Ghetto fighters, unconquered, with one last cynical word on the lips, ennobled by the radiance of innocence in an evil world."[38] Why Niehoff's resistance to Welles's "heroic" version of Josef K.? Kafka did not see fascism coming, she continues. Rather, he saw a world without God. However, Niehoff's discussion of her own sense of Kafka revealed a preoccupation with questions of guilt and its attribution that suggested history played a role in the "Kafkaesque" as much as did metaphysics and religion: "that which gets the heart beating while reading Kafka is the untragic triviality and how it insinuates itself; the absurd does not reveal itself as such; rather, it becomes the crystalline result of an unprotected Reality considered through to its logical conclusion; the complacent dailiness hides and releases in every moment the possibility, not only to be put on trial, but—what is even worse—to actually become guilty, guilt based upon an unknown and inaccessible law."[39] Despite her generalized language, Niehoff's bitter resistance to the "heroic" Josef K. and preoccupation with K.'s having become "guilty" indirectly revealed an awareness that the reality of the recent German terror dictatorship was the reality of collaboration rather than heroism. Karena Niehoff was a Jewish woman who had survived the Nazi period in the Berlin underground. After the war, she began her journalism career and wrote for the Berliner *Tagesspiegel* between 1952 and her death in 1992. She was also a witness in the postwar trial of the German filmmaker Veit Harlan, where she had been subject to some anti-Semitic violence. She was politically engaged, but refrained from talking about the past and did not draw attention to her status as a Jewish survivor in her work. Ironically, her ironic-associative style of writing reflected here in her critique of Welles's film, hinted at her own personal experience of persecution.[40]

For the conservative critic Walter Kaul, writing for the *Kurier,* Berlin, the "prophet of fascism" model also concealed a preoccupation with getting to historical essentials in aesthetic terms: "Every bitter association is quickly blended out through the hoaky flashing of a blade, at which point one yearns for Bunuel-Dali's (from *The Andalucian Dog*) shaving of the eyelid from the eyeball."[41]

One French critic, Alexandre Alexandre, writing for *Der Kurier* from Paris, noted that Kafka's texts were a means of coping with the terrors of the Gestapo during the war and that his texts continued to be relevant in a postwar world where "the deeply awaited Renaissance of freedom and human dignity did not immediately materialize."[42] Another French critic, writer and academic Jean-Louis Bory, also actively approved of Welles's linking Kafka to fascism. Welles had "modernized" Kafka. He wrote in *Arts* that Welles had "accused that which had made history even more Kafkaesque than Kafka: the world of the concentration camps and, in short visual allusions, had awakened the memory of the Nazi camps. This KZ world threatens to become our world as we continue on the road of progress." For Bory, Welles had detected two interrelated types of guilt. The first was the guilt of the accused who resists the accusation; he is guilty of being an individual. And as an individual, he is guilty of collaboration, of being a cog in a system, becoming frightened only when he is accused himself.[43] Bory, as a French critic, was surely not unfamiliar with issues related to French collaboration with the Nazis during World War II. His opinions, as well as the opinions of other French critics, were circulated widely in German film magazines.

Like Bory, German critics were preoccupied with questions of agency and guilt. Welles "modernization" of Kafka was about the state of "Josef K. in 1963":

> Today, whoever has experienced a trial, whether a political trial directed against war criminals all the way to civil cases involving traffic violations, notices again and again how in our secularized times the consciousness of guilt has either receded or been completely damaged. Particularly in treason cases, the familiar phenomenon may be observed, that fear of terror and its organizations is much stronger than the feeling that one is guilty of something ... In Welles's film, the conscience has long since been lost, and the terror of an authoritarian regime and its organizations liquidates the isolated, soulless human being.[44]

Despite the self-righteous tone, the analysis here of how in police states fear replaces conscience as a basis for action or agency hints at the relevance of such issues for an understanding of the (then) recent German past. Indeed, as the previous five years had seen a number of spectacular court cases, such as the "*Einsatzgruppen*" trial in the late-1950s, in which individuals brought suits against former SS members, and the 1961 Eichmann trial in Israel, which was closely observed by the German public, the courtroom had been transformed from a metaphysical symbol to a concrete, historical place. Welles's film thus encouraged viewers to link Kafka's *Trial* to the present moment.[45]

*   *   *

Making Kafka into a "prophet of fascism" was one thing, but transforming Josef K. into an active agent who resists the tyrannies of the court was quite another. Many German critics rejected this idea by way of a critique of the American actor Anthony Perkins's performance. German critics often framed Welles's casting of Anthony Perkins in the role of Josef K. as a type of misreading of the figure.[46] In Kafka, they claimed, Josef K. has two primary characteristics: he is passive and he is anonymous; Anthony Perkins did not fit either of these.

First, Perkins was a well-known star in the early 1960s, which made it difficult for viewers to understand the figure of Josef K. in the "authentic" Kafkaesque sense of anonymity. The German born, Jewish refugee François Bondy, Swiss citizen and political editor of the *Schweizer Monatshefte*,[47] described this notion of anonymity in his critique of the casting of Perkins, which again shed light upon the ways such apparently "neutral" notions as "anonymity" were being actively tied to more controversial—more politicized—concepts such as "complicity": "In *The Trial*, there is a tendency to self-destructiveness, to complicity in one's own destruction, to masochism ... Orson Welles does not pick up on this strain. Only for this reason could he choose an actor, to whom the grey anonymity of the Man without a last name does not fit, and in whom one can detect no traces of resignation or complicity with his own enemies."[48] Second, Josef K. is perceived to respond passively to the arbitrary charges of the court in the novel. In the final scene of the film, in particular, as well as in his response to the parable of the law, Josef K. actively resists the court's interpretation of the events, as well as his execution.

A number of critics attributed this resistance to an "Americanization" of Kafka through the figure of Welles. The director had projected his own identity as a "rebel against American conformity" onto Josef K., yet nonetheless remained an American.[49] In the film, Perkins assumes the contours of an "Americanized" resistance hero, taking on the court single-handedly and refusing to succumb.[50] American art had a tendency to exaggerate and overextend, another critic argued, citing such disparate examples as William Faulkner, Margaret Mitchell, Jackson Pollock, and Elia Kazan; Welles belonged in this company.[51] The link to Welles as an American made plausible the otherwise unconventional connection between resistance and Americanization and exemplifies how the figure of Welles as an American "auteur" could function as a "transnational mediator," in Uta Poiger's term, for rather unconventional notions of "Americanization," ones that went beyond the U.S as imperialist world power or purveyor of "mass culture."[52]

Resistance to the casting of Perkins functioned on another level as well: this particular Josef K. had a "past." As one German critic put it, Perkins's star image was so influenced by his previous roles, particularly that of Norman Bates in Hitchcock's *Psycho,* that his presence in the film functioned as an "*illusions-störende personelle Vordringlichkeit,*"[53] an obtrusive, illusion shattering persona. Thus, the content he gave to the form of the "anonymous" Josef K. was that of a murderous, neurotic cross-dresser. And even his later more romantic role as the young lover opposite Ingrid Bergman in *Lieben Sie Brahms?* (*Goodbye Again*) echoed the effeminate qualities of the character of Bates for a number of German critics. Thus, paradoxically, critics found Perkins too heroic, American, and protest oriented on the one hand and too neurotic, hectic, and jumpy on the other. This combination of qualities, bridging as it did conventional divisions of gender, was not suited to the characterization of an "anonymous" everyman.

However, other critics appreciated the dimensions Perkins brought to the role and did not necessarily collapse his previous performances into one stereotypical image: "Anthony Perkins has dispensed with the sophisticated ladies' man type.[54] He portrays the increasing confusion of Josef K. with great sensitivity and intelligence."[55] "Anthony Perkins," the *Augsburger Allgemeine* stated, "personifies the trembling soul of Josef K."[56] Critic Peter Körfgen offered a subtle analysis of why he thought Perkins performance fit to Kafka quite well by comparing Kafka with Hitchcock's films: "It has been criticized that Anthony Perkins's Josef K. does not go under the skin. But Kafka is not a Hitchcock. His intellectualism prevents him from leaving things at a reparable shock. The insinuating confusion of our time does not hit like a bolt of lightning. And psychologically it is much more likely that the crew of an anchorless ship would be subject to a paralyzing sense of horror than to spontaneous panic.[57] Significantly, Körfgen linked this empathy for Perkins's "*lähmendes Entsetzen*" (paralyzing horror) to his understanding that Kafka's works did indeed contain elements of resistance, an aspect that was regularly underplayed by German critics.

During their first meeting to discuss the possibility of Perkins's playing the role of Josef K., Welles said to Perkins that his taking the role was a precondition for his making the film.[58] Perkins was well-known in the early 1960s, and a number of German critics attributed Welles's (mis)casting of Perkins to have been undertaken largely for commercial reasons.[59] However, in later interviews, Welles revealed that it was precisely the qualities Perkins brought to his previous roles that Welles wanted in the part of Josef K. In addition, Welles also linked those qualities to Perkins's status as a closeted homosexual; Josef K.'s fears were thus linked to transgressive sexuality.[60] Thus, subjectivizing and "sexualizing" K.'s guilt was one of Welles's central strategies in his adaptation of Kafka. Indeed, Welles relied upon the intertextual quality of Perkins's image to lend to Josef K. a complex subjective dimension.

Interestingly, German critics did not directly comment upon the sexual dimensions of K.'s guilt; instead, they argued that the film parted company with Kafka, because it relied too much upon "psychological realism" where a star, not an anonymous hero, determines the action. "Biography", rather than "existence," was the film's main issue.[61] Thus, a genuinely Kafkaesque hero, in German eyes, was one whose primary characteristics were passivity and anonymity, not sexuality and not biography. To sexualize his crisis was to personalize it and thus make it less publicly significant to the question of the "plight of modern man." This was the essence of the problem with the film in the eyes of several German professors at the Technische Hochschule Stuttgart. In a panel discussion in a "large packed lecture hall" between humanities professors and a representative from the Schorcht Film Verleih, Rudolf Lubowski, the question was raised: "Was Welles's *The Trial* "Kafkaesque" or not?" Lubowski responded to the professors with the assertion that the film's psychological aspect had its purpose: to make "the nightmare of modern existence emotionally accessible to the average cultural consumer." The then critic of the *Deutsche Zeitung,* Hellmuth Karasek, countered with the response that culture was meant for the "happy few" and that to psychologize was "to vulgarize." By transforming Kafka into a mass cultural vehicle, Karasek implied, Welles had created a "dangerous forgery."

While not giving much space to the responses out of the "packed lecture hall" to this conservative reading of *The Trial,* the journalist of this piece nonetheless conveyed his or her own criticism of this old fashioned reading of Kafka in the sarcastic introduction to the article: "The apologists for literary purism and the unassailability of the literary work of art were in their element when it came to the issue of whether the film had either totally messed up or retained minimal traces of the "Kafkaesque" atmosphere ... Rudolf Lubowski quickly became the black sheep, upon which the conceited and the differentiated, the objective and the resentful reproaches against this film and against the film industry were unloaded."[62] Dietmar Schmidt, editor of the Protestant Information Services periodical *Kirche und Film* (Church and Film) and biographer of the controversial Protestant church president Martin Niemöller,[63] called attention to what he perceived as an anti-intellectual trend in the West Germany of the early 1960s that might well have described the elitist panel discussion at the TU Stuttgart. He suggested in an editorial in *Kirche und Film* that films like *The Trial* could provide models of *"heilsame Unruhe,"* forms of "healing restlessness," that might awaken the conscience of their viewers more effectively than most church sermons were doing. Additionally, Schmidt suggested that church leaders should take the critical capacities of their congregations more seriously and promote more complex cultural products that did not necessarily offer "positive images." In the area of literature, according to the well-known scholar Walter Jens, a one-sided emphasis on the "positive" had taken over, and the same seemed to be happening in film: "With a nonchalance, from which can only be assumed that there never was such a figure as Goebbels or such an institution as the Reichskulturkammer, or indeed, that both have again become definitive authorities, the familiar adjective pairs "nihilistic" and "positive," "corrupting" and "healthy" are thrown into the debate."[64] Schmidt linked the "either/or" criticism of films such as *The Trial* to the cultural politics of the Third Reich and called his readers to remember the function of "black and white" points of view on public culture in the past.

If many German critics preferred Josef K. as an anonymous everyman lack-ing sexuality and biography, and hence rejected Anthony Perkins's Josef K., they were more enthusiastic about the cast of female players, especially about the Austrian actress Romy Schneider's performance as Leni. Their discussion revealed the ways Schneider's image as the naive, charming Kaiserin Sissi, a holdover from her popular films of the 1950s, was shifting in the early 1960s. Schneider as "Sissi, the young Empress" embodied an archetypal female ideal of the 1950s in Germany and Austria. Sissi's dilemma as a foreign import into the royal Austrian house was that—unlike her mother-in-law, who iden-tified with the public function of ruling and insisted that her daughter-in-law do the same by giving her children to a royal governess—she wished to raise her children herself in classic, middle-class fashion and vehemently re-jected any claims or pretensions to power. The popularity of this image in the German-speaking world would haunt Schneider and "force" her—in a man-ner of speaking—into exile in Paris, where she took on other roles and was recognized by the critical establishment as a fine character actress.

German critics took note of the dramatic shift in Schneider's image in their response to *The Trial*. While many could not see beyond Perkins's previ-ous roles, Schneider had clearly shifted away from her 1950s screen image: Schneider's "bravado performance as the (sexually promiscuous) nurse has nothing more in common with the little Sissi soul she once was."[65] The *Frank-furter Allgemeine* wrote: "Romy Schneider has dispensed with the charming little goose Sissi. The svelt, high-heeled witch with the cat's eyes, quick steps, pressing gestures and whispers understands the elementary art of seduction. An excellent performance."[66] Often Schneider's performance was favorably compared with the performances of the other actresses, Jeanne Moreau, who played the nightclub dancer Miss Burstener, and Elsa Martinelli, who played Hilda, the court attendant's wife, in what seemed like a contest of European nation-states—West Germany, France and Italy—for the prize of who could play a Kafkaesque female most effectively.[67] In the eyes of German critics, Schneider's was the most convincingly Kafkaesque performance.

What exactly did this mean? More detailed discussions of Schneider's Leni revealed a key assumption some critics held about the role and place of women in a Kafkaesque universe: that they were not true "subjects": "Romy Schneider as Leni … is a doll in a double sense of that word, in her erotic submissive-ness and marionette-like impersonality. She represents completely the image of the women in *The Trial* who do not possess sufficient substance, who are too animalistic, ever to become the "accused" themselves."[68] Apart from draw-ing attention to the interesting fact that there are indeed no accused women in Kafka's universe, the critics' interpretation of this absence highlights the archetypal significance attached to forms of "submissive" female sexuality and the ways these apparently stood in deep conflict with notions of agency. Ironically, several critics praised Schneider's Leni as her first quality characterization, even as they defined her, tongue in cheek, as without character, a being "somewhere between a frog and a human," referring to Leni's physical defect: small webs between several of her fingers.[69]

Those critics who commented upon the clearly sexual, as opposed to "Kafkaesque," dimension of the female performances stressed the morally problematic nature of the behavior: "Kafka's reality is completely disconsolate—how dreadful then, that the 'deliverance through the woman' seems here always to be expected from some half-prostitute in a form of final confusion, which loses itself in empty sensuality."[70] This could not be Kafka, despite the fact that these sexually aggressive female characters all crop up in *The Trial*. Those critics who conceded that there were sexual dimensions to be found in Kafka and who liked Schneider's performance sarcastically attributed her shift of image to the "arts" the "little Vienna beast" had learned in Paris.[71]

Thus, Schneider's performance as Leni was, on the whole, considered quintessentially Kafkaesque, while Anthony Perkins's Josef K., with important exceptions, was not. What did this suggest about the changing functions of the Kafkaesque in postwar West Germany? One very interesting aspect is tied to gender. Despite Josef K.'s passive anonymity, his status as subject is reinforced as an "accused" party. Women in this world of passive anonymity occupy a space a notch below even this status, as their "sexuality" degrades them to animal status. German critics did not think to link the sexual aggressiveness of the female characters in *The Trial* to the more active dimensions of Josef K. that Welles creates, nor did they relate a Josef K. who resists his oppressors to the isolated moments of resistance in the Third Reich, as Niehoff suggested but then rejected, the Warsaw Ghetto fighters, or the Scholl siblings. Instead, the proper world of Kafka was a world where men were unjustly accused but did not resist and women were not "accused" at all. Therefore, the framework of the "Kafkaesque" essentially excluded women as agents and suggested the limits, as critic Reinhold Thiel argued, of using Kafka as a framework within which to analyze the dynamics of state power.

Nonetheless, the reception of Orson Welles's adaptation of Franz Kafka's *The Trial* in the West Germany of the early 1960s demonstrates that there had been a development of sorts in the ways Kafka could circulate in German society. If Kafka's works could be actively linked to German history and its terrors, as was argued by some German and French critics, during—in France—and immediately following—in Germany—the war, the "fashionable" pessimism of the Kafkaesque that could be linked to a suppression of the past, which followed in the first half of the 1950s, had now given way to the option of both. Whether active agents circulated in a "Kafkaesque" world was, on one level, the hubris of an isolated American film auteur, yet it provoked questions in West Germany that found something like a concrete historical agent, if not an active rebel, hidden away under the layers of metaphysical existence: "Persecution no longer emerges, as in Kafka, out of a metaphysical consciousness of guilt; rather, it is secret yet real powers that take a Josef K. to court leading to execution. The Josef K. of 1963 … this must be decisive."[72] It was then up to, among others, the New German cinema to interpret this historical agent and what he—and indeed, she—chose to do or not to do.

*   *   *

While Welles's *The Trial* did not become a popular blockbuster in 1963, its status in German film circles is well-established. Enno Patalas has described *The Trial* as a "Film Club Heuler," a film that was well-liked and appreciated in art film circles and that has since taken on a didactic aspect.[73] Pupils reading Kafka for the Abitur exams—Kafka is a regular on exam lists in German schools—might see the film as part of their coursework, or the film may be screened as a "classic" in what's left of small art cinemas in Germany today.

In hindsight, Welles's "sexualization" of Josef K., which several German critics linked to the vulgarity of mass culture, has proven to be prophetic. Four years after the film's German release, the publication of Kafka's *Briefe an Felice* (*Letters to Felice*) would reveal an intriguing connection between the "metaphysical" aspects of Kafka's *Trial* and his tormented engagement to Felice Bauer, the woman to whom Kafka was engaged twice but never married. This material was not yet available to the public when Welles made his film, though Felice Bauer had sold the letters to Kafka's publisher in New York in the late-1950s. Thus, both Welles and Perkins's attempts to give to Josef K. a dimension of sexual guilt would, to some extent, anticipate later revelations about the relationship between Kafka's biography and his work.[74] During his engagement with Felice Bauer, Kafka was engaged in an intimate correspondence with Bauer's best friend, Grete Bloch, at the same time that he was writing in a similar vein to Bauer. Bloch revealed this correspondence to Bauer, who subsequently called a meeting between herself, her friend, and Kafka at a hotel in Berlin to confront Kafka with what both she and Bloch perceived as his duplicity. Kafka's account of this "hearing" reveals that he remained completely silent throughout, unable to articulate an adequate "defense" on his own behalf and claiming to be completely unaware of a conflict between the two correspondences. Because he perceived his engagement as, in essence, an extension of his literary calling, which could or would not exclude any form of literary expression, Kafka had an acute awareness of a conflict between his writing and the bourgeois norms attached to marriage and founding a family. He began work on *The Trial* in August of 1914, shortly after the "hearing" in the Berlin hotel.[75]

These revelations suggest a completely different reading of Kafka's *Trial* from those that ultimately defined the contours of any historical or metaphysical "Kafkaesque" and certainly lend credence to the distinction between the pre- and post-fascist Kafka. Indeed, nearly 130 years after Kafka's birth, scholars of German literature are still battling with the metaphysical "Kafkaesque" first created by Max Brod and attempting to situate him in a historical and cultural context that today is more interested in "re"-constructing Kafka as a product of his time.[76]

However, in 1963, Kafka's status as a German language writer banned by the Nazis and his politicized function as a "prophet of fascism" enlisted Welles's film and the leitmotif of "Americanized resistance" in the continuing process of coming to terms with the past in West Germany. While receptive to the idea that fascism may have been anticipated by a Jewish writer, German critics preferred an "anonymous, passive" Josef K. to one who resisted his oppressors. Ultimately, this "preference" reflected less a more accurate reading of Kafka than it did a defensive, though basically accurate, perception of the increasing exposure of the "anonymous German everyman" to historical scrutiny as the 1960s progressed. Orson Welles cryptically suggested such an aspect in a statement quoted in the publicity material: "My film is not only about the conspiracy of the court against the innocent; it is much more a study of the corruptibility of the judicial process. My hero (Josef K.) is not innocent; he is capable of being just like the others. Yet none of the others comes to his aid. And neither does he do anything for those around him."[77]

Notes

1. See especially James Naremore, ed., *Film Adaptation* (New Brunswick, New Jersey, 2000), 1–16. Compare also with John Orr, "*The Trial* of Orson Welles," in John Orr and Colin Nicholson, eds. *Cinema and Fiction: New Modes of Adapting, 1950–1990* (Edinburgh, 1992), 13–27.

2. Paul M. Malone, "Trial and Error: Combinatory Fidelity in Two Versions of Franz Kafka's *The Trial*" in Deborah Cartmell, I.Q. Hunter, Heidi Kaye and Imelda Whelehan (eds.) *Classics in Film and Fiction.* (London and Sterling, Virginia, 2000), 176–193; 179.

3. Wolfgang Becker und Norbert Schöll, *In Jenen Tagen...Wie der deutsche Nachkriegsfilm die Vergangenheit bewältigte* (Opladen 1995); Christoph Classen, *Bilder der Vergangenheit: Die Zeit des Nationalsozialismus im Fernsehen der Bundesrepublik Deutschland, 1955–1965* (Cologne, Weimar, Vienna, 1999); Helmut Dubiel, *Niemand ist frei von der Geschichte: Die nationalsozialistische Herrschaft in den Debatten des Deutschen Bundestages* (Munich, 1999); Norbert Frei, *1945 und Wir: Das Dritte Reich im Bewußtsein der Deutschen* (Munich, 2005); Michael Geyer, "Cold War Angst: The Case of West German Opposition to Rearmament and Nuclear Weapons" in Hanna Schissler, ed. *The Miracle Years: A Cultural History of West Germany, 1949–1968* (Princeton, 2001), 376–408; Michael Th. Greven und Oliver von Wrochem (hrg.) *Der Krieg in der Nachkriegszeit: Der Zweite Weltkrieg in Politik und Gesellschaft der Bundesrepublik* (Opladen, 2000); Jeffrey Herf, *Divided Memory: The Nazi Past in the Two Germanys* (Cambridge, Massachusetts, 1997); Knut

Hickethier, "Der Zweite Weltkrieg und der Holocaust im Fernsehen der Bundesrepublik der fünfziger und frühen sechziger Jahre," in Greven/Wrochem, *Der Krieg in der Nachkriegszeit,* 93–112; Robert G. Moeller, *War Stories: The Search for a Useable Past in the Federal Republic of Germany.* (Berkeley, 2001) and Moeller, "Victims in Uniform: West German Combat Films from the 1950s," in Bill Niven, ed. *Germans as Victims: Remembering the Nazi Past in Contemporary Germany.* (MacMillan: Basingstoke, 2006), 43–61; Hanna Schissler, "Writing about 1950s West Germany," in Schissler, *The Miracle Years,* 3–15; Frank Stern, "Film in the 1950s: Passing Images of Guilt and Responsibility," in Hanna Schissler, ed., 266–280; Frank Stern, "Gegenerinnerungen seit 1945: Filmbilder, die Millionen sahen," in Greven/Wrochem, 79–91; Edgar Wolfrum (Hrsg.), *Die Deutschen im 20. Jahrhundert* (Darmstadt, 2004).

4. Habbo Knoch, "The Return of the Images: Photographs of Nazi Crimes and the West German Public in the "Long 1960s." in Philipp Gassert and Alan E. Steinweis, eds. *Coping with the Nazi Past: West German Debates on Nazism and the Generational Conflict, 1955–1975* (New York, 2006), 46.

5. All primary source materials are taken from the archival collections of the Deutsches Filminstitut, Frankfurt am Main, the press archives and library of the Film Museum Berlin, and the Deutsche Kinemathek, Berlin.

All references to Kafka's *The Trial* will be based upon the following edition: Franz Kafka, *Der Prozess,* (Frankfurt am Main, 1998); based upon the third edition: Franz Kafka, *Gesammelte Werke,* hrg. Max Brod. *Der Prozess. Roman.* S. Fischer Verlag. Lizenzausgabe von Schocken Books (New York, 1950).

6. All references to Orson Welles' adaptation of *The Trial* from: *The Trial: A Film from Orson Welles,* dir. Orson Welles, Paris-Europa Productions, 1963 [1962]; video release Fox-Lorber Associates, Inc., 1998.

7. Originally published in *Cahiers du Cinema,* No. 165 (April 1965); reprinted in *The Trial: A Film by Orson Welles,* Modern Film Scripts; Eng. trans (of interview) by Nicholas Fry (New York, London), 9.

8. USE, "Der Prozess," *Film-Dienst* (24 April 1963).

9. The still depicts an image—Josef K. seated beneath a row of meat hooks—that does not appear in the film. Bent and defeated, the Josef K. of the still appears much more the passive victim of a fascist system, represented by the meat hooks, than the Josef K of the film, who is seen quickly walking past a row of meat hooks, in flight from two of the court's henchmen.

10. Wolfgang Beutin, *et al. Deutsche Literaturgeschichte* (6th ed.) (Stuttgart, 2001), 612–613.

11. See, for example, Stanley Kauffmann, "Joseph K. and Orson W," *The New Republic* (2 March 1963), 34–35.

12. Jonas Mekas, "Movie Journal," *The Village Voice,* Vol. 8 (21 February 1963), 15.

13. Ernest Callenbach, "The Trial," *Film Quarterly,* Vol. 16, No. 4 (Summer 1963), 42.

14. Orson Welles and Peter Bogdanovich. *This is Orson Welles,* Jonathan Rosenbaum, ed. (New York, 1993), 285–86.

15. Karl-Heinz Krüger, "Kein Freispruch für Orson Welles," *Der Abend,* Berlin, (2 April 1963).

16. Enno Patalas, "Citizen Kay," *Frankfurter Rundschau* (8 June 1962); Ulrich Seelmann-Eggebert, "Franz Kafka als Citizen K," *Stuttgarter Nachrichten* (8 February 1963); "Der Prozess," *Rheinische Post,* Kreis Dinslaken (23 July 1964).

17. Walter Kaul, "Der Prozess," *Der Kurier,* Berlin, (1 April 1963). The film's soundtrack, which was entirely "looped," was characterized several times as difficult. The film contains no original dialogue.

18. Heide Fehrenbach, *Cinema in Democratizing Germany: Reconstructing National Identity After Hitler.* (Chapel Hill and London, 1995), 211–233.

19. Tim Bergfelder, *International Adventures: German Popular Cinema and European Co-Productions in the 1960s.* (New York, 2005), 73; "Schorcht-Film stockte auf," *Hamburger Abendblatt* No. 162 (14.07.1962), 14.

20. S.M.P (Siegfried M. Pistorius), "So leise fallen Dichter aus dieser Welt," Schorcht Filmgesellschaft m.b.H., Publicity Press Release, 2–3.

21. Alfred Maria Schwarzer, "Orson Welles verfilmte Franz Kafka," Schorcht Filmgesellschaft m.b.H. Publicity Press Release.

22. Sigfried M. Pistorius, "Orson Welles: nach fünf Jahren wieder ein Film," Schorcht Filmgesellschaft m.b.H. Publicity Press Release.

23. Sigfried M. Pistorius, "Der Prozess: Gegen die Zwangsjacke der Obrigkeit," Schorcht Filmgesellschaft m.b.H. Publicity Press Release.

24. Harry Järv. *Die Kafka-Literatur: eine Bibliographie* (first edition). Malmö [*et al*] : Cavefors, 1961.

25. Rolf Traube, "Das Pathos der Angst," *Deutsche Volkszeitung,* Düsseldorf (17 May 1963). Traube was one of the few critics to discuss Kafka's Judaism.

26. Andreas Huyssen, *After the Great Divide: Modernism, Mass Culture, Postmodernism.* (Bloomington, 1986), 191.

27. Oliver Passek, "Die Gruppe 47 im politischen Kontext," in Peter Gendolla und Rita Leinecke (Hrsg.) *Die Gruppe 47 und die Medien.* MUK, Massenmedien und Kommunikation, Nummer 114/115 (Siegen, 1997), 102–114.

28. *Welt am Sonntag,* Berlin (15 April 1962).

29. Andre Bazin, Charles Bitsch, Jean Domarch: Gespräch mit Orson Welles, in *Cahiers du Cinema,* No. 87 (September 1958); dt.Übersetzung in *Der Film: Manifeste, Gespräche, Dokumente.* Bd. 2 (Piper Verlag).

30. Georg Herzberg, "Der Prozess, *FilmEcho/Film Woche* 29 (10 April 1963): 8.

31. Karl-Heinz Krüger, "Romy's Erfolg im Prozess" (Berlin paper), 28 January 1963.

32. J.S. "Überall schimmert Wirklichkeit." *Westfälische Rundschau,* Dortmund (13 June 1963). "Das ist die Geschichte, die ein Traum ist, erfüllt von Traumlogik. "Losen Sie keine Rätsel!"-warnt Orson Welles. Trotzdem schimmert überall die Wirklichkeit hindurch. Die der Konzentrationslager und der Gestapo, die Kafka vorausschaute; die unserer Tage, die den einzelnen im Strudel der Masse versinken läßt…Ein Film der endlich wieder einmal zeigt, was Film sein kann und sein sollte."

33. Reinold E.Thiel (til), "Der Prozess," *Filmkritik* (May 1963):244–248.

34. Ibid, 248.

35. Volker Baer, "Nicht Kafka..." *Der Tagesspiegel Berlin* (4 April 1963).

36. Interview with Enno Patalas, Kino 46, Bremen, 24 January 2004.

37. Walter Kaul, "Der Prozess," *Der Kurier,* Berlin, 1 April 1963.

38. Karena Niehoff, "Geisterbahn auf dem Oktoberfest," *Christ und Welt,* (3 May 1963): 22.

39. Niehoff, "Geisterbahn auf dem Oktoberfest," 22.

40. *Karena Niehoff: Feuilletonistin und Kritikerin,* with an essay by Jörg Becker, "Wer das Schreiben liebt, wird es auch fürchten." (Munich, 2006), 9–77.

41. Kaul, "Der Prozess," *Der Kurier,* Berlin 1 April 1963. "Jede bittere Assoziation wird rasch durch kinntophaftes Messerblinken verwischt, bei dem man sich nach Bunuel-Dalis Augapfelrasur sehnt."

42. Alexandre, Alexandre (aus Paris) *Der Kurier,* Berlin, 10 January 1963.

43. Jean-Louis Bory, from *Arts,* 26 December 1962, Film Distribution Materials for Press(?), 111/11-12; 31.1.63.

44. USE. "Der Prozess," Film-Dienst, 24 April 1963. Another significant trial that took place during this time that was linked to the Cold War was that involving the federal government vs.

the magazine, *Der Spiegel.* Editor-in-Chief Rudolf Augsburg had been arrested for allegedly publishing "classified" defense information.

45. Konrad H. Jarausch. "Critical Memory and Civil Society: The Impact of the 1960s on German Debates about the Past." in Philipp Gassert and Alan E. Steinweis, eds. *Coping with the Nazi Past: West German Debates on Nazism and Generational Conflict, 1955–1975.* (New York, 2006), 20–22.

46. grg. "Der Prozeß," *Die Zeit,* Hamburg (19 April 1963); Dieter Strunz, "Kafka, von der Kamera gejagt," *Berliner Morgenpost* (4 April 1963).

47. R. Reich and B. Bondy, eds. *Homme de lettres.* (Rudolf Köser). Freundesgabe, (Zürich, 1985).

48. [François Bondy] "Im Entscheidenden kein Kafka," *Die Welt, Berlin* (4 June 1963).

49. Ulrich von Thuna, "Citizen K," *Film: Zeitschrift für Film und Fernsehen* (June/July 1963), 42.

50. Ulrich Kurowski, "Ein verfilmter Kommentar," *Echo der Zeit, Recklinghausen* (12 May 1963).

51. USE. 11904, "Der Prozess," *Film-Dienst* (24 April 1963), 153.

52. Uta G. Poiger, "Commentary: Beyond "Modernization" and "Colonization." *Diplomatic History,* 23.1 (Winter 1999): 45–56. See also Jessica C.E. Gienow-Hecht, *Transmission Impossible: American Journalism as Cultural Diplomacy in Postwar Germany, 1945–1955* (Baton Rouge, 1999).

53. Erwin Goelz, "Prozeß gegen Kafka," *Stuttgarter Zeitung* (25 May 1963).

54. Anthony Perkins's European image was linked much more closely to his role as the young lover of Ingrid Bergman in *Goodbye Again.* In contrast, in the United States, his image was always tied to the performance in *Psycho.*

55. Karl Korn, "Ein Exempel," *Frankfurter Allgemeine Zeitung* (1 July 1963).

56. Dr. T.L. "Neue Filme in Augsburg: Der Prozeß," *Augsburger Allgemeine* (11 July 1963).

57. Peter Körfgen, "Der Mensch braucht das Unzerstörbare…" *Mannheimer Morgen,* 8 June 1963.

58. Charles Winecoff, *Split Image: The Life of Anthony Perkins* (Raleigh, North Carolina, 2001 [1996]), 193–194.

59. Erwin Goelz, "Prozeß gegen Kafka," *Stuttgarter Zeitung* (25 May 1963); Ulrich Seelmann-Eggebert, "Franz Kafka als Citizen K," *Stuttgarter Nachrichten* (8 February 1963).

60. Edward Guthmann, "Repeat Performance: Welles' Rare Masterpiece Restored-Film Based on Kafka's *The Trial* opens at the Castro," *San Francisco Chronicle* (7 January 2000) .http://www .sfgate.com/cgi-bin/article.cgi.../chronicle/archive/2000/01/07/DD15381:DTL

61. Tm, "Prozess gegen Orson Welles," *Stuttgarter Zeitung* (21 June 1963).

62. Ibid.

63. Rudolf Joos, et al. eds. *Mosaiksteine: Zum 65. Geburtstag von Dietmar Schmidt.* (Frankfurt am Main, [no date]), 172–173.

64. Dietmar Schmidt, "Heilsame Unruhe," *Kirche und Film,* Nr. 6/ Jg.6 (June 1963): 2–3. "Mit einer Unbekümmertheit, die vermuten lassen könnte, es habe nie ein Goebbels und eine Reichskulturkammer gegeben—oder aber: beide sein heute schon wieder massgebliche Autoritäten—werden die vertrauten Adjektivpaare 'nihilistisch' und 'positive,' 'zersetzend' und 'gesund,' in die Debatte geworfen."

65. dt., "Der Mensch K. unterliegt der Macht," *Westdeutsche Allgemeine,* Essen (13 June 1963).

66. Karl Korn, "Ein Exempel," *Frankfurter Allgemeine Zeitung* (1 July 1963).

67. bm., "Genial an Kafka vorbei," *Kölnische Rundschau,* (25 April 1963).

68. François Bondy, "Kafka-Gesehen von Orson Welles," *Die Welt* (29 December 1962).

69. -be, "Filme der Woche: Nach Kafka: "Der Prozeß", *Westdeutsche Rundschau,* Wuppertal-Barmen (18 May 1963).

70. "Hitchkafka," *Die Welt* (Berlin-West) (18 April 1963).

71. Karl-Heinz Krüger, "Kein Freispruch für Orson Welles," *Der Abend, Berlin* (2 April 1963).

72. USE. Review of *Der Prozess, Film-Dienst* 17 (24 April 1963): 152–153.

73. Interview with Enno Patalas, Kino 46, Bremen, 24 January 2004.

74. Franz Kafka, *Briefe an Felice, und andere Korrespondenz aus der Verlobungszeit,* hrg. Erich Heller und Jürgen Born (Frankfurt am Main, 1976); see also Elias Canetti, *Der Andere Prozeß: Kafka's Briefe an Felice* (Munich, 1984).

75. Canetti, 60.

76. See, for example, Volker Weidermann, „Kafkas Welt in einem Kästchen." *Frankfurter Allgemeine* Sonntagszeitung, 20 April 2008, Nr. 16/ page 31, FAZ.NET, http://www.faz.net/s/RubC17179....; Friedmar Apel, „Mythengestöber", *Frankfurter Allgemeine* Zeitung, 3 December 2008, Nr. 283/Page 32, FAZ.NET; Friedmar Apel, „"Der war ja gar nicht kafkaesk." *Frankfurter Allgemeine Zeitung,* 11 August 2008, Nr. 186/Seite 34, FAZ.NET

77. Schorcht press and publicity release, S.M Pristorius, „Orson Welles: nach fünf Jahren wieder ein Film."

PART II

Postfeminist Relations between Classic Texts and Hollywood Film Adaptations in the U.S. in the 1990s

Barbara Klinger has made a case for developing and improving the field of reception study of film by paying closer attention to: 1) public combat over film meaning rather than unities, 2) historicizing inquiry beyond industrial practices, and 3) pursuing diachronic and synchronic meanings.[1] Implicit in her three points is a framework for an understanding of "the historical" in relationship to film studies and adaptation studies to which I subscribe: that a focus upon conflict rather than consensus can tell us more about relations between audiences and films in the past; that knowledge of the past should be sought beyond the privileged spheres of economics and politics to include such cultural phenomena as film and literature; and that focusing upon both diachronic and synchronic meanings can offer a richer sense of the relationship between context and meaning, in other words, what knowledge about the past can tell us about contemporary concerns.

Part Two will explore the relationship between the reception and adaptation of specific nineteenth-century "classic" texts, notably works by Jane Austen and Henry James. In the late-1990s, six film and television adaptations of nearly all of Jane Austen's novels, including *Sense and Sensibility*, *Pride and Prejudice*, *Emma* and *Persuasion* were produced. Not long after, a smaller but no less significant series of adaptations of Henry James's novels were released to film audiences: versions of *Washington Square*, *The Portrait of a Lady* and *The Wings of the Dove*. My focus on the Jane Austen and Henry James film "booms" of the 1990s reflects the traditional Hollywood tendency to mine nineteenth-century literature for its "realistic" and prestigious, i.e. canonical and thus easily identifiable, texts. However, this series of Austen and James adaptations also raises a key question: Why are certain canonical books interesting to Hollywood during certain periods?[2]

A recent study of "British Heritage Retrovisions since the mid-1990s" suggests that this question is best answered by paying attention to the industrial dimensions of these film productions; the Austen adaptations, for example, "were ... variants of the English heritage film—attempts by the industry to prolong the Anglo-Hollywood costume trend."[3] In other words, there was nothing distinctively "Jane Austen" oriented or, indeed, "Henry James" oriented about these adaptations. That the Austen and James films were part of a trend of film adaptations of classic literature—that was by no means exclusively British—was clear; however, close attention to the specific films, as well as to their reception, reveals an obsession with the figures of Austen and James, their literary personas and reputations, and the ways the films modified the novels. Additionally, the nature of the modifications in the films shows that the individual filmmakers were very much interested in both authors' works and paid close attention to those works. Thus, while the focus on long term film production trends is important, it is no less important to focus closely upon individual films and the ways audiences interacted with them.

In exploring this question in the case of adaptations of Austen and James, one dimension is particularly significant: the centrality of questions of changing conceptions of gender identity in the late twentieth century. Importantly, this contemporary dimension becomes most evident when comparing the film adaptation with the original work, not so much for the sake of rating the film's "fidelity" to the original but for analyzing how classic texts are enlisted by Hollywood in an intertextual discourse on gender. The popularity of Austen's works, tied as they are to a tradition of "female authorship" and to a focus on marriage and private life, is often explained by critics as representing a conservative perspective on gender issues in the films' critical reception; however, the adaptations negotiated ideological dilemmas such as conflicts between work and family, intimacy and autonomy for women and men in a postfeminist context. James's works were associated with the conservative—implicitly male—ideal of "Great Literature," even as the adaptations were very much preoccupied with a shift of perspective on male identity from conventional subject to the visual equivalent of admired object, a status heretofore held almost exclusively by women.[4]

Thus, these adaptations of Austen's and James's works can provide fascinating insights into shifting conceptions of gender identity when they are looked at in relation to both the original works and to each other. Additionally, there is a clear conflict that exists between the level of the reception of the films, which tends to remain wedded to conventional ideas of male and female authorship, respectively, and the different goals of the filmmakers involved in these adaptations, who tend to pursue—both consciously and unconsciously—a "postfeminist" agenda, or "reading strategy," in Janet Staiger's terms.

In using the term postfeminist as a framework within which to understand the sort of "collective agenda" of the filmmakers involved, as well as to explain at least a portion of the films' reception, I will define the concept broadly, relying upon such diverse theorists as Susan Bordo, Susan Faludi, Deborah Tannen, Gisela Bock, and Steven Cohan.[5] Though I find interesting Tania Modleski's well-known definition of postfeminism as being essentially in opposition to second-wave feminism, I do not rely on her negative definition.[6] Rather, I think the term is flexible enough to incorporate a number of different ways of understanding the relationship between feminism and postfeminism that are marked by intense creativity, as well as ambivalence, frustration as well as hope. Concretely, I would like to employ the term postfeminism as a means of calling attention to gender related issues that have emerged since the women's movement of the 1970s. Thus, the term will function as a means of drawing attention to a past movement in order to show both its contemporary influence and shifting focuses and emphases that have become significant since. As Charlotte Brundson has argued, "postfeminism has a considerable purchase in any approach to [certain kinds of film material], not least because of the way in which it attributes an historical specificity to the women's movement of the late-1960s and 1970s. It is a useful term historically, because it allows us to point to certain representational and discursive changes in the period since the 1970s."[7] No matter how conservative the conclusions of some of these films appear to be, no filmmaker or adaptor of the classic nineteenth-century literary text has remained untouched by the women's movement. And because nineteenth-century "realist" texts were first and foremost about issues of gender, they prove to be highly appropriate vehicles for efforts to redefine what gender means in the twentieth and twenty first centuries.

What were some of the issues that emerged since the 1980s that became part of a "postfeminist" agenda? Chief among them was the problem of articulating a specifically female identity that could reconcile public and private spheres and could combine economic autonomy with desires for personal intimacy. Media discussion of women's issues in the 1980s and 1990s often created oppositions between "radical feminism" and "conservatism," associating feminism with career-oriented women who prioritized accomplishment over intimacy, individual freedom over family commitment, and conservatism with "family values" that emphasized traditional female values of motherhood, nurture, and, by extension, patriotism.[8] Focusing on themes of "mediation" rather than economics, scholars and commentators such as Deborah Tannen sought to critique these oppositions by stressing new models of communication to overcome linguistic differences between men and women and to encourage men to develop more active, self-critical attitudes towards their own gender identities.[9]

The ever increasing influence of multi-media images and their impact upon gender identity also characterizes postfeminism. Feminist philosophers and film historians such as Susan Bordo and Steven Cohan became increasingly interested in questions of the body and how consumer culture mediated images of female and male bodies.[10] Rather than rejecting consumer culture for creating sexist images of women and men, as the second-wave feminist movement tended to do, Bordo and Cohan stressed the importance of analyzing and negotiating the realms of consumer culture in order to understand newly developing conceptions of gender identity linked to "ideas of performance, style, and desire"[11]

Thus, reconciling oppositions between public and private spheres through language and representation and utilizing consumer culture to understand gendered subjects as both "desired and desiring" became a hallmark of the post-feminist point of view, and filmmakers in the 1990s, such as Ang Lee, Emma Thompson, Jane Campion, and Agnieszka Holland, would enlist the works of Jane Austen and Henry James to draw attention to these issues. However, at the same time, critics and viewers of the Austen and James adaptations tended to remain wedded to traditional notions of adaptation as fidelity, and—with some exceptions—understood the Jane Austen and Henry James film booms as reactionary cultural phenomena that signaled modern women's increasing frustration with "postmodern liberation."

There is a conflict of sorts between the reception of the films and the ways the filmmakers attempt to invent new ways of adapting classic works while simultaneously attempting to appeal to a large market. In James Naremore's terms, there is a conflict that exists between the model of translation of text to film that demands "fidelity" on the one hand, and the model of performance that demands "a unique signature" on the other.[12] While audience expectation and market forces shape the films using a model of translation, comparing the films with the original novels and with each other shows a model of performance at work. However, these performances are not isolated, essentialized, "auteur" performances in the traditional sense. Rather, they reflect efforts to deal with cultural trends relating to gender issues through the vehicle of adaptation, suggesting the strategic cultural function of adaptation for negotiating different types of social and cultural change. The use of canonical literature by specific filmmakers will thus be a central issue even as the model for understanding the filmmaker as "auteur" is significantly revised, because it is between this dynamic of translation, performance, and response that important ideological dynamics emerge that both engage and reflect contemporary cultural politics.

In particular, some critics of the Austen films did not follow the traditional path of classifying the films solely in terms of preconceived notions of "Jane

Austen adaptations." The feminist playwright Wendy Wasserstein shifted the focus and indirectly linked Ang Lee's and Emma Thompson adaptation of Austen's *Sense and Sensibility* with the contemporary film *Thelma and Louise,* a film about two women fleeing the FBI after killing a potential rapist.[13] Between the analysis of the Austen and James film booms, respectively, I will follow up on this clue from the Austen film reception and offer a close comparison of the adaptation of the nineteenth-century Austen novel *Sense and Sensibility* with the actively debated, contemporary, Ridley Scott film *Thelma and Louise.*

If comparing *Sense and Sensibility* to its precursor text highlights the ways gender ideologies have changed over time, comparing such adaptations with a film about "contemporary women" clearly shows the specific ways the "historic" Austen characters in the films are in fact contemporary as well. This comparison is intended to draw attention to the ways the respective receptions of the two films created an opposition between the poles of "feminism" and "conservatism" that suggested the cultural politics of these two films were completely different. In fact, a comparison of the two films actively undermines this specific difference and locates that difference elsewhere. *Sense and Sensibility* shares with *Thelma and Louise* a similar literary structure that emphasizes the complexity of the female character by demonstrating the ways a relationship of equality between two very different women leads the one to take on some of the characteristics of the other. As this dynamic progresses in both films, it also calls attention to cultural tensions that characterized the "postfeminist" context of the 1990s, particularly, the tension between the unmet expectations of equality raised by the women's movement of the 1970s and the high level of self-reliance demanded of women by a postmodern economy. Hence, linking these two films offers yet another means of drawing attention to the ways Hollywood narratives can engage in intertextual dialogues with each other across genres that shed much light upon the relationship between female character development in popular narratives and changing late twentieth-century definitions of gender identity.[14]

* * *

All of these cases illustrate the ways a historical approach to adaptation can offer more illuminating possibilities than either ahistorical conceptions of "fidelity" or "intertextuality." Adaptation understood as a certain kind of reception can actively function to mediate the relationship between film and society and thus become a means of discussing significant political and social issues. Whether in West Germany in the 1950s or in the U.S. at the end of the twentieth century, film adaptation was never just about "fidelity to the original work" nor purely "infinite and open-ended." Rather, film adaptation functioned historically to mediate the relationship between culture and politics in different times and in different places.

Notes

1. Barbara Klinger, "Film history terminable and interminable: recovering the past in reception studies," *Screen* 38.2 (Summer 1997), 113.

2. James Naremore, ed. *Film Adaptation* (New Brunswick, New Jersey, 2000), 11. Jane Austen "booms" are not new to the late twentieth century. A boom in the publication of her works in the late nineteenth century U.S. and England triggered debates about the relationship between Austen and her status as a woman writer in the literary canon of "realism." See Anne-Marie Scholz, *An Orgy of Propriety: Jane Austen, and the Emergence and Legacy of the Female Author in America, 1826–1926*. (Trier, 1999). Quite a few studies of the Austen films emerged following the film boom, most of which emphasized questions of "infidelity." An interesting example is the volume edited by Linda Troost and Sayre Greenfield, *Jane Austen in Hollywood* (Lexington, KY, 1998). For a partial overview see Eckart Voigts-Virchow, "Corset Wars: An Introduction to Syncretic Heritage Film Culture since the Mid-1990s," in Eckart Voigts -Virchow, ed., *Janespotting and Beyond: British Heritage Retrovisions since the mid-1990s*, (Tübingen, 2004), 13–19.

3. Andrew Higson, "English Heritage, English Literature, English Cinema: Selling Jane Austen to Movie Audiences in the 1990s." in Eckart Voigts -Virchow, ed., *Janespotting and Beyond*, 39.

4. Steven Cohan, *Masked Men: Masculinity and the Movies in the Fifties* (Bloomington, 1997) and David Greven, "The Museum of Unnatural History: Male Freaks and *Sex and the City*," in Kim Akass and Janet McCabe, eds., *Reading Sex and the City*, (London, 2004), 33–47.

5. Susan Bordo, *Unbearable Weight: Feminism, Western Culture and the Body* (Berkeley, 1993); Susan Faludi, *Backlash: The Undeclared War Against American Women* (New York, 1991); Deborah Tannen, *You Just Don't Understand* (New York, 1990); Gisela Bock, "Challenging Dichotomies in Women's History," in Mary Beth Norton and Ruth M. Alexander, eds. *Major Problems in American Women's History* (2nd ed.) (Lexington, MA, 1996); Steven Cohan, *Masked Men*: (Bloomington, 1997); A recent study of *Buffy the Vampire Slayer* also offers a more inclusive version of "postfeminism": see Kristin Lenk and Franziska Korthals, "Macht und Weiblichkeit in *Buffy the Vampire Slayer*: Auseinandersetzung mit einer postfeministischen Ikone," (Magisterarbeit, University of Bremen, Germany, 2004), 8–11.

6. Tania Modleski, *Feminism without Women: Culture and Criticism in a "Postfeminist" Age*. (London, 1991).

7. Charlotte Brunsdon, "Post-Feminism and Shopping Films," in Joanne Hollows, et al, eds. *The Film Studies Reader*, 290.

8. Faludi, *Backlash: The Undeclared War Against American Women* and Bock, "Challenging Dichotomies in Women's History."

9. Deborah Tannen, *You Just Don't Understand*. (New York, 1990).

10. Judith Butler, *Gender Trouble: Feminism and the Subversion of Identity*. (New York, 1999). Butler's arguments have influenced the works of Bordo and Cohan.

11. Brundson, 291.

12. Naremore, "Introduction: Film and the Reign of Adaptation," in James Naremore, ed. *Film Adaptation*, 1–16.

13. Wendy Wasserstein, "The *Premiere* Review: *Sense and Sensibility*" (February 1996): 17.

14. Robert Stam, "Beyond Fidelity." In James Naremore, ed. *Film Adaptation*, 64.

Chapter Four

Jane-Mania

The Jane Austen Film Boom in the 1990s

Throughout 1995 and 1996, a series of film adaptations of Jane Austen's novels were released to audiences around the world. Beginning, as one critic put it, "almost subliminally" with *Clueless*—a loose adaptation of *Emma* set in a contemporary Beverly Hills high school—written and directed by Amy Heckerling (*Fast Times at Ridgemont High*), the trend continued with *Persuasion,* a British production adapted for the screen by Nick Dear and directed by Roger Michell, *Sense and Sensibility,* adapted by Emma Thompson and directed by Ang Lee, *Pride and Prejudice,* adapted by Andrew Davies and directed by Simon Langton for British television, and finally, British and American versions of *Emma.*[1] Although adaptations of Austen's novels with varying degrees of quality had been produced throughout the previous two decades, notably, Fay Weldon's fine adaptation of *Pride and Prejudice* for the BBC in 1980, it was clear to many critics that this sudden spate of Austen dramatizations could not have emerged out of a cultural vacuum.[2]

Despite the fact that the last decades of the twentieth century saw a consistent trend toward highly aestheticized "historical" dramatizations, notably the many Merchant/Ivory productions beginning with *A Room with a View* and moving on through dramatizations of Edith Wharton and Henry James, critics nonetheless chose to define the series of Austen films largely as an isolated phenomenon, best interpreted not within the larger context of recent historical dramatizations but in terms of the author, the female author, herself. The reviews dealing with the films carried titles such as "Jane Reaction," "Jane Mania," and "Jane Addiction," suggesting two things: that the films could only be understood in terms of the person of the female author—"Jane" rather than Austen—and that an interest in this figure—mania, addiction, etc.—was irrational, subjective, but above all, personal and private in nature, unrelated to the public world of business, law, and politics.[3] These two key assumptions comprise the legacy of the concept of the female author, whose sphere of authority, that is, of public knowledge, is radically circumscribed. Analysis of the reception of the Austen films by the American and, to some extent, German reviewing establishments reveals the ideological aspects of this legacy, which shaped the central question raised by practically all the reviewers of the film adaptations of Austen's novels: why are we in the midst of a "Jane Austen film boom" at the end of the twentieth century?

Responding to this question, Evan Thomas wrote in *Newsweek* magazine: "People have become accustomed to vulgarity, as well as other common indignities—their neighbors threatening to sue them, their colleagues incessantly whining, their former lovers spilling their secrets, and perfect strangers insulting them or, worse, confiding in them. Possibly, they are growing sick of it. The cult of Jane Austen, with its nostalgia for a more decorous and polite age, is one small sign."[4] Thomas's glib rhetoric of boundary transgression conceals an important subtext: that the reason behind the Jane Austen boom is a desire to reestablish conventional distinctions between public and private life. This presumption directly links Jane Austen to the legacy of female authorship, the legacy that equated female authority with authority over the private sphere alone. Moreover, Thomas reads this "nostalgia" as a fundamentally apolitical desire, a rather amorphous longing for more polite social interaction. Other critics, less sanguine than Thomas about the implications of reestablishing conventional notions of public and private, nonetheless equate the dramatizations of Austen's novels with the desire to do so: "What could possibly account for this Jane mania? ... I thought I understood the Victorian revival ... But Regency England? And not *really* Regency England of a distinctly weird George III but these Cinderella idylls about it—in which, to paraphrase Nina Auerbach, before a novel or a life could properly begin, the women must wait at the door for the gentlemen to enter. Is it an aspect of antifeminist backlash?"[5] George III represents the public world, whereas Austen's Cinderella idylls represent private life, a life to which the forces of "antifeminist backlash" would like to see women return. Thus, Leonard links the films to the reactionary politics of the New Right: to return women to the private sphere where they presumably belong. Whether critics politicize the nostalgic longing for order—women are flocking to Jane Austen films, because they are frustrated with postmodern liberation[6]—or not—the films are constrained by the emphasis upon who or who will not marry whom[7]—, by associating the Austen dramatizations with precisely this "nostalgic" impulse, all the critics link the films to the legacy of female authorship that associates women's domestic writing with writing about private life alone. This association more or less guarantees that the films will function either as reaffirmations of conservative values or as apolitical romantic idylls.

It is worth noting that when critics pay attention to specific films, without linking their discussions to the above question, very different readings emerge, readings that, in emphasizing questions of production and adaptation, raise provocative issues about the relationship between text (film) and context (the late twentieth century). For example, Wendy Wasserstein's review of *Sense and Sensibility* did not situate the film within an overarching "Jane Austen boom." Rather, she compared it to "contemporary" depictions of "intelligent women" in Hollywood:

> It's not that Hollywood isn't aware of female intelligence. Recently we've had an onslaught of supporting role lawyer babes, psychologist cat woman babes, and of course, the nicest wife who ever lived and also happens to be a surgeon babe. What is stunning about *Sense and Sensibility*, and Emma Thompson's knowing screenplay, is that when all the latter twentieth-century 'you've come a long way, baby' trappings are removed, we're left with the heart of the matter: character. The Dashwood sisters' intelligent life is internal and can't be roughly sketched in with threatening, high powered jobs and Armani suits. Attention to the personalities, therefore, must be paid.[8]

Wasserstein argues that *Sense and Sensibility* arrives in a contemporary context that has a difficult time depicting female intelligence as real or believable. What all of the above Hollywood renditions of female intelligence have in common, after all, is that they are "babes" at heart or private, sexual beings. By rendering intelligent life internal rather than external, *Sense and Sensibility* shows that female intelligence cannot be understood strictly within the boundaries of the public world of work, but must also be understood in relationship to a woman's personal life and sexuality. Thus, Wasserstein suggests that Austen's focus upon intelligent female character actually undermines distinctions between public and private life, distinctions which continue to associate women's deepest character with her private sexuality, or "babeness."

However, overall, even as critics focused closely upon the film as text, their assumptions about Austen as a female author often marred otherwise insightful analysis. Discussing the significance of the relationship between Elinor and Marianne in *Sense and Sensibility*, Martin Amis put forth: "When Elinor addresses Marianne as "my dearest," we are moved, because the endearment is literally true—and may well remain true, for life. For the unmarried, no reconfiguration awaits the pattern of their love; their nearest are their dearest and that is the end of it ... And we naively console ourselves that Jane Austen, whatever else she lacked, at least had Cassandra."[9] Addressing a seemingly feminist issue, female relations in the novels of a canonical British author,

Amis situates himself squarely within the tradition of female authorship by linking his reading of the scene to the personal maladjustment of the female author herself. "We fancy ourselves perfectly placed to pick up the distress signals sent out by *Persuasion,* with its tartness and well-trimmed melancholy," Anthony Lane wrote in *The New Yorker,* "We cannot conceive that anyone as long suffering as Jane Austen could also be so funny. Her balance is beyond us; however good a person we may think she was, she was better."[10] According to David Ansen in *Newsweek, Persuasion* "is a comedy tinged with the melancholy and the ache of missed opportunities ... it's the closest she came to revealing her own yearning soul." [11]

Given the history of efforts to privatize the public authority of the female author, the above attempts to link the Austen film adaptations to the female author's private "long-suffering yearnings" may be more a sign of backlash than the films to which they are presumably a response. Here, we see how Austen's reception draws attention away from the public significance of the film adaptations by claiming to situate their meaning within a naturalized, ahistorical, but above all, privatized notion of female yearning. But if this is not the right context in which to situate the Austen boom of the 1990s, what is?

In an insightful review of the Austen boom in the *New York Review of Books,* critic Louis Menand suggests an alternative conceptualization of context for the Austen films. "These films have all come out at the same time, it's true," Menand writes, "but they were all put together at different times, and the impulse to make them must have been much stronger than the mere impulse to watch them. The shortage of leading roles for women in contemporary screenplays," Menand suggests, "is probably a better explanation for the appearance and the quality of these films than some imagined cultural turn."[12] But surely it is less a question of the quantity—shortage—of women's film roles than of their quality, that is, their content. Susan Faludi has suggested that the portrayal of women in film in the 1980s took a sharp turn from the celebration to the vilification of female independence, that is, women's public roles: "The backlash shaped much of Hollywood's portrayal of women in the 1980s. In typical themes, women were set against women; women's anger at their social circumstances was depoliticized and displayed as personal depression instead; and women's lives were framed as morality tales in which the "good mother" wins and the independent woman gets punished."[13] Films such as *Fatal Attraction, Broadcast News, Crossing Delancey,* and *Baby Boom* all manifested aspects of this trend toward vilification, emphasizing the ways in which women's quest for public recognition and independence was presumably directly related to their inability to create and sustain intimate relationships with men. Women's public roles were thus represented as being fundamentally at odds with their private beings and thus wholly unrelated to them.

I want to argue that several of the Austen films of the 1990s, notably *Sense and Sensibility* and *Persuasion,* attempt to reforge a link between public and private spheres for both women and men and thus can only be understood as a response to, rather than as a manifestation of, the society-wide backlash of the 1980s: the New Right's efforts to reprivatize male and female relationships.[14] That response, in turn, has been very much shaped by the women's movement and its profound ideological effects on the late twentieth century, even as it shows itself to be ambivalent about that influence. To best understand the Jane Austen boom of the 1990s is to disassociate the films from the cultural myth of Jane Austen as a female author and instead to locate them squarely within what might be called the postfeminist context of the late twentieth century, a context preoccupied, as was Austen, with the "discourse rather than the representation of politics."[15]

Critics generally agreed that two productions stood out in the series of Austen films that came to the screen: *Sense and Sensibility* and *Persuasion. Sense and Sensibility,* adapted for the screen by Emma Thompson and directed by the Taiwanese director Ang Lee, became a hit production in 1996 and received an Academy Award for Best Screenplay.[16] One of the least popular, and certainly the least dramatized of all of Austen's works, the novel was reworked extensively for the screen. Always situated in the shadow of *Pride and Prejudice,* the choice of *Sense and Sensibility* as fare for an expensive Hollywood vehicle itself signaled what might be called an "Americanized" change of approach to the Austen canon, one that privileged one of Austen's "minor" novels, because it had, according to the U.S. producer of the film Lindsay Doran, the "qualities in a book ... that would translate into a good film: ... wonderful characters, a strong love story ... relevant themes, and a heart-stopping ending." When Doran later "found" herself working "as an executive at a Hollywood studio," her first priority was "still to make a movie out of my favourite book." Emphasizing her Hollywood pedigree: her father, D.A. Doran, had been a studio executive for forty years, Doran legitimized bringing a minor Austen novel to the screen in terms of the democratic priorities of the Hollywood entertainment industry as opposed to the more elite criteria of the literary establishment[17] (see Figure 4.1).

The publicity surrounding the film centered around its star, Emma Thompson functioning both as female lead and screenwriter, its director, Ang Lee, as a foreign element seemingly unsuited to an Austen dramatization, and its costar, Hugh Grant. Much of what made the film such a success was the attention it received as a result of its stars, but shrewd marketing emphasizing the connections between the film and the legacy of Austen as female author also played an important role. New editions of *Sense and Sensibility,* with the film's stars gracing the cover, put Jane Austen's least respected canonical work on

Lose your heart
and come to your senses.

Figure 4.1. Publicity poster for *Sense and Sensibility* depicting Elinor (Emma Thompson) and Marianne (Kate Winslet). (Courtesy: Photofest)

many a bestseller list. In addition, the publication of Emma Thompson's production diaries along with her screenplay further fueled the new Jane Austen
mania.[18] Some critics even compared Thompson to Austen as a female authorial figure, and producer Doran actually suggested that the screenplay should
be "novelized" and marketed as the Austen novel.[19] Asked what she would ask
Jane Austen if she were to come back to life, Emma Thompson only somewhat
facetiously replied: "What percentage she wants of the gross."[20]

To understand the ways in which the film breaks with the legacy of female authorship is to focus less on its reception than on the ways in which
Thompson modified the text of the novel to suit the screen. In the novel, two
genteel but impoverished sisters, Elinor and Marianne Dashwood, represent
two opposing emotional strategies in the task of surviving their sole chance of
access to solvency and public esteem: the marriage market. Elinor, the elder
sister, represents the strategy of sense, in that she believes that feelings must
be controlled for the sake of society, whereas Marianne believes feelings and
passions should take precedence over societal norms. Their attitudes about
emotions reflect the way each deals with the excitement, uncertainties, and
risks of courtship. Their suitors, Edward Ferrars and John Willoughby, each
represent a seeming complement to the female roles: Edward, suited to Elinor,
is rational; Willoughby is emotional and passionate. In the novel, both suitors
disappear from the scene fairly early on, leaving the ideal of complementar-
ity in the air. It is now the women who must work out the implications of
their differing emotional structures for their own lives. An older, more rational
suitor, Colonel Brandon, is waiting in the wings for Marianne in case the
match with Willoughby does not turn out. The novel concludes with two marriages: between Elinor and Edward, and Marianne and Brandon.

In the *New York Review of Books,* critic Louis Menand noted how Thompson solved the narrative problem of the "disappearing suitors" in her screenplay. She fleshed out the role of the third, younger sister, Margaret, who is not
at all developed in the novel, in order to create a friendship between her and
Edward at the beginning of the film, thus rendering Edward more interesting
and memorable enough to survive his early disappearance.[21] Yet by situating
Margaret in relation to Edward, rather than in relation to the other two sisters,
Menand dismisses the possibility of Margaret as a viable third party. Another
critic saw the possibility of a connection but then rejected it due to age: "A
third sister, Margaret, played by Emilie François, is, at eleven, too young to
stand for anything."[22]

However, close attention to the role of Margaret in the film reveals a function that goes beyond a mere aesthetic modification for purposes of narrative
interest. A review of Thompson's screenplay shows that the character of Margaret was to provide a third dimension of female identity: the independent,

modern woman no longer a pawn of her own emotions. An opening scene, later cut from the film, is a dialogue between Mrs. Dashwood and her dying husband outlining the marital futures of the three daughters: Elinor as sensible, Marianne as romantic, and Margaret as independent.[23] This triangular theme runs throughout the film, but the omission of the opening scene renders it largely implicit, a "modern" subtext that mediates between the predominant Austenian themes of "sense" and "sensibility"[24] (see Figure 4.2).

On one level, the character of Margaret in the film suggests the immaturity of a young girl who must grow up to learn her sister's, Elinor's, coping mechanisms. However, on another level, she is clearly a harbinger of the future. She is the future of women, representing their desire to enter the public world: Margaret wishes to go to sea and become a pirate. Her way is openly to question unjust laws, fleeing out of doors when Elinor insists she "come inside." Throughout the film, Margaret always insists upon speaking directly about public injustice. She questions the laws of entail and manages to get Elinor to speak openly as well:

Elinor: Margaret, are you there? Please come down. John and Fanny will be here soon.

Margaret: Why are they coming to live at Norland? They already have a house in London.

Figure 4.2. The three sisters in *Sense and Sensibility*: (from left) Marianne (Kate Winslet), Margaret (Emilie François), and Elinor (Emma Thompson). (Courtesy: Photofest)

Eleanor: Because houses go from father to son, dearest—not from father to daughter. It is the law ... If you come inside, we could play with your atlas.

Margaret: It's not my atlas any more. It's their atlas.[25]

Likewise, Margaret questions the norms of silence governing public discussion of desire and romance. Like the neighborhood gossip Mrs. Jennings and unlike her family, she prefers to "talk about things."[26] Whereas even Marianne clearly subscribes to norms of polite discourse, attempting to shield Elinor from the embarrassment of having her suitor's name made public, Margaret's request for more frankness is clearly not satirized within any of the scenes where she offers her third viewpoint. The viewer recognizes that, unlike Mrs. Jennings, Margaret is requesting not gossip but open communication.

Thus, Elinor's "sense" cannot be understood merely in opposition to Marianne's sensibility: repressing one's emotions rather than expressing them within a fundamentally passive relationship to the public world. Instead, Elinor's "sense" is updated, so to speak, to function as a model of female comportment existing somewhere in between the poles of autonomy (Margaret) and affiliation (Marianne). This renders Elinor a very modern, perhaps even postmodern, entity for contemporary audiences, as public conceptions of female identity tend to situate women ideologically either in terms of independence or affiliation, resulting in a double bind for many women that has made it difficult for them to discuss publicly both aspects of their identities without being classified either as neo-traditionalist or "radical" feminist. Thus, the fact that Elinor's sense triumphs with Margaret, as well as it does with Marianne at the end of the film, acquires a different meaning than it had for Austen. For Thompson, Elinor's sense must come to mediate between the demands of Margaret and the desires of Marianne.

How does Elinor mediate between the two poles of independence and affiliation? Within the female triad Thompson creates, all of Elinor's actions acquire significance insofar as they serve as models for both Margaret and Marianne. Elinor's knowledge of Lucy Steele's engagement to Edward and her unwillingness to make it public, for example, exemplifies a form of female heroism: honorable behavior vis à vis her rival, who has more ancient claims upon her lover.[27] As Thompson pointed out in an interview with the German magazine, *Der Spiegel*, female heroism in Austen cannot be demonstrated by actions, as with men, but rather by way of character.[28] If, for Marianne, Elinor's behavior might appear to demonstrate too much discipline and self-control of heartfelt emotions, for Margaret, it represents precisely the type of behavior necessary for success in the public world. Elinor exemplifies a model for public conduct, or what Thompson refers to as female heroism, within the central dilemma of patriarchy, the conflict between love (affiliation) and money (independence). Yet, particularly in her relationship to Marianne, Elinor illustrates an affiliative nature that several critics patronizingly misread in terms of the "crucial heaviness of ... sisterly love," that is, love unable to be channeled into the conventional direction of heterosexual bonds.[29] In the deathbed scene with Marianne, Elinor reveals a powerful capacity for emotion which calls attention to the sensible aspect of her nature. Thus, combining characteristics that serve as models both for independence and affiliation, Elinor demonstrates that female character consists of both independence and affiliation, sense and sensibility.

What sort of a man can accommodate such a female personality? Thompson's rendition of Edward takes on particular significance in the late twentieth century:

> Elinor: Margaret has always wanted to travel.
>
> Edward: I know. She is heading an expedition to China shortly. I am to go as her servant but only on the understanding that I will be very badly treated.
>
> Elinor: What will your duties be?
>
> Edward: Sword-fighting, administering rum, and swabbing.
>
> Elinor: Ah.
>
> Edward: All I want—all I have ever wanted—is the quiet of a private life, but my mother is determined to see me distinguished.[30]

To posit a man with no ambition who just wants to have a "private" life as a fit partner for Elinor is to suggest a new male type as well, one not conventionally associated with romance. The notion of "private" meant something different for Jane Austen than it means today: it was a term not yet gendered female. For Edward to desire a private life suggests a male identity not beholden to the conventional sexual division of labor. Correspondingly, the marriage of Elinor and Edward does not represent a validation of private female identity. Rather, it is a modern ideological validation of Elinor's particular virtues: her self-reliance and her intellectual and practical capacity to mediate between independence and affiliation.

Yet the powerful ambivalence regarding this "resolution" is demonstrated in the response to Elinor's "breakdown" when she learns Edward is free to marry her. The scene triggered two types of responses in many viewers: either laughter or a reserved silence. Those who responded with laughter felt the emotion conveyed in the scene was happiness, the conventional response to the "happy end." However, the "silent" group used very different adjectives, primarily of relief. This group did not see the marriage as a reward for good behavior. Rather, the final breakdown suggested that acquiring a partner willing to accommodate women's public and private dimensions cannot be effected by will or by virtue; it is simply a matter of luck. This factor calls attention to the not so perfect role the "sensible" woman will play at the end of the twentieth century, in the absence of luck: taking full responsibility for both public life and private life, the modern variation on the dilemma of love and money that so interests Thompson in *Sense and Sensibility*.[31]

If Elinor's sense represents less a private means of coping than it does a way to reconcile both public and private, Emma Thompson's emphasis on the themes of love and money in the plot of *Sense and Sensibility* stresses the interrelationship of public and private life for women in the early nineteenth century and, more generally, an insistence upon demonstrating the connection between the personal and the political for women in the present. While critics tended to focus on the personal female relationships in *Sense and Sensibility*, Thompson emphasized instead that for Elinor and Marianne, their "private" pain is clearly linked to their "public" exclusion from entail, and this interconnection is reinforced throughout the film; indeed, it is highlighted much more directly in the film than in the novel. In the novel, for example, the description of the cottage the Dashwoods rent after leaving the estate of Norland emphasizes largely its aesthetic deficiencies, whereas the cottage in the film is grey, stark, and unfurnished, symbolizing the loss of wealth and status the family has experienced.[32] Director Ang Lee made every attempt to emphasize themes of social class throughout the film by way of attention to the spaces the Dashwoods inhabit. Discussing the ballroom scene where Elinor and Marianne confront Willoughby's betrayal, Thompson writes in her diaries: "I could never have imagined the scene occurring in so many different rooms, but Ang's (director Lee's) vision is full of movement—and notions of class."[33] The different rooms in the ballroom scene emphasize the class differences of the participants; the more lavish and ornate room where the sisters discover Willoughby, for example, symbolizes the wealth for which Marianne has been abandoned.

The dilemma of love and money, as understood in Austen's time, highlighted the centrality of "good" marriages for the economic and emotional standing of women in the early nineteenth century, that is, for both their public and private standing in society. Critics who spoke of the dated nature of this theme—after all, women today can earn their own money and no longer need to rely on men for their economic well-being[34]—missed the larger point Thompson and Lee wished to convey: that presumably private questions of love and romance were inextricably linked to public issues of law and economics. Moreover, the subtextual presence of Margaret Dashwood further suggested that the connections between private and public realms had a clear

relevance for the late twentieth century, not because women like Elinor Dashwood—women who mediated the conflicting demands of independence and
affiliation—were excluded from the realms of law and economics as they had
been in Austen's day but because they were now included in them, largely
on an unequal basis. Indeed, the dilemma of love and money had acquired a
different meaning for women in the late twentieth century; it had become a
"both/and" rather than an "either/or" problem. Not, as Thompson said in one
interview and as was the case in the nineteenth century, "if you haven't any
money, you can't get married, and if you don't get married, you'll never have
any money."[35] Rather, as she more aptly put it in a German interview: it may
be wonderful to fall in love, but can women today "afford" to do so?[36] As those
still made primarily responsible for emotional and family life even as they have
entered the men's public world and those most financially disadvantaged by
divorce, women must come to recognize that "love" is as pressing an issue of
public concern for them as "money."

Why choose a Jane Austen novel to convey such a message? Claudia Johnson has suggested that the novels of Jane Austen are best understood not in
relation to the legacy of female authorship but rather in relation to the English
reaction to the French Revolution at the beginning of the nineteenth century.
Austen's novels, she argues, attempted to use aesthetic strategies to question
the ideological polarities the reaction to the Revolution had wrought.[37] As
artists from very different cultures, both Thompson and Lee nonetheless share
Austen's method of using representations of family life as a means to make social and political points about a contemporary society ideologically polarized
as a result of the combined legacies of the sexual revolution of the 1960s and
the free market counterrevolution of the 1980s. Yet crucially, both were situated in relation to the tradition of female authorship in such a way as to make
the collaboration seem almost miscegenous. "You certainly wonder," one critic
dubiously wrote in *Time* magazine, "how a Taiwan born director ... managed
to reach across time and cultures to deliver these delicate goods undamaged."[38]
Indeed, Ang Lee was viewed by many critics as an anomalous choice for an
Austen film, presumably because of the difference between Eastern and Western culture. Yet his other films, notably *The Wedding Banquet* and *Eat Drink
Man Woman* clearly employ aesthetic strategies very similar to Austen's. And
Thompson, ironically, is viewed as a perfect mediating vehicle for an Austen
novel not because she is interested in Austen's original aesthetic strategies as
a means of "uncovering the ideological underpinnings of cultural myths" but
because she "has always been good at the cadences and muffled sobbiness of
rebuked love." "In Thompson as in Austen, sense and sensibility are not so very
far apart."[39]

Yet *Sense and Sensibility* is ambivalent about itself and its political subtexts as well, no doubt due to the importance of producing a successful, profitable film, and its tapping into the nostalgic associations surrounding the legacy of female authorship was by no means accidental. Although critics generally noted a marked difference between the way Lee worked with lavish and scenic "high culture" themes and materials, in comparison to, for example, Merchant/Ivory productions, clearly much of what is affecting about *Sense and Sensibility* is its rich and ornate costumes and scenery, cues that would draw attention less to concrete themes of social class and gender inequality than to the status of "high culture." While Thompson tried at times to draw attention away from the high culture elements of the film, as when she insisted that production designer Luciana Arrighi's aristocratic picnic arrangement during a key scene should be replaced by "cheese, bread, apples, and beer," because the Dashwoods are "poor," the trappings of high culture in *Sense and Sensibility* are difficult to overlook.[40]

Moreover, Emma Thompson's star status, particularly the effort to link her person to Austen's as a female authorial figure, tended again to promote Anglophilic associations with British high culture. That Thompson, the author of the screenplay, doubled as one of the characters in the novel she adapted for the screen also highlighted the collapse of the vital distinction between the female author and the text (film). Indeed, Thompson's published diaries on the making of the film, along with the screenplay were marketed as high culture, seemingly removed from the distant world of contemporary cultural politics.

But perhaps the most conservative dimension of the film is that, at bottom, its overall aesthetics do not reinforce its political subtexts, a theme I will explore in greater detail in *Persuasion*. It was not just Jane Austen Society members who pointed out that the physical attractiveness and eroticism of cast members such as Hugh Grant reinforced a reading of the film as just another "love and romance" plot, where aesthetic signals trigger from the outset who is meant for whom in the private world of romantic relationships. In conforming so precisely to Hollywood standards that associate the cues of high culture so completely with idyllic beauty and lavish scenery, *Sense and Sensibility* succeeded, unfortunately, in camouflaging its most innovative dimensions.

* * *

Persuasion, adapted for film by Nick Dear and directed by Roger Michell—"two men of the British theatre," as one critic put it—was the first "period" Austen dramatization when it was released in the fall of 1995.[41] Highly praised by practically all major film critics, the film nonetheless received little publicity and disappeared quickly from public attention after the release of the much more popular and talked about *Sense and Sensibility*.[42] Like *Sense and Sensibility*, *Persuasion* lags behind *Pride and Prejudice* in popularity, though it is considered one of the finer, and certainly the most romantic, of Austen's six novels. In *Persuasion*, the heroine, Anne Elliot, was persuaded by a trusted and established mother surrogate, Lady Russell, to reject an offer of marriage from Frederick Wentworth on account of his lack of fortune and gentility. The story begins seven years later when Anne, at the age of twenty-seven, still ensconced in her loveless and negligent aristocratic family of origin, reencounters Frederick Wentworth, now an established captain in the British Navy. Wentworth still resents the rejection, and Anne regrets it, but because neither speaks of their feelings directly, most of the action involves indirect communication between the former lovers via dialogue with the other characters or various types of exchanges of gesture or gaze with one another. The plot is thus driven by silence, or an absence of verbal communication.

Critics tended to associate the "silence" exclusively with Anne, attempting to link it to her status as an over-the-hill spinster. It is Anne, not Frederick, who "nurses her silent hopes," as she is a "twenty-seven year old Cinderella who has lost her prince the first time round and who no longer has her looks."[43] Critics generally overemphasized the role of Anne Elliot in the film and underemphasized that of Frederick Wentworth, largely due to their assumption that *Persuasion* was best understood within the legacy of female authorship and its emphasis on the female heroine/female author. As *Persuasion* is commonly interpreted as the autumnal novel Jane Austen wrote on her deathbed, it is misread as autobiographical, the story of a lonely, dying female author "revealing her own yearning soul."[44] The film is interpreted in similar terms. John Bowman in the *American Spectator*, for example, read the film as a model of "every woman's romance: the need to be loved for herself alone and the fulfilment, after many false steps and near misses, of that need."[45] Yet *Persuasion's* silences are not Anne's exclusively. They are in fact, integral to her relationship with Frederick, who is likewise silent, even as he is entitled to the prerogative of speech.

Persuasion's silences can thus be linked to the politicized themes of gender and (mis)communication in late twentieth-century life and the great difficulty in bringing this "transparent communication" about.[46] Indeed, communication between men and women has become a potent theme in contemporary cultural studies. Linguists such as Deborah Tannen in *You Just Don't Understand* have attempted to define gender difference less in terms of biology—gender difference is grounded in nature—or politics—men dominate women—and more in terms of differing communication patterns between the sexes which, when rendered transparent, might be less a source of tension than of understanding. While this definition of gender difference might strike some as notoriously depoliticized, its intent is decidedly political: to undermine the association of gender difference with hierarchy or nature and, in the process, to bring men into the task of reforming the relationship between public and private life. While contemporary gender difference may have its modern roots in the doctrine of separate spheres, the differences created by the separation can be broken down via communication.

This thesis might sound idealistic, but Dear and Michell take it very seriously on two fundamental levels: that of what I will call "the mind," or point of view of the camera, and of the body, or what the camera "sees." Several critics noted that we, the audience, see the developments in *Persuasion* from the heroine's point of view, that is, the point of view of a subjected female. As men of the British theatre, Dear and Michell's regendering of the eye of the camera is a first step in breaking down its conventional male gaze.[47] Several critics noted the strikingly innovative use of the camera to "refurbish the conventions of the costume drama,"[48] but did not link that innovation to gender. How did the filmmakers manage to capture the subjective, internal viewpoint of the novel with the "'objective' eye of the camera?," as the German critic Patrick Bahners diplomatically put it.[49]

If *Sense and Sensibility* broke with Hollywood norms in portraying the "intelligent female character,"[50] *Persuasion* goes a step further, offering the entire narrative from Anne Elliot's point of view. Despite her elite social standing, Anne's position in her family is strikingly marginal. We see with Anne's eyes, as Bahners noted, but Anne is not seen. *Persuasion* thus dramatizes a particular instance of female subjection and, simultaneously, offers the audience the point of view of a female subject.[51] Given that both director and screen adaptor were "men of the British theatre," *Persuasion* might be "understood," like Tannen's efforts, as an attempt to deconstruct gender difference by way of a communication medium.

The political implications of another of Michell's aesthetic strategies is particularly striking: his reconfiguration of the body. In an early scene, Sir Walter Elliot is shown holding forth on the subject of physical attractiveness in men. He is surrounded by women: Elizabeth, the eldest daughter, Anne, Lady Russell, and Mrs. Clay. None of these women are "made up" in the conventional Hollywood manner and thus do not conform to Hollywood beauty standards. Devoid of make-up and flattering lighting, none of the female characters offer the audience a conventional cue as to who the subject of romantic interest will be in the film. Indeed, all of the conventional Hollywood beauty that the film offers belongs to the most heartless and mercenary characters: Sir Walter Elliot and his nephew, Sir William Elliot, who will inherit the Elliot estate due to Sir Walter's lack of male heirs. By severing the connection between beauty and virtue, as well as that between beauty and sexual desirability, Michell succeeds in disrupting just about every aesthetic convention associated with the tradition of "costume drama," and even Western art in general.

Susan Bordo has argued that a feminist politics of culture must take into account two dimensions of mass cultural imagery of gender: the tendency to homogenize, that is, to "smooth out all racial, ethnic, and sexual 'differences' that disturb Anglo-Saxon, heterosexual expectations and identifications" and the tendency to normalize, or create images that "function as models against which the self continually measures, judges, 'disciplines,' and 'corrects' itself."[52] She further suggests that, to remedy these two tendencies, it is necessary to conceptualize the body not as a sight of the play of cultural differences but as a battleground. She provides a concrete example: a pro-choice advertisement offering a woman's face split into halves, the left half a conventional photo, the other half its negative. Superimposed over this divided image is the text "Your body is a battleground."[53]

Michell's *Persuasion,* clearly distances itself from the tendencies of homogenization and normalization, and its reception reveals the "battle" over the female body and its right to intimacy and authority if it is not perceived as "normalized." Many critics, reading *Persuasion* as a "conventional romance," actively resisted identifying with the characters portrayed by Amanda Root, Susan Fleetwood, and even Ciàran Hinds, because they simply could not overlook this "break" with Hollywood beauty norms: "A few anachronisms [in *Persuasion*] can be overlooked, but there is no getting around that not-to-be-overlooked, or looked-at, heroine." Simon continues: "A few years before," we read in the novel, Anne "had been a very pretty girl, but her bloom had vanished early. Miss Root, manifestly a different part of the plant, has no bloom whatsoever, and seems never to have had."[54] "In their attempts to purify the movie [*Persuasion*] of Hollywood sheen and give it an air of naturalism, the producers ... have too zealously ripped away the romantic gauze: the distressing results are an unappealing Anne Elliot, a pockmarked Captain Wentworth, a greasy-locked Benwick, and a slovenly-looking Lady Russell."[55] "Even more disturbing ... is the Lady Russell of Susan Fleetwood, an actress I could never abide, and who, besides looking slovenly ... towers physically over the tiny Miss Root. You feel that to stop Anne from marrying Wentworth, she might not so much have persuaded her as merely sat on her."[56] Various other demeaning adjectives were used to describe Amanda Root: "with her pursed mouth and shoe button eyes;" "plain and sad-eyed;" "prim and tight-lipped"[57] (see Figure 4.3).

By structuring the film around the point of view of a romantic heroine who is "not seen" and "not to be looked at," that is, not seen not only by her family and the looks conscious patriarch who heads it but also by the so-called critical film establishment of late twentieth-century culture, unwilling or unable to imagine romantic attachment outside the powerful homogenizing and nor-

Figure 4.3. The two lead characters from Roger Michell's BBC adaptation of Jane Austen's *Persuasion*: Anne Elliot (Amanda Root) and Frederick Wentworth (Ciàran Hinds). Anne and Wentworth consult in a crisis situation involving the injured Louisa Musgrove. Captain Benwick (Richard McCabe) looks on helplessly. This still shows clearly the unglamorous and "naturalistic" depiction of the characters that was criticized by many critics. (Courtesy: Photofest)

malizing forces of popular culture. Michell's adaptation of *Persuasion* "deepens and confuses our apprehension of Jane Austen," because "the novel, too, does something comparable."[58] Michell retains Austen's critique of male vanity in his adaptation, as well as Austen's critique of the critical male gaze, as embodied in Sir Walter, who judges human beings based almost solely upon their physical appearance. Perhaps it is something like an instance of "Austenian irony" when late twentieth-century film critics assume the point of view of the characterological object, Sir Walter, of some of Jane Austen's "most withering satire."[59] That irony points to the important distinction between Jane Austen's works and the literary and generic categories in which she has been classified—categories that have been appropriated by the visual expectations of Hollywood formulas for the "costume drama" that demand the same physical perfection as does Sir Walter.

Like *Sense and Sensibility, Persuasion* also emphasizes the importance of social class and hierarchy via use of the camera. However, as with its choice of actors, *Persuasion* departs from *Sense and Sensibility*'s reliance upon the "conventions of the costume drama." While *Sense and Sensibility* limits its filmic explorations of class difference to those aspects relevant only to the happiness of the genteel but impoverished sisters and glamorizes "high culture" via costumes and lavish scenery, *Persuasion* highlights crass divisions of social class in general, showing anonymous farmers laboring around the estate and focusing the camera upon their facial expressions and profiles. Thus, the infrastructure of the narrative is made visible to the audience, and it is significant, because Anne's gender marginality is linked to the class marginality of her servants. For example, in a scene showing Anne leaving the estate of her father, a scene which one critic objected to on the grounds that it must be historically inaccurate, Anne is shown riding in an animal cart.[60] Clearly, this is the mode of transportation to which her servants are entitled, yet to place Anne in such a cart is to represent the parallels between gender and class marginality.

However, it is not just the lower class world but also "the upper-middle-class Regency world [*Persuasion*] evokes [that] feels scruffed and lived-in," according to David Ansen in *Newsweek*.[61] Michell "made it his business," according to Anthony Lane, to "roughen and dampen the Austen world into a state of nervous desperation."[62] With this demythologizing of the upper class dimension of the costume drama, Dear and Michell attempt a most unusual endeavor in *Persuasion*: to gender the world of Jane Austen *male*. This "regendering" functions on two levels. What Anne Elliot witnesses—what we witness by way of the camera—is a world of men. We begin, for example, not in the company of women but of men, a room full of sailors toasting the defeat of Napoleon.[63] Throughout, we are confronted with the sense that this world of *Persuasion* feels, above all, "scruffed and lived in." However, it is the second level that is most intriguing. The weather beaten faces of the sailors, along with the unmade up and physically imposing female characters, Mrs. Croft and Lady Russell, suggest a world where women who exercise power do so along lines conventionally defined as male: directly and forcefully, rather than passively and indirectly, as would be the case during the Victorian period of "separate spheres." Characters in *Persuasion* who anticipate the model of "separate spheres," particularly Mary Musgrove, are satirized by Dear, as they are by Austen. The world of the proto-Victorian female is, above all, claustrophobic; the world of the "self-made" sailor is, decidedly, open. By demythologizing the costume drama visually, Dear and Michell actively regender it, thus rendering the presence of men in the world of domestic fiction plausible.[64]

However, this is not a world where the "masculine" principle of activity dominates the female principle; it is not the male side of separate spheres. Rather, it is a world where we witness male presence in a domestic world from the heroine's point of view. In turn, we are made to see the divided nature of the "self-made" male subject: On the one hand, the uniform that symbolizes that in 1814, an officer in the British Navy "was pretty much the most exalted being on the planet,"[65] that is, a static, fixed entity with public authority but no inner life. On the other, not the uniform but the face of Captain Wentworth, along with the faces of other Navy men, all distinguished in their ability to express very dynamic emotions through their decidedly imperfect features. If Anne's silence is a product of her gender role, Frederick's silence is the product of the division between what he represents to the world and what he desires.

"Women need to reaffirm they have equal power with men," actress Amanda Root, commenting on *Persuasion,* said in an interview. "Austen deals with that, pretty positively. My character faces a life of spinsterhood, yet she gets on with it and not in a weepy way. She deserves the kiss we gave her at the end of the film. But I think it says something that that kiss, because it isn't in the book, made a lot of people go completely mental."[66] Indeed, in *Persuasion* a scene showing Anne Elliot and Frederick Wentworth kissing briefly on a public street was included in the adaptation, and it did trigger critical commentary. Anthony Lane, for example, writing in the *New Yorker,* had the following to say: "There are times when [the film's] clutching at modern sensibilities makes scant historical sense; if you're going to show Anne and Frederick kissing in the *street*—a street in *Bath,* of all places—you might as well go the whole hog and have them perform oral sex in the Pump Room, but the kiss is just a romantic sop"[67] In line with many Austen purists, Lane resists the scene because it's not in the novel and thus "historically" inaccurate.[68]

Yet Root's implicit association of that kiss scene with feminist concerns of equality between men and women is interesting, because so much feminist literature associates the culmination of romantic novels, marriage, with the central validation of female identity and the containment of female power within a male defined and dominated institution.[69] Why should this scene be any different symbolically? One major reason is that, in both *Sense and Sensibility* and *Persuasion,* marriage is conceived as a reward for female virtue, not a validation of female identity. When they receive their marriage offers, the lead heroines in both films have already come to terms with the possibility of "spinsterhood," recognizing that their identities are not based solely upon the acquisition of a partner. They have each done so by different routes. Elinor's identity consists in learning to mediate between the poles of independence (Margaret) and affiliation (Marianne), demonstrating or symbolizing women's capacity and need for both dimensions, while Anne must learn to assert herself against the authority of her female guardian, Lady Russell.

What sort of men do these women marry? Edward, as we have seen in *Sense and Sensibility,* wants the comfort of a "private life" but is clearly unwilling to fight for it. Indeed, he is the figure Mrs. Jennings implicitly refers to when she tellingly declares: "I do not know what the young men are about these days—are they all in hiding?,"[70] suggesting that the Elinors of the world may very likely not be rewarded for their virtue. Contemporary cultural criticism focusing upon issues of male identity first raised by the feminist movement have answered Mrs. Jennings's query with a variety of theories, notably Barbara Ehrenreich's illuminating *The Hearts of Men,* where she argues that Western male identity is no longer predominantly shaped by the ethic of the breadwinner, thus releasing men from the cultural obligation to marry, even as they continue to earn higher wages than women. She refers to men's increasing identification with consumer culture in terms of a "flight from commitment" to women as wives and mothers. Moreover, she defines the "backlash" of the 1980s not in terms of a male reaction against feminism but rather in terms of a female reaction to men's increasing rejection of the role of breadwinner.[71]

If *Sense and Sensibility's* key subtext is about contemporary female identity, *Persuasion's* is about contemporary male identity. If Anne represented the dying aristocracy and Wentworth the up-and-coming democratic classes of entrepreneurs and independent agents in Austen's day, in the late twentieth century, the figures clearly represent something very different. Frederick Wentworth's silence after his return to Anne's circles is, after all, what must be explained, since it is certainly he who must raise the issue of their previous engagement and reacquaintance publicly. His silence is best understood within the ideological force fields represented by the three central women in the film: Lady Russell, Mrs. Croft, and Anne Elliot.

Lady Russell's stature and bearing, commented upon so disparagingly by certain critics, is a central symbolic statement in the film, because it is not meant to be understood in relation to Anne's physical presence but rather to Wentworth's. A brief but critical scene where Lady Russell and Frederick Wentworth confront each other, and which is not part of the plot of the original novel, clearly marks them as equal contenders for power and influence, and Lady Russell's insistence that Frederick Wentworth is not grounded, one might say, outside the confines of his own person—he had, as she puts it in the film, "nothing but himself to recommend him"—is the key prejudice Wentworth knows he has to overcome. Given that she sees only his presumed growing partiality for Louisa Musgrove, she is evidently confirmed in her suspicions that Wentworth is as incapable of "constancy" as he is wanting in birth and breeding. Clearly, Lady Russell is wrong, but her instincts are on behalf of Anne, whose public stature will be based upon whom she marries. That Lady Russell prefers to see Anne publicly distinguished rather than privately "happy," represented by her preference of Sir Walter's heir, William Elliot, can be read ideologically as a clear defense of what might be called the "male as breadwinner" model. That Wentworth is now rich suggests he has overcome the obstacle; nonetheless, Lady Russell's point of view symbolizes the powerful interconnection between masculinity and social class.

If Lady Russell represents the link between male identity and social class, Mrs. Croft offers another challenge. She questions his masculinity insofar as she accuses him of what can only be defined as sexism. In a dialogue between her and her brother, Mrs. Croft's insistence that women are "rational creatures" rather than "fine ladies" is fielded by Wentworth via hasty retreat. Michell chose an actress whose stature and bearing was comparable both to that of her husband, the Admiral, as well as to Wentworth's. Neither does Mrs. Croft think too highly of her brother's powers of differentiation in matters of love and commitment when she remarks that, now that he is rich, any charming young woman between the ages of fifteen and thirty might do for him. In the novel, the line is uttered not by Mrs. Croft but by Wentworth himself, and there he means it sarcastically—"He said it, [Anne] knew, to be contradicted"—whereas in the film, Mrs. Croft does not expect to be countered.[72]

Finally, there is Anne Elliot's challenge, her assumption that women are more emotionally constant than men. This is, of course, reflected in her dialogue with Captain Harville, who insists that men are quite capable of constancy, that is, lasting emotional commitment. Thus confronted with the central challenges to masculine identity posed by women in the late twentieth century: that they have fled from commitment to women economically, politically, and emotionally, Wentworth's "silence" acquires a particular significance. The kiss scene in Bath thus represents a good deal more than just a "romantic sop," for insofar as Anne has been influenced—indeed, persuaded—by both Lady Russell and Mrs. Croft, she contains all three dimensions of the critique. The scene can thus be read as a defense of the idea of male constancy, rather than a validation of female identity and a symbolic insistence upon the idea that men and women can overcome the silences those challenges have created.

I would conclude that the film's central message of male "constancy," combined with the "regendering" of the domestic milieu as male, offers a response of sorts to that dimension of both conservative and feminist discourse that suggested the realms of the emotional and affective belong exclusively to women. And indeed, unlike the "men's movement" of the 1990s, led by Robert Bly and others, which tended to stress—implicitly though not explicitly—separate spheres of male and female activity, the men in *Persuasion* and the women whom they marry share one another's worlds.[73] Correspondingly, women are not placed in the position of assuming responsibility for teaching men to "feel" their emotions, the conventional cultural function of the female associated with the ideology of separate spheres.

Although *Persuasion* was critically acclaimed, it was not a particularly popular film. Certainly budgeting and marketing constraints played an important role. Unlike *Sense and Sensibility, Persuasion* did not have the advantages of star status in its direction or its cast. However, more critical is the relationship between the films' aesthetic and political dimensions. In *Sense and Sensibility,* the basic aesthetic strategies of the film conform with major strains of the legacy of female authorship: the glamorization of high culture and the physical idealization of the main cast members. These signals encourage a conventional reading that emphasize that the relationships the film portrays are strictly "private" in character, with no significance outside the confines of the personal. *Persuasion,* in contrast, violates fundamental genre expectations and, in the process, exposes more fully its fundamentally political intention: to question the separation of public and private worlds along gendered lines.

Notes

1. David Ansen, "In This Fine Romance, Virtue is Rewarded." *Newsweek* (9 October 1995): 78.

2. See, in particular, the volume edited by Linda Troost and Sayre Greenfield, *Jane Austen in Hollywood* (Lexington, Kentucky, 1998 [2001]) for insightful, though very different, readings of the Austen film boom.

3. James Collins, "Jane Reaction," *Vogue* (January 1996): 70; "Jane Addiction," *Show Sunday, Orange County Register* (14 January 1996): 1; John Leonard, "Jane-Mania," *New York* (15 January 1996): 55.

4. Evan Thomas, "Hooray for Hypocrisy," *Newsweek* (29 January 1996): 61.

5. John Leonard, "Jane-Mania," *New York* (15 January 1996): 55.

6. Elaine Rapping, "The Jane Austen Thing," *Progressive* (July 1996): 37–38.

7. John Simon, "Novel Distractions," *National Review* (23 October 1995): 58.

8. Wendy Wasserstein, "The *Premiere* Review: *Sense and Sensibility*" (February 1996): 17.

9. Martin Amis, "Jane's World," *New Yorker* (8 January 1996): 35.

10. Anthony Lane, "Jane's World," *New Yorker* (25 September 1995):108.

11. Ansen, 78.

12. Louis Menand, "What Jane Austen doesn't tell us," *New York Review of Books* (1 February 1996): 15.

13. Susan Faludi, *Backlash: The Undeclared War Against American Women* (Doubleday: New York, 1991), 113.

14. Rosalind Pollack Petchesky, "Antiabortion and Antifeminism," in Mary Beth Norton and Ruth M. Alexander, eds., *Major Problems in American Women's History* (Lexington, Massachusetts, 1996), 508.

15. Claudia L. Johnson, *Jane Austen: Women, Politics, and the Novel* (Chicago, 1988), 27. See also *Equivocal Beings: Politics, Gender and Sentimentality in the 1790s, Wollstonecraft, Radcliffe, Burney, Austen* (Chicago, 1995) and "Austen Cults and Cultures," in Edward Copeland and Juliet McMaster, eds. *The Cambridge Companion to Jane Austen* (Cambridge, England, 1997), 211–226.

16. According to boxofficemojo.com, since 1995 *Sense and Sensibility* has grossed over $43,000,000 on the domestic front and over $91,000,000 overseas. See http://boxofficemojo .com/movies/?id=senseandsensibility.htm.

17. Lindsay Doran, "Introduction" in Emma Thompson, *The Sense and Sensibility Screenplay and Diaries* (New York, 1996), 11.

18. Emma Thompson, *The Sense and Sensibility Screenplay and Diaries* (New York, 1996).

19. Thompson, 215.

20. Jan Stuart, "Emma Thompson, Sensibly," *Los Angeles Times Calendar* (10 December 1995): 85.

21. Menand, 14.

22. Terrance Rafferty, "Fidelity and Infidelity," *New Yorker* (18 December 1995): 124.

23. Thompson, *The Sense and Sensibility Screenplay and Diaries,* 27–29.

24. For a different reading of the significance of Margaret, see Julian North, "Conservative Austen, Radical Austen: *Sense and Sensibility from Text to Screen*" in Deborah Cartmell and Imelda Whelehan, eds. *Adaptations: From Text to Screen, Screen to Text.* (London, 1999), 38–50.

25. Thompson, 34.

26. Thompson, 74.

27. "Verflucht harte Arbeit": Interview mit Emma Thompson. *Der Spiegel* 10 (4 March 1996): 230–231.

28. "Verflucht harte Arbeit," 230–231.

29. Amis, "Jane's World," 35.

30. Thompson, 48.

31. Ruth Sidel, *On Her Own: Growing Up in the Shadow of the American Dream* (New York, 1990), 219–243. Jan Stuart, "Emma Thompson, Sensibly," *Los Angeles Times Calendar* (10 December 1995): 8–9; 85. In her insightful essay, "Piracy is Our Only Option: Postfeminist Intervention in *Sense and Sensibility*," Kristin Flieger Samuelian offers a different reading by linking Thompson's version of *Sense and Sensibility* to a "postfeminist consciousness [that] demands a reconciliation between female independence and marriage." (151) Though I agree with Samuelian that *Sense and Sensibility* is clearly ambivalent about its own feminism, her definition of "postfeminism" would seem to exclude Austen's novels as vehicles for feminist critique by definition, since all of them attempt to reconcile "female independence and marriage" in one form or another. See her essay in Troost and Greenfield, eds. *Jane Austen in Hollywood,* 148–158.

32. Jane Austen, *Sense and Sensibility* (New York, 1966), 23–24.

33. Thompson, 261.

34. See, for example, Stanley Kauffmann, Review of *Emma, New Republic* (19 and 26 August 1996), 38–39.

35. "Emma Thompson, A Close Reading," *New Yorker* (15 November 1993): 47.

36. "Verflucht harte Arbeit," 230–231.

37. Johnson, *Jane Austen*, xiii–xxv, 1–27.

38. Richard Schickel, "Kissing Cousins," *Time* (18 December 1995): 73.

39. Johnson, 27; Review of *Sense and Sensibility, Los Angeles Times Magazine* (January 1996): 108.

40. Thompson, *Diaries*, 234.

41. Ansen, 78.

42. Since its release *Persuasion* has grossed $5,269,757 in the United States and was ranked 146th for the year 1995. This is well below *Sense and Sensibility* but considerably more than other adaptations would gross, particularly the James adaptations *The Portrait of a Lady* and *Washington Square* discussed in Chapter 6. See http://boxofficemojo.com/movies/?id=persuasion.htm.

43. Menand, "What Jane Austen doesn't tell us," 14.

44. Ansen, 78.

45. James Bowman, Review of *Persuasion, American Spectator* (December 1995): 69.

46. Deborah Tannen, *You Just Don't Understand* (New York, 1990).

47. Graeme Turner, *Film as Social Practice, 2nd ed.,* (London, 1993), 114–121.

48. Ansen, 78.

49. Patrick Bahners, "Das Herz hat seine Gründe," *Frankfurter Allgemeine Zeitung* (3 December 1996), 39.

50. Wasserstein, "The *Premiere* Review: *Sense and Sensibility*" (February 1996): 17.

51. Gisela Bock, "Challenging Dichotomies in Women's History," in Mary Beth Norton and Ruth M. Alexander, editors, *Major Problems in American Women's History, 2nd ed.,* (Lexington, Massachusetts, 1996), 8.

52. Susan Bordo, *Unbearable Weight: Feminism, Western Culture and the Body* (Berkeley, 1993), 24–25.

53. Bordo, 263–64. Bordo's argument is compelling, but the ad she selects is a weak defense of her thesis, for close inspection of the face itself reveals the conventional symmetry associated with Hollywood beauty standards. The representation itself is thus not an example of Bordo's thesis, but rather another abstract rendition of it. To see the battle over the body in action, so to speak, it is necessary to review responses to instances when the norms of "normalization" are violated.

54. John Simon, "Novel Distractions," *National Review* (23 October 1995): 59.

55. Brooke Allen, "Jane Austen For the Nineties," *New Criterion* (September 1995), quoted in Simon, 58–59.

56. Simon, 59.

57. Menand, 14; Ansen, 78; David Denby, Review of *The Scarlet Letter* and *Persuasion, New York* (23 October 1995): 57–58.

58. Anthony Lane, "Jane's World," *New Yorker* (25 September 1995): 107.

59. Jane Austen, *Persuasion.* (1817) with an Introduction (1965) by D.W. Harding, (Harmondsworth, 1970): back cover.

60. Denby, 57–58.

61. Lane, 108; Ansen, 78.

62. Lane, "Jane's World," 107.

63. Though, in this early scene, Anne herself has not yet been introduced; nonetheless, the camera's point-of-view assumes the position of Anne, and thus can be defined as representing her throughout the entire film. Moreover, to depict scenes where no women are present is a major modification of Austen's texts, where there are no such scenes.

64. Louis Menand noted a seemingly analogous phenomenon in the British redramatization of *Pride and Prejudice*, that is, an emphasis upon Darcy's [male] body. Director Simon Langton and scriptwriter Andrew Davies added scenes of Darcy bathing, etc., attempting to emphasize his male physical presence. This "added Darcy" was, however, precisely that—a rather intrusive addition to a profoundly conventional reading of the novel. The world of Jane Austen is first and foremost a world gendered female in *Pride and Prejudice*, with the male body (i.e. Darcy's body) given, at best, a symbolic "bodice-ripper" function.

65. Menand, 14.

66. "Austen Anew," *New Yorker* (21 and 28 August 1995):56.

67. Lane, 108.

68. In *Sense and Sensibility*, rather oddly, a kiss scene between Edward and Elinor—also not in the novel—was included as a film still in the published diaries/screenplay but *not* included in the film. See, Thompson, *Diaries*, 34.

69. See, for example, Julia Prewitt-Brown, "The Feminist Depreciation of Austen: A Polemical Reading," *Novel: A Forum on Fiction* 23(1990): 303–313 and Johnson, "Austen Cults and Cultures," 211–226.

70. Thompson, 140.

71. Barbara Ehrenreich, *The Hearts of Men: American Dreams and the Flight From Commitment* (New York, 1983). See also Alan Deutschman and Jennifer Brown, "Men at Work," *Gentlemen's Quarterly* (January 1997): 101–107.

72. Jane Austen, *Persuasion* (Harmondsworth, 1970), 86.

73. Robert Bly, *Iron John: A Book About Men* (New York, 1992).

Chapter Five

Thelma and Sense and Louise and Sensibility

Challenging Dichotomies in Women's History through Film and Literature

While filmmakers were engaged in postfeminist explorations of identity issues in their adaptations of Jane Austen's works, the critical reception of the films tended to frame the "Austen boom" as a conservative response to postmodern liberation. However, the feminist playwright Wendy Wasserstein's review of *Sense and Sensibility* stood out by linking the Austen films to questions of contemporary Hollywood depictions of female character: "Precisely 200 years ago, Jane Austen was writing great parts for women. She didn't have to meet with a creative executive with a post–*Thelma and Louise* agenda or a Hollywood agent with a client list of impatient, over-thirty females to get the idea. In Jane Austen's world, women's choices, marriages, yearnings, and economic status were the stuff central storylines were made of."[1] Following this small clue from the reception of the Austen adaptations, I would like to explore some implications of recontextualizing the Austen boom not as a conservative but rather as a postfeminist phenomenon, that is, one that seeks to engage questions of the relationship between gender and culture not only within the genre of the "Austen adaptation" but also across genres, in order to address issues of gender identity that have become relevant since the women's movement of the 1970s.

What distinguishes Wasserstein's perspective from more conservative commentators is her assumption that popular films like *Sense and Sensibility* (1995), directed by Ang Lee and starring Emma Thompson and Kate Winslet, and *Thelma and Louise* (1991), directed by Ridley Scott and starring Geena Davis and Susan Sarandon, actually have something in common in their focus upon female intelligence or female character, in spite of the completely different categories into which each film was placed.[2] And indeed, a close reading of both films in relationship to each other reveals an active challenge to the conventional dichotomies of public/private and feminism/conservatism associated with the conservative reception of the Austen boom. *Thelma and Louise* is a particularly noteworthy point of comparison, because it shares with *Sense and Sensibility* a fundamentally similar plot structure: two women with very different personalities confronting a challenging situation that leads each protagonist to take on some of the characteristics of the other (see Figure 5.1; compare also Chapter 4, Figure 4.1).

Figure 5.1. Publicity poster for *Thelma and Louise* with Susan Sarandon (Louise) and Geena Davis (Thelma). (Courtesy: Photofest)

In this chapter, I would like to compare the two films in order to show exactly how they challenge these conventional dichotomies. I would also like to show why it is that such films are generally not understood in relationship to each other, but rather in relation to specific genre categories which perpetuate, at the level of reception, conventional notions of "separate spheres." This will become clearer when comparing the differing receptions the two films received when each was released.

When *Thelma and Louise* was released in 1991, it was often compared to the "buddy film" genre associated most notably with *Butch Cassidy and the Sundance Kid,* thus acquiring the somewhat oxymoronic label of "female buddy" film, a label that did not particularly capture the reviewing establishment's imagination.[3] What did capture its imagination was the assumption that the film had a "feminist" message, best understood in terms of the following questions: "Are Thelma and Louise feminist role models?; are the violent actions exhibited in *Thelma and Louise* morally reprehensible?; and, is the movie's male-bashing unfair to men?"[4] All of the questions, structuring the discussion of the film in terms of a radically feminist, i.e., separatist agenda, failed to emphasize the differences between the two women, or that their differences as characters was the motor of the film, not their similar genders. Critics offered viewers a "radical feminist" framework in which to situate both Thelma and Louise, which could then be fruitfully invoked as an implicit contrast to more conservative, well-behaved women.[5] The background critics used to understand the film's characters was not the particular social and cultural context in which these two very different women find themselves; rather, the background became the implicitly conservative, non-male-bashing woman less violently inclined. Which isn't to suggest that feminist dimensions do not shape the film; it is rather—as I'll note later—to ask why certain dimensions of the film are defined as feminist and others are not. According to most critics, the feminist dimension in *Thelma and Louise* turned out to be the aggressive behavior of the women themselves and not the point of view of the camera regarding the significant differences between the two women.[6]

If *Thelma and Louise* was thus situated on the radical left with reference to possible "female" attitudes, *Sense and Sensibility* was situated on the right. Defined at the outset either as a "romantic domestic comedy" or, more frequently, as a dramatization of a "Jane Austen novel," meaning roughly the same thing, critics were preoccupied with the potentially reactionary implications of the Jane Austen film boom in the mid-1990s, rather than with the significance of the character differences between the two female leads—though Wasserstein's review is a notable exception here in at least drawing attention to the issue. Fixating largely upon the historical period of the film rather than on the female characters, critics pondered the meaning of the Jane Austen film boom in a postfeminist age, offering such acute analysis as the suggestion that the Austen films may well indicate a "frustration" with "postmodern liberation."[7]

Therefore, by comparing the receptions of the two films briefly, we can see that an opposition has been created in relationship to the approaches critics use to understand films dealing with female character. Either they are linked to the radical feminist left or the conservative, family values right, obviously obscuring the complexity of the question of female character in the films and, by extension, the question of the future and problem of gender identity as a cultural issue. Moreover, the nature of this particular opposition functions to limit the relevance of the films to women alone, as review blurbs such as "sisterhood is powerful" for *Sense and Sensibility* and speculation over whether Thelma and Louise "may" be "lesbian" would suggest.[8] Moreover, these categories of classification actively function to obscure the important similarities between the two films, namely, the relationship of different female characters to the modern patriarchal contexts in which they develop. My essential point is that when films do focus upon the question of female character, that "character" tends to be framed within the opposition discussed above, which works against the task of actually evaluating the nature of female character as it is presented in the films.

To begin to understand both films in terms of their focus upon the development of female character, it is important to look in an obvious place: at their plots. The plots of these films suggest a context within which to evaluate the women very different from not only the opposition between "feminism" and "conservatism" suggested by the reception but also from a prevalent popular mythos of postmodern "women's liberation" in the 1990s: "having it all."[9] Neither Thelma, Louise, Elinor, or Marianne "have it all." But what do they have? If having it all very concretely refers to the myth that a modern liberated woman has both a committed personal relationship with a man (married, if at all possible), a family, and a successful career, as well as an unlimited array of possible lifestyle choices, all of the female characters in the films fall abysmally short. Thelma has a lousy marriage, no children, and no career. Louise has a problematic relationship and a lousy career as a waitress; she got what she "settled for," as she puts it in the film, suggesting that she blames herself for not living up to this mainstream ideal. Elinor and Marianne are manless and moneyless. The dilemma of "love and money," as it is articulated by Austen in her novels and experienced by Elinor and Marianne, is updated by Emma Thompson in her screenplay to resonate with the contemporary version of this dilemma as it is understood by modern audiences, the conflict between home and work, family and career, or the lack of family (love) and lack of career (money) all of these female characters experience in one form or another. Thus, these women are basically on the margins of what their respective societies consider the "ideal woman": solidly middle class and married "well."

Why are these women so marginalized despite the clear potential, charm, intelligence, attractiveness, and strength of character each manifest? Both films offer clear answers. Their marginality is directly related to their gender and must be understood not as personal fault but rather as a structural relationship to specific social institutions: the law, the economy, and the family, or rather, men. In both *Thelma and Louise* and *Sense and Sensibility*, women's problematic relationship to the law is foregrounded. The implicit assumption that it is the law that encourages male violence against women and refuses to recognize its own double standard involving most crimes of violence against women, or the nature of the genesis of that violence in "normal" male gender roles, leaves women with little recourse when they are victims of that violence. The recourse they do find in *Thelma and Louise* is not in the law but in female solidarity against their marginal status in the law. Critics tended to focus upon the violent actions the women engage in and not upon the development of their mutual agreement that they are both outcasts. Thelma and Louise attempt to circumvent the law not so much by "running away," but through female solidarity, i.e., agreement on their similar structural relationship to the law, a solidarity that develops "on the road" between the two lead characters, but that is also participated in by a third party, the waitress Lena (Lucinda Jenney) at the country and western bar, whose remark to Detective Slocum (Harvey Keitel) that Thelma and Louise "weren't the murdering types" is meant to be understood literally and sympathetically, rather than ironically and confrontationally, despite the fact that it is factually wrong.

This theme, female solidarity as a means of defense against legal marginality, has a pedigree in American literature going a long way back. Stories such as Susan Keating Glaspell's "A Jury of Her Peers," written in 1917, likewise dramatize women agreeing to an alternative understanding of justice based upon the different relationship of men and women to the law. After the murder of her farmer husband, the former Minnie Foster is suspected of the deed but cannot be pinned down with evidence. When the representatives of the law come to search the scene, the male members of the party go upstairs while their wives remain in the kitchen. What the wives find is a strangled canary, suggesting Minnie Foster's psychic, emotional, and domestic strangulation by her husband, as well as a motive for the murder. The women agree to hide the canary from the men, because they realize that the violence committed against Minnie is not recognized by the law, whereas the violence committed against her husband is. The women thus offer an alternative standard for judging Minnie, and she is presumably released.

Like Thelma and Louise, the women in "A Jury of Her Peers" make a decision to agree that it is their gender that unites them in their marginality. Moreover, the moment of recognition is offered to the audience/reader in a similarly passionate, somewhat sentimental, and personal way: sharing a gaze of "mutual recognition." Therefore, it is not a recognition firmly anchored in mainstream cultural traditions but rather situational and essentially personal in nature, perhaps corresponding to the relative decline of the women's movements in each respective era.[10] Significantly, in Glaspell's story, the women cannot count on any understanding—sympathetic or otherwise—from the men folk. Asked in the story whether she thinks the men would recognize the implications of the dead canary, Martha Hale replies ambiguously, "maybe they would ... maybe they wouldn't," (304) meaning essentially that the women have decided to take the law into their own hands. Like the women in "A Jury of Her Peers," Thelma and Louise intuitively grasp that even the—now—greater personal sympathy for their plight exhibited by the FBI agent Slocum (Harvey Keitel), does not translate into support at the more significant structural level of the FBI as a public agency. Hence, they too, like the women in Glaspell's story, choose not to confide in the men.

Women's legal marginality in *Sense and Sensibility* is also a central dimension of that film. When the Dashwoods find themselves ousted from their home due to the death of their father, Elinor clearly articulates women's marginality from the law to her youngest sister, who fails to accept the dictum: "Houses go from father to son, dearest, not from father to daughter. It is the law."[11] While the early nineteenth-century historical setting might encourage audiences to think this particular type of legal marginality is an arbitrary thing of the past, what is critical to note is the way it is articulated as a structural relationship based upon gender, a structural relationship that—theoretically—determines how the women will behave toward potential marriage partners and what sorts of partners they choose, because it is that particular economic and legal arrangement that will allow them a less marginal status in society. The private, personal pain they experience as a result of the death of their father is thus linked to their "public" exclusion from entail, and this connection is reinforced by way of a number of aesthetic strategies throughout the film, notably, Lee's emphasis upon the declining social status of the women and the increasing sparseness and modesty of the spaces they inhabit. To a great extent, both films clearly situate their main characters on the margins of the central social and cultural institution of the law and use various filmic strategies to highlight this marginality. Implied, of course, are the structural, rather than personal, origins of their particular conflicts.

Likewise, both films highlight the connections between the economic circumstances of the female characters and the presumably "personal" and highly problematic relationships they have with men. While in *Thelma and Louise,* Thelma's status as a housewife makes her economically dependent on her husband, a dependence foregrounded in the film by her need to ask her husband for permission, as well as to insist that her relationship to him should not be based upon dependency—"you're my husband, not my father"—, in *Sense and Sensibility,* it is clear that the women's poverty has a clear impact upon the nature of the personal relationships they choose to enter into. When Fanny, Edward's sister, arrogantly suggests to Elinor's mother that Edward is "entirely the kind of compassionate person upon whom penniless women can prey," she has articulated the connection between public and private very succinctly, as Elinor's poverty and gender render her personal motives suspect by definition.[12] Marianne's aborted engagement to Willoughby is also a result of economic considerations on his part: his public standing in society will be insupportable without the foundation of a "good," i.e., lucrative, marriage. Seduction and abandonment, with the man either leaving a woman with the burden of a child without support, as was the case involving Willoughby and Colonel Brandon's ward, Eliza, or sexual manipulation linked to theft, as with Thelma and J.D., further draw attention to the interconnections between personal and financial realities. Thus, economic marginality and volatile, noncommittal, and damaging relationships with men are shown to be related to one another. Therefore, it is not just a question of "male-bashing," as most critics saw it. If we venture to see the connection between the economic marginality of the women—and men—and the decidedly problematic nature of their personal relationships, the social rather than individual dimensions of the gender themes in the films become much clearer.

Given this structural marginality within which the women find themselves, how do they cope with their marginality? This is the essence of the question of female character. Before I launch into that discussion, let me say a few words about the concept of female character and how it is understood in contemporary cultural studies. As a tool of literary analysis, the concept of character was usually situated in terms of the conflicts individual characters in the tradition of realist and modernist literature experienced in relationship to themselves, their society, and each other. Critics in the 1950s and 1960s formulated the notions as follows: man vs. man, man vs. society, and man vs. himself.[13] The obvious gendering of character here has given way to more neutral terminology, such as "person vs. person," "person vs. environment," and "person vs. self," as a result of the women's movement and its impact on the academy.[14] Nonetheless, recent scholarship has reintroduced gender in relationship to character, emphasizing not the presumed neutrality of gender—man vs. himself—but rather its clear influence upon character as such; hence, there are male characters and female characters, each influenced by the social contexts that either limit or enable their development within or against the norms of gender identity in any given context.[15]

Indeed, "female character," or women's social, personal, and cultural development as an idea in literature, was always construed to have political as well as personal implications, although the genrefication of literature has tended to stress female character in so-called private contexts alone.[16] For example, Jane Austen's works are still very much defined as "novels" dealing more or less exclusively with women's personal quest for happiness, marriage, romance, etc. However, as Claudia Johnson and other scholars of Austen have demonstrated, Austen was clearly interested in the implications of different types of female characters for the future development of society at large and, to an extent that scholars disagree on, with the relationship of the status of women to the public realm.[17] Emma Thompson's screen adaptation of *Sense and Sensibility* recognizes this dimension clearly and makes effective, though not unproblematic, use of it.[18]

However, it is important to note that since the women's movement the question of female character has become an issue "for its own sake," so to speak. Female character no longer is interesting exclusively for how it is related to the general order of society. Rather, female character is interesting, because contemporary women must carve an individual niche out for themselves, create "an own" identity, an own story in the context of the narrative of individualism and democracy that has been the legacy of the modern world since the French Revolution, and that has, until quite recently, been exclusively gendered male. Yet, on an even more significant level, the question of female character today draws explicit attention to the question of male character as a gendered phenomenon, meaning that questions of female character are, by definition, also questions about male character and hence about the possible future of gender identity. It isn't just about women anymore, even though critics continue to make every effort to limit the relevance of films such as *Thelma and Louise* and *Sense and Sensibility* to women alone. Indeed, it is important to note that both films were scripted by women and directed by men, suggesting a collaborative model on the level of film-making, at any rate.[19]

Thus, if we take Wendy Wasserstein's very inclusive notion: "women's choices, marriages, yearnings, and economic status" as a broad definition of female character conceptualized in terms of the legacy of the term discussed above, that is, how women deal with their marginality in relationship to the social, political, and cultural institutions of modern life, especially those of the law and of economics, is there anything new we can learn by comparing the two films?

One particularly significant coping mechanism all of the women have at their disposal is friendship, that is, a relationship of basic equality with one

another. They may have other relationships that unite them, such as biologi-
cal sisterhood in *Sense and Sensibility*, but the bases of their relationships are
those of friendship, and the nature of their friendship is based upon the characteristics each brings to the relationship. However, this element of equality
is less a utopian model for all relationships than it is a context against which
the differences between the women become meaningful. What is most significant and noteworthy is that the bases of the women's relationships are not
their similar characteristics, that is, their gender and structural relationship to
society, but decidedly different ones, situated along precisely the poles represented by the Austen novel: sense and sensibility. All the female characters are
situated along the poles of rationality, or sense, on the one hand and passion,
or sensibility, on the other. Louise and Elinor share a fundamentally rational,
skeptical approach to the world around them and do not reveal their emotions particularly readily. In a key mise-en-scène at the beginning of *Thelma
and Louise*, Louise is characterized as neat, meticulous, and controlled, shown
getting ready shortly before the big trip in an unusually clean, well-organized
kitchen and packing her clothes for the weekend like a military man. Like
Louise, Elinor is orderly and meticulous, which is shown in the way she deals
with new acquaintances and negotiates the power games of their social lives.
She is ever diplomatic and attuned to the needs of others, calm, and disci-
plined. Her counterpart, Marianne, minces no words and is prepared to sacrifice a pleasant social atmosphere to express a thought, feeling, or conviction,
even if it is not particularly sound. Like Marianne, Thelma is passionate and
too "open" to strangers, disorganized, and impulsive, marvelously shown in
both her packing scene and the bar scene, when the two women first encounter the potential rapist. As the women in *Thelma and Louise* move in a much
less confined, though a good deal more atomized, society, their manifestations
of rationality and passion take on different forms, but the internal dynamic is
clearly similar.

What is the significance of this opposition between rationality and passion
today? While the reception of the two films suggests they can only be classified in terms of the tension between conservatism and feminism, the dynamics
between the characters undermine this opposition by demonstrating the complexity of female character. For example, in *Sense and Sensibility*, the tensions
between the three lead characters draw attention to a highly relevant contemporary opposition suggested by Deborah Tannen in her work on gender
and linguistics: that between independence and affiliation.[20] However, while
Tannen defines this opposition along gendered lines, in *Sense and Sensibility*,
it is best understood in relationship to the three lead characters, Elinor, Marianne, and Margaret. Notably, Elinor functions as a model for both Margaret,
the independent younger sister, and Marianne, the more passionate, affiliative

nature, in that her actions—keeping her knowledge of Lucy Steele's engagement a secret for reasons of honor and exhibiting strong emotions, particularly in relationship to her sister—demonstrate that she possesses both dimensions. Instead of falling neatly into either the "conservative" or "feminist" category, Elinor's contemporary appeal is precisely her manifestation of both tendencies toward independence and affiliation, tendencies that are defined as oppositional within even the most progressive debates.[21]

However, within this model, it is nonetheless the more rational woman who occupies a privileged vantage point, because she is more self-reliant in relationship to her society and therefore more likely to survive the dangers of her marginal status. In this schema, rationality, in general, is a strategy women must develop to survive as marginal entities, because their marginal status renders their passions profoundly dangerous. This is demonstrated first in their greater awareness of the connection between sexuality and power. Louise and Elinor question the seemingly benign romantic and sexual attentions of men and attempt to point out the dangers to their more passionate counterparts. In *Thelma and Louise*, Louise attempts to enlighten Thelma about the motives of the would-be rapist while they are still "having fun" in the bar and insists, after telling Harlan to leave by blowing cigarette smoke in his face, that Thelma should not be too open in what she communicates:

> Thelma: Geez, Louise, that wasn't very nice.
>
> Louise: Can't you tell when somebody's hittin' on you?
>
> Thelma: Oh, so what if he was—it's all those years of waitin' tables that's made you jaded, that's all.
>
> Louise: Maybe.
>
> Thelma: Well, just relax, will ya, you're makin' me nervous![22]

Elinor likewise cautions Marianne about Willoughby:

> Elinor: Mr. Willoughby can be in no doubt of your enthusiasm for him.
>
> Marianne: Why should he doubt it? Why should I hide my regard?
>
> Elinor: No particular reason, Marianne, only that we know so little of him.[23]

Unlike their more passionate counterparts, the rational women also have a greater awareness of the importance of financial independence. Elinor is preoccupied with economy, whereas her mother and her sister tend to overlook such matters, and Louise, the "breadwinner" in the friendship, repeatedly emphasizes the importance of money as a basis of the two women's flight to "freedom."

This greater emphasis upon self-reliance on the part of the more rational women must be understood less as an absolute opposition to the greater passions of the other, that is, one woman is always passionate whereas the other is always rational. Rather, it makes more sense in the context of the fundamentally unequal relationship the women have in relationship to the larger society. Thus we have what might be called a tension, rather than a clear-cut opposition, between self-reliance and equality, because the equality of their particular friendship exists in the context of their inequality as women in relationship to men and the larger society. The apparent opposition between rationality and passion for contemporary audiences is that friction between women's increasing self-reliance in society and their continued inequality in relationship to major social and cultural institutions such as the law, the economy, and the family. I would like to put forth that it is this forceful cultural dynamic that drives the films forward, more than the car and the violent behavior in *Thelma and Louise*[24] and more than the costumes in *Sense and Sensibility.*[25] Ultimately, Thelma and Louise have much more in common with Elinor and Marianne than they do with Butch Cassidy and the Sundance Kid.

Two further dimensions of female rationality in relationship to female characterization in the two films should be noted, because they contribute to the task of challenging the dichotomous views the opposition between radical feminism and conservative true woman imply. The first and most obvious point is that rationality as such is not gendered male in the films, as not only are most of the male characters decidedly non-rational but neither woman is offered to the audience as a "sexy babe" with the external intellectual dimensions such as business suits and high powered jobs suggested by Wasserstein. Their intelligence is "internal" and hence not gendered. While a number of critics have argued that Louise and Thelma mimic or invert the male buddy role and shed their accoutrements of femininity, such as clothes and make-up, over the course of the film, the changes of appearance and behavior seem to draw attention to their actions as efforts to establish a self-reliant identity as women rather than a metamorphosis into maleness. Moreover, their rationality does not render them asexual. Both Louise and Elinor have their share of sexual passions, obviously more openly displayed in the former but nonetheless legitimated in the context of the story. Finally, and this is by extension, passion as such is not equated with female sexuality. Marianne's and Thelma's more open displays of feeling do not make them more sexual in relationship to their counterparts. The issue for Thelma, in particular, is learning to deal with her sexuality in a more rational, less impulsive manner, so she can avoid exploitation in the future. Marianne must learn this as well, though her society's conventions necessarily link female sexuality with marriage.

But more than survival-in-marginality is at stake for the women in the films, especially for the rational women. In both *Sense and Sensibility* and *Thelma and Louise,* the more rational women have a secret, a secret they can share neither with their more passionate counterpart nor with men. Louise, for example, cannot and does not tell Thelma about having been raped in Texas or tell her boyfriend Jimmy about the murder. In *Sense and Sensibility,* Elinor's greatest challenge is not revealing her knowledge of Edward's engagement to Marianne and not revealing her true feelings to Edward. Controlling their impulse to convey this information even under the most high pressure circumstances is a highly significant and meaningful similarity between the two films. What is the significance of this secret for female character?

One function of the secret is a clear effort at a type of heroic behavior, that is, a type of behavior that has public relevance beyond the personal, subjective conflicts of the individual. As Emma Thompson thoughtfully pointed out in an interview, in literature as in life, women rarely have a chance to demonstrate their agency by way of actions, as men do in situations of war and conflict, for example. Rather, they must demonstrate their agency, their independence, by way of character. Elinor's secret is such an example of female heroism, according to Thompson, keeping a promise to a rival for reasons of honor, even if it interferes with her potential happiness.[26] Certainly Louise keeps her secret from Jimmy out of similarly honorable motives, a desire not to make him an accessory to the crime, which also makes it impossible for her to marry Jimmy, hence he is "not an option." Therefore, her private happiness is likewise jeopardized by her honor, further buttressing its status as heroic gesture.[27] The notion of honor is significant, because it signifies an effort on the part of the women to establish a relationship to the public sphere, that is, to the institutions from which the women are, in essence, marginalized: the law in particular. They give a more significant meaning to the nature of their experiences and transform them from strictly personal dilemmas into actions of much greater public significance; the secrets of both rational women suggest efforts to forge an independent niche for themselves, a space for independence and self-reliance apart from their marginalization.

Both women guard their secret with great vigilance, keeping it not only from the men but also from their closest female counterpart. The meaning of this aspect of the women's silence functions on a number of significant levels. First, both Elinor's and Louise's secret jeopardizes their implicit claims to greater rationality vis-à-vis their counterparts. For Elinor to reveal Lucy's engagement to Edward to Marianne or for Louise to reveal the rape in Texas to Thelma would draw attention to the limits of female self-reliance, or female independence and rationality in the context of institutional marginality, suggesting the ultimate bankruptcy of the strategy of female rationality in the face of gender marginalization. Each woman's secret would be interpreted less as evidence for her structural marginalization than evidence that personal, subjective motives are the primary source of her actions.[28] The only way for the women to forego this particular ambiguity is either to keep it out of circulation completely or else to bond in "personal" female solidarity against the mainstream society.

On one level, both films' conclusion highlights the problematic nature of female rationality or heroism. While Thelma and Louise's suicide draws attention to the limits of female self-reliance, while simultaneously manifesting it, the marriages of Elinor and Marianne, particularly that of Elinor, has a good deal less to do with the women's honorable behavior and a great deal more to do with simple luck. Elinor's breakdown scene after Edward finally turns up to tell her he is free to marry her elicited ambivalent responses from audiences who weren't sure whether Edward's return was a reward for Elinor's virtue or else a happy coincidence, since Lucy's decision to marry Edward's brother instead of Edward was unrelated to Elinor's heroic "secret." Thompson's emotional response, noted by several critics as "a moment of superbly honest filmmaking," was labeled as such precisely because it drew attention to Elinor's vulnerability and ultimate dependence on circumstance despite her heroism.[29] Without structural equality in their relationships to men and institutions, women's self-reliance, whether economic, political, emotional, or otherwise, is on shaky ground.

Closer attention to the similarities between the conclusions of both films will shed light upon the tension-ridden relationship between female self-reliance—female rationality, in more conventional terminology—and the marginality that continues to characterize their relationship to institutions such as the law and the economy, thus rendering them fundamentally unequal, despite their heroism, rationality, and self-reliance. If the conclusion of *Thelma and Louise* is interpreted as a suicide at the level of narrative realism, at the symbolic and aesthetic level, it is clearly a marriage between the two women, not unlike the marriages that conclude *Sense and Sensibility*.[30] The vow to drive off the cliff together, sealed by a kiss and a clasp of hands, marks the women's entry into the idyll of lifetime partnership as the only really viable realm for genuine equality. Therefore, rather than addressing the tension between female self-reliance and inequality at the social level, which both films clearly raise in their focus upon the gender marginality of the two women, the films rely upon the dimension of marital closure to ensure an aesthetic resolution of sorts, as well as a retreat back into the private realm.[31] This is their core similarity as narratives of female character development and, to a large degree, signals the limits of that genre as a means of articulating structural inequalities.

However, the strength of this genre is its capacity to dramatize the complexity of the problem of female character outside the antagonistic opposition used to understand so many questions of "femaleness" in the cultural debates of the 1990s: the opposition between radical feminism and conservative, domestic family values.[32] Moreover, each film's focus upon the complexity of female character draws attention to the limits of female self-reliance in a context of institutional marginality. For even as women offer gestures of heroism, that is self-reliance, those gestures will be of limited value unless recognized as public statements by the social and cultural institutions that continue to marginalize women.

*   *   *

While the critical establishment's response to *Sense and Sensibility* and *Thelma and Louise* suggested a deep-seated ideological opposition between conservatism and feminism, comparing the two films in terms of their approaches to female character locates the dilemma of postfeminism in more complex tensions between women's increasing self-reliance and continued institutional gender inequalities.[33] Emma Thompson's adaptation of *Sense and Sensibility* draws attention to the characteristics Elinor and Marianne actually share with Thelma and Louise and suggests why filmmakers in the 1990s continued to rely on the nineteenth-century literary imagination to understand contemporary gender dilemmas rather than making films about the present. In the final chapter, I will explore how the works of Henry James were enlisted by filmmakers, female filmmakers in particular, to steer a course beyond such oppositions as feminism and conservatism and to take a closer look at issues of contemporary male and female identity.

Notes

1. Wendy Wasserstein, "The *Premiere* Review: *Sense and Sensibility*" (February 1996): 17.

2. *Thelma and Louise,* like *Sense and Sensibility,* did very well at the box office—the film has grossed over $45,000,000 since its release in 1991 (with a production budget of $16.5 million) and was ranked #28 among films released that year. See http://boxofficemojo.com/movies/?id=thelmaandlouise htm.

3. See, for example, Natasha Yong, "Sexism and a Female Buddy Connection: Review of *Thelma and Louise,*" *Cyclone FilmsMovie Reviews*: http://www.swiftech.com.sg/~natvic/cr_telma.htm; [anon, Review of *Thelma and Louise*]: http://xochi.tezcat.com/~annoir/thelou.htm.

4. [Anon, Review of *Thelma and Louise*] and Richard Grenier, "Killer Bimbos," *Commentary* (September 1991): 50–52.

5. See, in particular, the discussion of the reception of *Thelma and Louise* in Sharon Willis, *High Contrast: Race and Gender in Contemporary Hollywood Film* (Durham, N.C., 1997), 98–104.

6. See, for example, Margaret Carlson, "Is This What Feminism is All About?", *Time* (24 June 1991): 57; John Leo, "Toxic Feminism on the Big Screen," *U.S. News and World Report* (10 June 1991): 20.

7. Elaine Rapping, "The Jane Austen Thing," *Progressive* (July 1996): 37–38. See also: John Leonard, "Jane-Mania," *New York* (15 January 1996): 55; Evan Thomas, "Hooray for Hypocrisy," *Newsweek* (29 January 1996): 61.

8. "Sisterhood is powerful" appears next to the illustration on the Wasserstein review. The suggestion that Thelma and Louise might be lesbian was offered in John Simon, "Movie of the Moment," *National Review* (8 July 1991): 48–52.

9. For a discussion of the concept of popular or "celebrity feminism," see Jennifer Wicke, "Celebrity Material: Materialist Feminism and the Culture of Celebrity," *South Atlantic Quarterly* 93 (Fall 1994):751-778. See also Susan Bordo, *Unbearable Weight: Feminism, Western Culture and the Body* (Berkeley, 1993).

10. Susan Keating Glaspell, "A Jury of Her Peers," in *Lifted Masks and Other Stories,* edited by Eric S. Rabkin (Ann Arbor, 1993): 279–306.

11. Emma Thompson, *The Sense and Sensibility Screenplay and Diaries* (New York, 1996), 34.

12. Ibid, 57. That the comment comes very close to accuracy if we think of it in relationship to Lucy Steele underscores the structural nature of its significance, for it is Elinor's financial circumstance and her gender that make it possible to place her in the same category as Lucy Steele, another penniless woman.

13. Nancy Glazener, *Reading for Realism: The History of a U.S. Literary Institution,* (Durham, 1997), 18.

14. Ralph F. Voss and Michael L. Keene, *The Heath Guide to College Writing: Annotated Teacher's Edition* (Lexington, Massachusetts, 1992), 521.

15. See, for example, Linda Troost and Sayre Greenfield, eds. *Jane Austen in Hollywood* (Lexington, Kentucky, 1998).

16. Claudia Johnson, *Jane Austen: Women, Politics, and the Novel,* (Chicago, 1988): xiii–xxv. Nancy Armstrong, *Desire and Domestic Fiction: A Political History of the Novel* (New York, 1987).

17. Johnson, *Jane Austen,* and Julia Prewitt-Brown, "The Feminist Depreciation of Austen: A Polemical Reading," *Novel: A Forum on Fiction* (Spring 1990): 303–313.

18. Insightful, though very different, readings of the extent to which Emma Thompson's rendering of *Sense and Sensibility* is or is not feminist include Kristin Flieger Samuelian, "Piracy is Our Only Option: Postfeminist Intervention in *Sense and Sensibility,* Devoney Looser, "Feminist Implications of the Silver Screen Austen," and Deborah Kaplan, "Mass Marketing Jane Austen: Men, Women, and Courtship in Two Film Adaptations," all in Troost and Greenfield, eds. *Jane Austen in Hollywood,* 148–158, 159–176, and 177–187, respectively.

19. The screenplay for *Thelma and Louise* was written by Callie Khouri.

20. Deborah Tannen, Ph.D. *You Just Don't Understand: Men and Women in Conversation* (New York, 1990.)

21. See esp. Chapter 4 of this work.

22. *Thelma and Louise.* Writer Callie Khouri. Director Ridley Scott. With Susan Sarandon and Geena Davis. MGM/UA, 1991.

23. Thompson, 101.

24. Sharon Willis, *Race and Gender in Contemporary Hollywood Film,* 108.

25. A further interesting aspect of the films is the function of their respective symbolic landscapes, the English countryside and the Southwest's Route 66, in relationship to the conflicts between the two lead female characters. For a discussion of the concept of "symbolic landscape,"

see D.W. Meinig, "Symbolic Landscapes," in D.W. Meinig, ed., *The Interpretation of Ordinary Landscapes* (New York, 1979): 164–192.

26. "Verflucht harte Arbeit": Interview mit Emma Thompson *Der Spiegel* 10 (4 March 1996):230–231.

27. Needless to say, men have not had to sacrifice personal affiliations to the opposite sex in order to demonstrate the public relevance of their gestures and behaviors, except insofar as the male counterparts to our two women, Edward and Jimmy, would have to.

28. Again, not unlike the dilemma depicted in Glaspell's "A Jury of Her Peers."

29. See, for example, Wasserstein, 17.

30. The political relevance of the idea of a marriage between the two women, as well as the clear homoerotic dimension of the relationship between them, both seem less central to me than the assumptions that precisely the symbolic power of this type of relationship closes down the tensions the film raises between self-reliance and equality. Glenn Man also takes note of this "symbolic marriage" (42) in *Thelma and Louise,* though he gives it a more progressive meaning, interpreting it as a gesture of female bonding "that seals their relationship off from the hetero-sexual conventions of their former lives." (45) Glenn Man, "Gender, Genre, and Myth in *Thelma and Louise,*" *Film Criticism* 18(1) (Fall 1993): 36–53. For discussions of *Thelma and Louise* with a focus upon lesbian sexuality, see, for example, Lynda Hart, *Fatal Women: Lesbian Sexuality and the Mark of Aggression* (Princeton, New Jersey, 1994).

31. See Claudia L. Johnson's essay, "*Sense and Sensibility*: Opinions Too Common and Too Dangerous," in *Jane Austen: Women, Politics and the Novel* (Chicago, 1988), 49–72.

32. And one might say that this also accounts for its *resilience,* as Wasserstein suggests in the opening sentences of her review: "Two hundred years ago, Jane Austen was writing great parts for women." (Wasserstein 17)

33. Ruth Sidel, *On Her Own: Growing Up in the Shadow of the American Dream* (New York, 1990), 219–243; Christie Farnham, "The Position of Women in the Slave Family," in Norton and Alexander, eds. *Major Problems in American Women's History,* (2nd ed.): 145–155.

Chapter Six

Jamesian Proportions

The Henry James Film Boom in the 1990s

Close on the heels of the Jane Austen dramatizations came a series of adaptations of novels by the Anglo-American novelist Henry James: *The Portrait of a Lady,* directed by Jane Campion, *Washington Square,* directed by Agnieszka Holland, and *The Wings of the Dove,* directed by Iain Softley.[1] Whereas all of the Austen dramatizations had been directed by men, two of the three James adaptations were directed by women, a fact that sparked commentary from several critics, emphasizing the extent to which they as "foreign" (non-U.S.) directors might be overly intimidated by so illustrious a modernist as James.[2] However, the release dates of the three films—*The Portrait of a Lady* in December 1996 and *Washington Square* and *The Wings of the Dove* nearly a year later—obscured this important dimension; *The Portrait of a Lady* was discussed in relationship to the Austen films, while the other two tended to be discussed as a pair with comparatively little reference to the earlier film.

None of these films achieved the popularity or acclaim of the best of the Austen dramatizations, *Sense and Sensibility* and *Persuasion,* nor were they discussed in the context of a "Henry James film boom" in the way the Austen films had been discussed in the context of a "Jane Austen film boom."[3] Certainly the gap in the release dates played a major role; however, it also had to do with the assumption that the Austen adaptations were more explicitly linked to a political—read: conservative—imperative by critics that associated an interest in Austen with a desire on the part of "liberated" women to return to conventional "private" relationships. In the case of James, the line between the art of his novels and politics is less clear precisely because he has been associated with an apolitical, "universal" aesthetic tradition of modernism, a tradition he both represents and helped to establish.[4]

If the reception of the Jane Austen dramatizations was shaped by the legacy of female authorship, that is, the tendency to link the films to the private authority of the female author, the James dramatizations are best understood in relationship to the reception of the Austen films and to the legacy of "Great

Authorship," which James helped to create,[5] emphasizing the concepts of "complexity" and "ambiguity," and situating the theme of "renunciation" as a universal moral value.[6] With few exceptions, critics tended to discuss the films in relationship to their success or failure at capturing Jamesian "complexity and ambiguity." However, intriguingly, the terms "complexity" and "ambiguity" were associated less with the films' actual similarities or differences to James's texts, which turn out to be quite different from those discussed in the reception, and instead functioned as an overarching terminology by which to distinguish the "complexity" of Jamesian literary modernism from the club footed medium of film, and hence to suggest that the films had no relevant contemporary tale to tell. Moreover, the rhetoric of elitist high culture, the absolute opposition between film and literature, belied the affinity of James's stories and novels to the cinema, an affinity reflected both in analyses of the relationship between cinema and James's fiction, as well as the extent to which filmmakers all over the world have used James's texts as a basis for their films.[7]

The rhetoric of "complexity" also served to distinguish the James dramatizations from the Austen dramatizations, or Henry James the "'modernist" from "costume dramas" in general, and hence to reinforce the authoritative gap between male and female authorship. However, the films reveal a continued experimentation with the costume drama genre begun with the Austen films, that is, an effort to historicize the aesthetic tradition of each author and, by extension, a preoccupation with cultural politics related to the questions raised by the Austen films: the status of contemporary male and female identity.[8] However, the more pessimistic strain in the James dramatizations must not be understood in relationship to the opposition between the light-hearted "happy end" of the female author and the high modernist themes of renunciation of the great author. Rather, the films are best understood in relationship to the ways they attempt to transform the presumably universal and humanistic themes associated with the concepts of "complexity" and "ambiguity" into more historically oriented themes related to issues of contemporary gender identity. This historicization of "Jamesian Modernism" is best evaluated in relationship to the reception of the films, the context within which they are understood, and to the changes and continuities apparent in the transformation from novel to film.[9]

Attention to the James adaptations of the 1990s and the ways they were received will also reveal the affinity between James's works and the imperatives of contemporary consumer culture. In particular, all three adaptations are clearly preoccupied with the relationship between gender and sexual objectification and suggest that the increasing sexual objectification of the male body will have cultural ramifications for contemporary gender identity. If defenders of the idea of classic texts define the notion of "Jamesian Proportions" in literary terms, the 1990s film adaptations lend to this idea an intriguing "bodily" twist.

*   *   *

If the Austen films were discussed in terms of the person of the writer, with an emphasis upon the "Jane" and not upon the "Austen," the James films were discussed in the more general terms of the "tradition" of a particular oeuvre. "Jamesian" was a commonly used adjective, referring to whether the adaptation had been wrought in "some sort of Jamesian proportions"[10]; or that the "Jamesian tradition" represented "hard" reading, even in the days when reading wasn't rare.[11] James's works were referred to as "classic" and "monumental,"[12] as well as "rich, strange, and complex."[13] Other critics from times past were used to buttress these various claims.[14]

What meanings did critics give to these concepts? For some, "Jamesian" ultimately referred to "deep explorations of character,"[15] though this was not discussed in any specific terms. Indeed, very few critics actively connected their discussion of James's depth or complexity with the goings on in the films themselves, even when they felt the films were well made; they tended to offer such comments as a sort of mystifying device, claiming that they knew what made James deep and complex, but that the filmmakers had, to a large degree, missed the mark. A typical mystifying generalization about James was that offered by the reviewer in the *Neue Zürchner Zeitung*: "Jamesian" meant to her "the catastrophic insight into the complexity of all being."[16] The films, needless to say, didn't meet the standard, even when they were praised. Thus, the overriding tone of the reception was that the James adaptations were not as "Jamesian" as they ought to be, that they did not "get," as Louis Menand put it in his review of *Washington Square* and *The Wings of the Dove*, "the Lesson of the Master."[17]

This dominating current all but suppressed those critics who saw similarities of theme and tone between the James and the Austen dramatizations, for example, themes of conflict between love and money, the importance of marriage, female independence, or the inability to express what one has on one's mind.[18] If anything, critics and filmmakers such as Jane Campion made active efforts to differentiate their productions from the Austen films, insisting that James was "modern" whereas the Austen films were "soft."[19] Eroticizing James, as Campion does, was interpreted as a means of differentiating James from Austen rather than what it obviously was: an interpretation of James by Campion. Suppressing the erotic is common to both James and Austen. Why, then, insist on the difference? In the case of Campion, attempting to distance her film from the legacy of female authorship and to associate it instead with the tradition of "modernism" was surely a means of legitimating her directorial authority by disassociating it from the tradition of female authorship—her film was to have more than private significance: claiming James, and thus the literary tradition of modernism, for a critique of patriarchy. It was precisely this equation that critics tended to reject. As Stanley Kauffmann put it: "this would be a better film than we can think it if the novel didn't exist." By giving Henry James a feminist spin, Campion only succeeded in reducing the "complexity" of the original.[20]

A number of commentators, including the filmmakers themselves, framed their endeavor as one of "modernizing" or "updating" Henry James. While Campion linked this modernization to a difference from Austen, others were less concrete, associating "modernizing" with moving the date of the action in the story up eight years—from 1902 to 1910—as was done in *The Wings of the Dove*.[21] "Modernizing" James was linked generally to making the plots relevant to contemporary audiences, though this relevance was not made as clear or as political in *The Wings of the Dove* as it was in *The Portrait of a Lady*. It was also an indirect form of justification for "meddling" with the novel, either through lack of understanding or simply because the producers probably hadn't read it in its entirety.[22] Of the three works, *Washington Square* was generally found to be the most "faithful" to James. Most of the talk about the films related to their affinity to or distance from the original work, as if this was the only relevant basis for discussion of the dramatizations. Moreover, this point of view was sustained regardless of how familiar the critic was with the original work and with very little attention to the question of the significance of the perceived differences between the novels and the films. Insofar as they were "interpreted," it was in broad terms of "modernizing" or "updating," neither of which was explained at any length.

Overall, the James films tended to be discussed individually, whereas the Austen films were more frequently discussed as a group, in keeping with the assumption that what they had in common—uniting the protagonists in marriage, a happy end—was more important than what differentiated them. The first James dramatization, *The Portrait of a Lady*, directed by Jane Campion, was released in late December 1996. In the film, a young, independent minded, American woman, Isabel Archer, comes to Europe to "experience life." She turns down a series of eligible, archetypal male suitors—the English Lord, the American Breadwinner, and, insofar as Ralph Touchett might be considered a suitor, the sensitive, if somewhat voyeuristic, Modern Male—along the way, and after unexpectedly inheriting a fortune that might make it possible for her to "realize the requirements of her imagination," she falls for and marries an expatriate aesthete and fortune hunter named Gilbert Osmond, who turns out to be cruel and dominant, transforming Isabel into little more than a precious object in his fine collection (see Figure 6.1).

Figure 6.1. Nicole Kidman (Isabel) and John Malkovich (Gilbert Osmond) in *The Portrait of a Lady*. (Courtesy: Photofest)

The film was discussed primarily in contrast to the Austen adaptations and to costume dramas in general. The stylistic dimensions of the film—the introductory scene of young women dancing, along with various erotic and surrealistic scenes, as well as the more open-ended conclusion—were discussed as either innovative ("bold modern touches")[23] or irritating ("deliberately arty")[24]; on the one hand the product of an artist and auteur, on the other pretentious and, to a certain degree, sacrilegious. Critics were also divided over whether the film was feminist or antifeminist; whether Isabel was a "victim" or an "idealist."[25]

However, the point of greatest resistance was not Campion's stylistic touches or her putative feminist framework but rather her casting of John Malkovich as Osmond. This was deemed a major flaw, because audiences were incapable of understanding what it was about him that attracted Isabel. Even critics more or less conversant with James, such as Roger Ebert, attributed this "error" to a misreading of the character in the novel, i.e., Osmond in the novel is more complex, sympathetic, and attractive than he is in the film.[26] While Malkovich does exhibit a sort of indirect physical brutality in the film, as in the scenes where he steps on Isabel's dress so that she falls or when he forces her to sit on a pile of pillows, neither of which takes place in the novel, overall Osmond's dark character was a point of convergence between novel and film, as the character of Osmond is taken for a charlatan by all the other characters in the novel except the protagonist, Isabel. Summarizing the plot of the last third of *The Portrait of a Lady,* even Henry James considered Isabel's "sweet delusion," i.e., her love and esteem for Osmond, to be the most difficult part of the story to render believable: "oh, the art required for making this delusion natural!"[27] Nina Baym, in her 1976 study of the differences between the earlier and later versions of *The Portrait of a Lady,* noted that Isabel's choice of Osmond is the major thematic problem in the later version of the novel, troubling to many critics, and the result of James's revisions of Isabel from an emotional, fearful, and humanly misguided character to a more cerebral, subtle character in the later version, in keeping with the aesthetic imperative of his "late works."[28]

All of which demonstrates that, in this regard, Campion was quite "faithful" to the novel, and that audience response to the film in many ways resembled critical response to the novel: how could an independent, thoughtful woman be so utterly wrong in her choice of mate? While film critics such as Richard Schickel and Roger Ebert deemed it a form of antifeminism,[29] Campion's interpretation of James, that Isabel's "sweet delusion" is based neither upon idealism nor masochism, but upon the patriarchal assumption that a woman can only find personal and emotional fulfillment through complete identification with and sexual capitulation to a male partner, in effect historicizes her "quest," linking it to the role and place of women in contemporary society and placing into relief the underside of the rational "postfeminist" subject: the needful, dependent, privatized female self, whose feminism has become little more than a fashionable label on the postmodern marketplace of "choice." The fact that Isabel happens to identify with Osmond rather than with the other suitors is less important to Campion than that this particular form of identification is the goal of her quest. By making it difficult for audiences to identify with Isabel's choice, Campion highlights the extent to which the seemingly free and independent feminist, i.e., the woman who professes feminist beliefs about freedom and choice, is not nearly so much her own mistress as she believes herself to be but that she must find that out, so to speak, "on her own."

Ruth Sidel's study of young, working women and their conceptions of their futures, *On Her Own: Growing Up in the Shadow of the American Dream,* is relevant to Campion's interpretation of James. Isabel must learn from her mistakes, learn that the choices offered to her by her culture have limits, even if she feels entitled to something more. But most importantly, she must learn this for herself, because she will not receive help from either women (i.e. feminism) or men (a supportive mate). Consequently, her assumption that she is entitled to support in her quest for fulfillment in public and private life is a painful delusion she must dispense with.[30] In this regard, Campion is a good deal harsher in her judgment of the inner and outer obstacles women face than even James. Evidence for this resides in her depiction of Henrietta Stackpole.

Perhaps the more problematic modification of *The Portrait of a Lady* Campion makes is less the casting of Malkovich as Osmond than the reduction of the character Henrietta Stackpole to a noisy side-kick. Though she is certainly a very funny character in the film, her loud voice, off-center spectacles, and "vulgar" American habits, such as sneaking hotel breakfast food out in a bag labeled "waste not want not," render her slightly absurd in comparison to Isabel. Interestingly, in portraying her this way, Campion follows the ideology toward Henrietta proclaimed by James in his preface to the New York edition of *The Portrait of a Lady,* but not the actual characterization of Henrietta herself.[31] Though she was reduced in significance in the revision of *The Portrait of a Lady* for the New York editions, she nonetheless offered a consistent counterpoint to Isabel's peculiar quest, both in her active involvement on the marketplace and in her decidedly unglamorous relationship to Mr. Bantling, who, presumably as Henrietta's suitor, is given one brief gratuitous scene at the end of the film, but whose presence is not woven into its plot. Henrietta in the film is alone, slightly neurotic, and preoccupied with little more than Isabel's choice of mate. It is as if she, the independent career woman, is condemned to idolizing Isabel for being such a man-magnet.[32] In contrast, even in the later version of *The Portrait of a Lady,* James gives Henrietta a variety of preoccupations and a suitor who treats her very well. Why Campion did not see fit to do likewise may have to do with formal considerations pertaining to focus in the plot, but it also may have to do with the sense of isolation that runs as a powerful aesthetic current throughout the film. While much of Campion's symbolism is tied to a sense of entrapment,[33] Isabel's isolation is reinforced metaphorically and symbolically throughout the film as well. Campion's opening sequence foreshadows this through the image of young women dancing and fantasizing. These young women are profoundly isolated in their "collective" fantasy, gazing into the camera but rarely at each other. When the story begins, overly close, off-center close-up shots, frequent images of Isabel gazing into a mirror, and indeed, the concluding scene renders Isabel's world one that isolates and separates her from those around her. This isolation is linked to contemporary women's sense of "postfeminist" isolation, where liberation is ostensibly a product of "self-motivation" and "self-creation," rather than a social and political project. Paradoxically, the film represents the dangers of this isolation in the form of the relationship between Isabel and Madame Merle. As the quintessential, self-created subject, Madame Merle's fascination for Isabel is precisely her ability to move in the world without attachments or commitments of any kind. Ultimately, there is no female figure who offers Isabel any kind of social or emotional support as, for example, Henrietta offers in the novel.[34] Indeed, Henrietta, the active career woman, in being deemed vulgar, loud, and tasteless, symbolizes the absolute gap perceived by women between personal intimacy and public accomplishment. Furthermore, Isabel does not feel a significant connection to Osmond's daughter, Pansy, the link that takes her back to Rome in the novel. Isabel is radically isolated from women as much as she is isolated from men, much more so in the film than in the novel.

Men do not fare much better than women as alternative sources of support in Isabel's quest, as she is so fixated upon her search for a mirror, a reflection of herself and her own desires, that she overlooks those who would offer support rather than identification. What is intriguing is that, in her choice of Osmond in the book, Isabel essentially sought an escape from her sexual impulses into an ideal world of art and culture. In the film, Campion defines Isabel's attraction to Osmond in exclusively sexual terms; she is seduced by him, in a manner not unlike the young aristocratic woman who is seduced by Valmont in the film *Dangerous Liaisons.*[35] Whereas in the novel, Isabel's sexual side is triggered more by Caspar Goodwood than it is by Osmond, in the film, it is presumably Osmond's taste and style that seduce Isabel, literally. This association of style with sexuality—that Isabel's "stupefaction" is, as one critic put it, "sexual, moral, aesthetic"[36]—is indeed a very contemporary dimension of *The Portrait of a Lady,* as it reflects the imperatives associated with contemporary advertising and postmodern consumer culture: the aestheticization of sexuality through external form and style.[37] Isabel's seduction is less a form of masochism than it is the result of the peculiar idealism of contemporary advertising, one that binds style and sexuality so closely together that it is only the constrained and stylized body that can represent the sexual; in the film, we clearly witness her transformation into an aesthetic—sexual—object at the hands of Osmond. Yet more often, this imperative has come to dominate ideals of both maleness and femaleness, and for contemporary audiences, John Malkovich did not correspond in their imaginations to a desirable male object. Viewers could not understand what Isabel—especially Isabel in the form of Nicole Kidman—saw in Osmond (Malkovich).

Indeed, what Isabel "sees" is, for Campion, the principle metaphor for Isabel's misguided quest, and it overrides the alternative approach to female choice the film offers, Henrietta Stackpole's more pragmatic vision. In her observation of various figures and situations, Isabel's gaze seems to fluctuate between the vampiric and voyeuristic as, for example, in the intriguing close-up where she is watching Mr. Touchett die, always curious but rarely sympathetic, always just a bit out of focus. It is an immature gaze, one that is in an experimental mode and that must learn the limits of its own voraciousness. For Campion, Isabel's gaze is a female gaze, both in the form of her own role as director of Isabel's gaze, which is also a new form of "looking" for women, as female directors continue to be a rarity on the movie-making scene and in the sense of a vulnerable gaze, one that has not had much practice in the art of analyzing her environment, even as she feels entitled to more maturity—or knowledge—than she actually has. For Campion, Isabel's quest, i.e., James's novel, functions as a sort of "founding text" for the female gaze. However, Campion is intensely critical of this gaze, because it derives its impetus solely by way of the dynamic of identification and significantly confuses erotic desire with identification and both with freedom. That she chooses a narcissistic aesthete, a male object over a British Lord, an American Breadwinner, or even a Sensitive Lover, all variations on the outmoded concept of the male subject, signifies her equation of a postmodern consumer culture of style with feminist liberation, where her gaze is on par with the male gaze and hence subject to similar "chances and dangers." However, this is not quite all, for Isabel's gaze is not competing with that of the men but rather transforms the male characters into types; they are, in other words, transformed into objects of her gaze. An interesting and significant problem is thus introduced in the film, which will be developed further in the following James adaptations, *Washington Square* and *The Wings of the Dove*: the complement of the female gaze, namely, the male object or male narcissist.

The transformation of men into sexual objects within mainstream culture has a relatively long history, going back, according to Barbara Ehrenreich, to the founding of *Playboy* magazine and the glorification of men as middle class consumers along with the eroticization of the male body in some of the most significant films of the 1950s. However, even as late as 1966, when films such as *Harper* made male preoccupation with aging, exercise, appearance, and beauty a leitmotif while simultaneously carting out Paul Newman's body and "laser blue gaze" for audience appreciation, the central theme of the tale was nonetheless the hero's absolute rejection of male narcissism. Indeed, the degree of criminal intent and culpability is allotted to each male character in direct proportion to the extent to which he identifies himself in narcissistic terms. Our hero, in contrast, though structurally an object of the viewer's gaze, rejects narcissism and promiscuity, pining instead for the wife who has left him and telling his lawyer pal he shouldn't be so obsessed with aging. While Harper may very well have been America's more upstanding answer to the sybaritic James Bond in the 1960s, this production leaves no doubt that male narcissism is rejected as an ideal male type.[38]

In *The Portrait of a Lady*, Campion's reading of Osmond suggests the male narcissist is not only a card-carrying member of the group of male types depicted in the film but that he has become the preferred type for women. However, what critics could not identify with was Osmond's sadistic cruelty and arrogant contempt for all around him; Malkovich portrayed him in a Jekyll and Hyde manner with only moments separating the metamorphoses—he also seemed to be hiding a vicious temper. This underside of Osmond's temperament is not in the novel; Osmond is a passive aggressive aesthete and a narcissist—he is psychologically not physically brutal. In addition, he is described by James as genteel and handsome, whereas Malkovich's persona is that of a "snaky, sinister poseur."[39] Nonetheless he is, of all of Isabel's suitors, an extension of the objects he owns and the one least endowed with a sense of character, and his type, both as an eminently desirable type for women and as a fraud, is a major aspect of James adaptations in the 1990s.

* * *

Agnieszka Holland's adaptation of *Washington Square*, released in the U.S. in October 1997, tended to be compared with *The Wings of the Dove* rather than *The Portrait of a Lady* because of their similar release dates; however, their literary history suggests important connections between them. James wrote *The Portrait of a Lady* on the heels of *Washington Square* and considered *Portrait* to be "more spacious, more human, more sociable" than *Washington Square*, a work he dismissed on the grounds that it had been too subject to the forces of "condensation." For example, he did not consider the character of Morris

Townsend to have been a genuine "portrait." "The only good thing in the story is the girl," he wrote to his brother William in November 1880.[40] In the story, loosely based upon an actual incident related to James by a friend, Mrs. Fanny Kemble[41], a young American heiress, Catherine Sloper, is held in contempt by her father for her lack of style, charm, and attractiveness. Soon she is pursued by and falls for an attractive young man, Morris Townsend, who, as her father suspects, is primarily interested in her fortune. While her love for Morris helps Catherine to achieve psychological independence from her father, he ultimately abandons her, because she does not come with her father's money. However, when Morris returns to Catherine after her father's death to renew the acquaintance, Catherine sends him away.

Critics tended to either compare Holland's film to the simultaneously released *The Wings of the Dove* favorably, or unfavorably, to William Wyler's 1949 adaptation, *The Heiress,* based upon a stage adaptation of the novel. However, few took an extended interest in comparing Holland's film with Campion's and how differently each chose to deal with the central problem of female self knowledge and independence and male objectification. Why, for example, did Campion choose to make the object of her heroine's affections less attractive in the film than he was in the novel, while Holland chooses exactly the opposite strategy: making Morris more attractive and sympathetic? How did each modify the endings of their respective novels, that is, their interpretations of their heroine's fate? And what might their differences in interpreting James have to do with their different approaches to feminism, a characteristic attributed consistently, though not terribly sympathetically, to both of these films?

Both Campion and Holland, as female directors, might be said to be reappropriating James's heroines, Isabel Archer and Catherine Sloper, from James's own appropriation of them, "his tendency to transform the social psychology of women into the formal aesthetics as well as the psychohistory of the literary author."[42] This process of transformation also pertains to the transition from novel to film, and if James ultimately subordinated his critique of phallocentric structures to a literary model,[43] Campion and Holland, in their task of adapting the novels, surely faced a similar, indeed much more personal, challenge in the ways they sought to combine, rather than to subordinate, their feminism with their sense of the literary. If both works were flawed, both must nonetheless be taken seriously as pioneering efforts to combine these two significant imperatives.

Campion and Holland begin by historicizing the journeys of their respective heroines: they are, in their essence, profoundly female journeys and must be taken seriously as such. Critical of the liberal feminist stance that suggests women are rational, feminist actors on an equal opportunity, equally rational marketplace, Campion and Holland focus upon heroines financially independent from the outset in order to highlight what they see as the more significant problem: psychological dependency. Both films offer an interpretation of this dependency and by doing so suggest alternative models of independence.

For Campion, Isabel's quest for "her clearest mirror" renders her vulnerable and dependent from the outset. While James proposed the question, "what will she do?," as though it was a great mystery, Campion knows what Isabel will do, as she reveals in the opening sequence of *The Portrait of a Lady*; Isabel will search until she finds a relationship in which she "goes under" or subordinates her independent nature to the whims of another person. In contrast to figures such as Henrietta Stackpole, Isabel sees the goal of her quest for independence as dependence upon someone else, a complete identification, which is what it is that she feels with both Madame Merle and Gilbert Osmond. While this is a quest that Campion sympathizes with and takes very seriously as a significant portion of most female biographies, her major point in *Portrait* is that it is a quest that is destined to fail. Campion does not see fit to show an alternative quest, because in keeping with James's preface to the New York edition of *The Portrait of a Lady*, she reduces the representative of such an alternative quest—Henrietta Stackpole—to an absurd comic figure. The flaw in *The Portrait of a Lady* is that, in making Isabel a symbol for all women or sort of universal female figure, Campion disowns the possibility that many women may have already learned this particular lesson; indeed, apparently, it is a lesson Campion has learned.[44] However, what is striking about Campion's film is the extent to which she elevates this particular problem of female psychology to an aesthetic level, exploring it by way of metaphor and thus making it a significant public issue.

However, the reception of the film suggests that audiences could not identify with Isabel's object of identification, Gilbert Osmond, and hence did not take seriously the relationship between the meaning of her quest and her choice of object. In short, audiences had a difficult time imagining Nicole Kidman falling for John Malkovich. Yet, how do you convey a critique of female romantic illusions without risking either alienating your audience, which is obviously what happened with the casting of Malkovich, or legitimizing the quest for identification by making audiences able to identify with Isabel's object of desire? This is the dilemma *The Portrait of a Lady* confronts, and by choosing to "alienate" her audience, so to speak, Campion's exploration of a particular form of female psychological dependency encountered significant resistance.

In contrast, Holland's strategy in *Washington Square* is exactly the opposite: render the object of female identification highly desirable and sympathetic in order to highlight an alternative path to female psychological independence. This is the main reason why she made the character of Morris Townsend more sympathetic and complex, not, as Louis Menand argues rather obtusely, to

highlight parallels between Morris's character and Dr. Sloper's and thereby explain the latter's unwillingness to bless the union.[45] In addition, Holland posits,
if only metaphorically, an alternative form of female quest: one that privileges
creative relationships outside the heterosexual ideal. Indeed, the theme of music as a form of relating to others, as it is developed and sustained in the film,
accompanies Catherine's maturing emotional life—she moves from being so
afraid of singing in public out of fear and nervousness toward her father that
she urinates on the carpet to achieving, through Morris, a form of sanctuary
through music in their musical duets, finally playing solo for the neighborhood
kids she now cares for and teaches to love music as a form of self-fulfillment.
This is the central point of the song the children sing at the close of the film:

> There once was a plain little piece of string,
> all alone and with nothing to do.
> Each night it would wish more than anything
> for a someone to tie itself to.
> Then one day a fiddler came wondering by,
> and the plain little string quickly caught his eye.
> The fiddler said just come along with me,
> I can tell you how happy you'll be....
> You've made a mistake said the little string,
> I have never made music before.
> The fiddler said I'll teach you how to sing,
> And you won't be alone any more.
> He played on the string
> at a fancy dressball,
> and the song filled the dancers and filled the hall.
> So sometimes a plain little piece of string
> Makes the prettiest music of all.[46]

Through this narrative, the former goal of the female quest, the desired object,
Morris, becomes a means or perhaps a stage along the way to a sense of one's
own significance in relationship to a larger community. Needless to say, this
parallel narrative is a modification of the original novel. Catherine's renunciation of Morris is thus neither a form of vengeance, as was the case in the
film, *The Heiress,* nor is it symbolic of her father's success in "killing off ... his
daughter's capacity for love,"[47] nor indeed, a form of universal moral vindica-
tion, as it seems to be in the original novel. Instead, it becomes a rejection of
the typical female quest as defined by Campion: the search for one's "clearest
mirror" in the form of a male object. Campion's ending to *The Portrait of a
Lady,* in contrast, leaves the audience uncertain about Isabel's next move. As

she does not promise Osmond's daughter, Pansy, to return to Rome, she is free at the end of the film, in contrast to the novel, to choose another road. Campion may have left the path open, but in isolating Isabel so profoundly, both narratively and symbolically, the audience is left to assume that she may well continue on the same road as before, if not to Rome, then toward another party willing to take from her the burden of her freedom.

What neither film posits as a viable possibility is a committed, monogamous relationship between members—two subjects—of the opposite sex, neither as a means nor as an end. In this, of course, the films stand in stark contrast to the Jane Austen dramatizations, which even in the more complex and experimental adaptations, did not question the possibility of reconciliation between female independence and marriage. The "happy end" marriages of the Austen adaptations were criticized as a conservative response to postmodern liberation by many critics and rejected as a model of "modernity" by filmmakers such as Jane Campion, who explicitly wished to highlight the difference between James and Austen. However, one of the problematic aspects of this opposition between the Austenian happy ending and the Jamesian depressing ending is that it universalizes the ideological meanings of specific narrative conclusions to the disadvantage of texts that do not insist upon an absolute opposition between female independence and marriage; it universalizes the myth of absolute gender incompatibility in the name of Literary Modernism, which ignores the social and cultural function of marriage in a society where women striving for psychological independence nonetheless marry men, and vice versa.

Without insisting that James's novels should all end like Austen's, I would nonetheless like to suggest that the ideology of renunciation, a characteristic of so many Jamesian conclusions, has ideological functions just like the happy endings of Austen's texts, and an interesting aspect of the newest James dramatizations is to explore what the cultural function of this renunciation of marriage, family, and long term relationships is in these films. James was more modern than Austen, Campion stated in an interview: "he breaks apart the fairy tale: no one is going to find the right person."[48] This is an interpretation of James on Campion's part, reinforcing a cultural myth that separates the two writers in order to gender the public relevance of their works. I am not persuaded that James, a life-long bachelor, did not believe in or condone marriage and family any more than Jane Austen, a life-long spinster, did. Indeed, both their oeuvres, as a number of critics saw, are obsessed with it, preoccupied with it, and unable to imagine human society without it for good or ill.[49]

What then, to repeat the question, is the ideological function of marital renunciation in Campion's and Holland's films? I think it is a symbol for a powerful cultural conflict that has developed over the last two decades in response to a significant shift in ideals of femaleness and maleness, respectively. That shift is essentially an inversion of the cultural model of femaleness and maleness that has shaped the imaginative depictions of gender in film, if not in literature, over the last century: the assumption that women appear, while men act.[50] In more and more films, and particularly in these James dramatizations, the situation is radically reversed, on a number of levels: women act and men appear, women function as subjects, while men function as objects. Or, perhaps more specifically, the female heroines, operating in a context where they are attempting to assert their subject status in the face of norms that insist upon their object status, witness the increasingly divided consciousness of their male counterparts, whose movement is in the opposite direction: from subject to object. Within this configuration—the logic of these James adaptations—no committed relationship is possible. How does this dimension manifest itself?

In Campion's adaptation, we witness an Isabel who is "all eyes," her quest is centered in her ability to "see and imagine," to analyze life as though it were an artwork.[51] This clearly places her in the position of a subject, a possessor of a distinctive gaze. Campion's film stands or falls, as does James's original, on our ability to "see the world through Isabel's eyes." Yet of all the suitors who knock at her door, Isabel chooses the one who is in his being—if not his countenance—most the object of appreciation, an aesthetic object, indirectly, through the aesthetic objects he owns. Osmond is also an erotic object; indeed, this is what he most represents to Isabel, a fusion of the aesthetic and erotic. He is, in essence, a male object or narcissist, which in his movements and gestures—perpetually lounging and reclining—he seeks to reinforce. That is what Isabel sees and falls for. From this perspective, Osmond might be viewed as a symbol for postmodern consumer culture, a culture whose market driving force is motored by the collaboration between the aesthetic or the stylish and the erotic. However, this male narcissist cannot accommodate a female subject, and it is here that the relationship between Isabel and Osmond founders, as viewers and audiences did not see Gilbert Osmond in the same way Isabel saw him, a desirable sex object fusing lust and form/art (see Figure 6.2).

In contrast, in *Washington Square,* the viewer is one with Catherine in finding the object of her affection "beautiful." Morris does indeed go beyond the type of the attractive fortune hunter as James conceived of him. He is, as Louis Menand put it, "a young man whose narcissism is unembarrassed and perfectly understandable. Catherine adores him, his sister adores him, the camera adores him; why shouldn't he do the same?" (see Figure 6.3). This candid self-identification as a desirable object informs Morris's logic of why he won't marry Catherine without her money, a logic that is not in the novel: Morris "just can't imagine life without the fortune he considers his due for allowing himself to make love to such a plain woman. Her money, as he tells Catherine

Figure 6.2. John Malkovich as Gilbert Osmond in *The Portrait of a Lady*: the male lead as the "reclining" consumer and aesthete. (Courtesy: Photofest)

when the crisis comes, is her "attribute": his attribute, he says, is this and points to his own gorgeous face." Menand calls this plot twist, "quite Jamesian," even as it has little to do with what James saw in the story.[52] Indeed, for all of Catherine's "plainness" and passivity, she shamelessly appropriates the gaze that has heretofore been an exclusively male prerogative—that of viewing the other as a desirable object—expressing openly in the film ("you are so beautiful") what she only thinks to herself in the novel. We know Morris's beauty and charm are important aspects of what makes him appealing to Catherine. When asking Dr. Sloper for Catherine's hand, Morris even suggests that Catherine's devotion—her willingness to listen to his stories and "be charmed"—outdistances that of other women he's known and even his own. Catherine links his charm and style to his moral worth, just as Isabel does in the case of Osmond. However, by defining this dimension of himself as a market commodity, akin to Catherine's money, Morris in effect severs this link. Catherine refuses Morris when he later returns, still handsome and charming—very different from the novel, where more time has passed and the years have not treated Morris well—not because he had "trifled with her affection" as James says[53] but because she no longer needs his beauty and charm to give herself value, when beauty and charm are all, indeed, he has to offer. Catherine Sloper, the female subject, does not require or desire a lifelong relationship with Morris Townsend, a male narcissist or male object.

Figure 6.3. Film still from *Washington Square* with Ben Chaplin (Morris Townsend) and Jennifer Jason Leigh (Catherine Sloper). (Courtesy: Photofest)

With regard to Morris's status as a desirable object, the film's reception reveals a certain uneasiness about Catherine's attraction to Morris, one that suggests that men are increasingly viewing themselves as potential sex objects. In response to Morris's argument one critic wrote: "[Catherine] can't see the converse of what [Morris] is telling her, that without his looks, she wouldn't be interested in him. Like her father and unlike her aunt, she doesn't see that perfectly good marriages have been built on less."[54] The assumption here that women are increasingly demanding that men "appear," much as women have been expected to do, rather than to "act" very much informs this critic's interpretation of Morris's argument, as he simply ignores the fact that Catherine turns Morris away at the end.

Catherine's significant relationship with what can only be defined as a representative of the male subject is, of course, with her father, and her psychological separation from him and his image of her as undesirable reinforces the film's strong insistence on women's psychological separation both from the old model of masculinity, the male subject, and the new model, the male object. The female subject has no choice but to look to the future for alternative, more compatible male types, which, as yet, do not exist. However, the central message for women is quite clear: an inversion of the conventional relationship between a male subject and a female object, where men appear and women act, is as unacceptable as was the traditional version. In exploring this dimension of sexual inversion as a political subtext in their films, both Campion and Holland offer a persuasive critique of the imperatives of postmodern consumer culture rather than watering down the "complexity and ambiguity" of James's original novels.

Unfortunately, films such as *The Portrait of a Lady* and *Washington Square*, which directly or indirectly address such imperatives, such as the assumption that object status is a prerequisite for acceptance and love for men and women, tend not to acquire a popular audience, probably less as a result of their ambiguous status as both "popular" and "elite" than because they confront viewers with the limitations of their "cinematic" norms and the extent to which such norms affect their values and beliefs.[55] These "cinematic" norms are often made explicit in the reception of such films and offer clues as to the reasons why they do not garner popularity. For example, in the adaptation of Jane Austen's *Persuasion*, perhaps the finest and least popular of the Austen adaptations, critics lamented the casting of a "plain" heroine—unkempt and overly "naturalistic" lead actors—arguing that they were unable to "identify" with such figures.[56] Much the same dynamic is apparent in the receptions of *The Portrait of a Lady* and *Washington Square*, although, interestingly, the language used to express this "cinematic norm" is much more diplomatic in the discussion of

male actors than female actors, suggesting that the norm of the male object is
something relatively new.

In *The Portrait of a Lady,* critics' rejection of John Malkovich as Osmond
tended to emphasize his interpretation of the role rather than his appearance,
but the distinction was not always clear: "No Miltonic Satan vital with glamour
and active evil, Isabel's ravisher is a lesser devil, a cold collector of fortunes"[57];
"Had Malkovich given Osmond a shred of ambiguity, *Portrait* would have
gained the dramatic logic and power it lacks. True villains always have their
charms, which is why they compel us"[58]; "he [Malkovich] fails to establish the
character's vampire-like charm. If you found Malkovich less than convincing
as an irresistible seducer of young women in *Dangerous Liaisons,* you'll have
the same problem here."[59] In contrast, critics' discussion of *Washington Square*
tended to emphasize the physical appearance of the cast members, especially
that of the heroine, played by Jennifer Jason Leigh: "Her father's callous as-
sessment of the girl as without charm, wit, or beauty seems entirely warranted,
especially when Holland places Leigh's sharp, unadorned features next to natural beauties"; "If the production lacks the emotional sweep and passionate fire
of Softley's interpretation (*The Wings of the Dove*), it is because Holland consciously refuses to cast beautiful people on a grand stage ... her clinical camera—elsewhere described in terms of "unforgiving close-ups"—records warts
and all."[60] Other critics sympathized with Dr. Sloper and Morris Townsend:
"This version scraps the juicy revenge theme concocted for *The Heiress* ... but
does show us why the doctor feels as he does"[61]; "the film encourages us to ask
what, in fact, draws him [Morris] to the colorless heroine."[62] Thus, although
the story calls for a "plain heroine," critics tended either to criticize the film on
these grounds or else to identify with the male characters rather than with the
heroine. Also interesting is the sense in which "the casting of beautiful people"
is equated with "emotional sweep and passionate fire," as though emotion
and passion can be realized only through specific external forms. That both
films, in effect, tampered with cinematic norms, or the creation of images that
"function as models against which the self continually measures, judges, "disciplines," and "corrects" itself,"[63] explains—to some degree—viewers inability
to identify with the situations depicted in the films. Yet in confronting viewers
with the dynamic of those norms more fully by showing how these norms of
selfhood—of objectification—have been extended to men, these films contribute to an analysis of postmodern consumer culture that encourages reflection and contemplation rather than situational identification.

*   *   *

The Wings of the Dove, a film directed by Iain Softley, was released almost
simultaneously with *Washington Square.* An adaptation of one of James's late

works, the film's reception was dominated by the issue of whether it had managed to capture the "complexity" of James's "late style," with critics being more or less evenly divided. In contrast to the two previous adaptations, both directed and scripted by women, *The Wings of the Dove* was directed and scripted by men. From the outset, the producers of the film insisted that they had radically altered James's work in order to "modernize" or "update" him for contemporary audiences, as though this was the premiere challenge the adaptation of the novel posed and as if to anticipate this particular criticism from reviewers and critics.[64]

The story centers around Kate Croy (Helena Bonham Carter), a young woman who has acquired a spot in British high society through the patronage of a wealthy aunt (Charlotte Rampling). However, her aunt disapproves of her relationship with an unambitious journalist, Merton Densher (Linus Roache). To preserve her affiliation to wealth and her relationship, Kate schemes to collect from a dying American orphan and heiress, Milly Theale (Allison Elliot), by throwing Merton—with whom Milly has fallen in love—in her way, in the hopes that she will bequeath her wealth to him. In the end, Merton is transfixed with the memory of the dead heiress, who has left him her money, and his relationship with Kate is poisoned.

The Wings of the Dove was by far the most widely discussed, highly praised, and financially lucrative of the three James adaptations.[65] Why was this so? If Campion and Holland modified certain dimensions of James's plot but maintained the basic plot structure and dialogue in their adaptations, in *The Wings of the Dove,* a radical shift takes place in the relationship between the novel and the film: in the film, pictures and scenery are substituted for James's dialogue. The pictures that are meant to replace James's dialogue are essentially eroticized gazes, sumptuous dress, and attractive actors who say very little, creating, as Louis Menand put it, "an atmosphere of relative lubricity."[66] Some critics praised this dimension of the film, calling it "sexy and spectral," while others were suspicious of its function, linking it not to James but rather to the film, *The English Patient,* and its essentially "formulaic" dimensions or to Dashiel Hammett and his formulaic dimensions, the film noir love triangle.[67] The pictures in the absence of the dialogue are meant to convey the tensions among the three characters and so to "suggest" James's "complexity and ambiguity."

What sort of story do these pictures of eroticized gazes tell us about the characters? In the case of Kate, "conniving" as she is, it was important to the filmmakers to make her "sympathetic," to make her "more modern." As Menand argues, the notion that James made her unsympathetic suggests a lack of understanding of the novel and the character[68]; however, what is more interesting is how Kate's character is made to be sympathetic in the film. We know of her dependence upon her aunt's patronage for the support of her

family in both the novel and the film, so this could not have been the primary aspect. How to be plotting and sympathetic simultaneously? For one,
according to Richard Corliss, she had to look the part: "at thirty-one, Bonham
Carter is up to the challenge, physically and technically. She is, for a start, fully
ravishing now. Her dramatic coloring—black eyes, ivory skin—is splashed on
a tauter canvas. Maturity has made her chipmunk cheeks swankily concave, allowing her, as Kate, to mull her plotting as if it were a fine port." Corliss never
does discuss the technical aspect of Bonham Carter's performance, so we are
made to assume that it is her looks that manage the feat of reconciling good
with evil, testifying to the importance the film attaches to the physical attractiveness of its characters. It is interesting to note that Bonham Carter does not
quite see things in these terms. Asked why she likes to play characters from
the early twentieth century she replies: "women tend to be the protagonists,
not the ornamental love interest," suggesting the self-perception of subject
rather than object.[69]

However, another more significant aspect of her sympathy is that, unlike
Kate in the novel, from the outset of Merton's first encounter with Milly's gaze,
she—Kate—is "afraid of losing him." This fear plagues her throughout the film
and it is what accounts for the absence of dramatic suspense, in short, the reason
why we are not surprised by the film's end. On account of Kate's conniving, the
dynamic among the three characters is set up in such a way as to favor a relationship between Milly and Merton. When Milly announces to Merton at the
dinner table that she "believes in him," it's clear that she will win the contest of
virtue between the good and bad woman. In the novel, several characters request
others to believe in them, most notably, Kate requesting such of Merton—that
he should believe in her "plan" for their future. Throughout the novel, characters
express the need that others believe in them, but at no time does Milly say
to Merton that she believes in him.[70] This statement has powerful ideological
implications in the film, as it is a remark that apparently shifts the tide in favor
of Milly for Merton and explains the last scene of the film, showing Merton
returning to Venice with a voice-over of Milly repeating her line about believ-
ing in him. Kate's prophesy that Merton will "grow tired of her" transpires as
predicted and Merton, returning to Venice "to live on Milly's money and Milly's
memory," as one critic put it, has the last laugh.[71] If James posited Kate's fascination for Merton in terms of her "talent for life," Merton in the adaptation has no
need of such talents. James gives Kate the last word, whereas the film gives it to
Merton, essentially punishing Kate for her dominance.

The film thus posits a contest over which woman is the ideal for Merton,
"the sort of weak, handsome man strong women are attracted to and know
how to use."[72] Here again, is a variation on the male object, an object that one
woman finds "beautiful" (Milly) and another is afraid to "lose" (Kate). Though

Milly is meant to symbolize a woman "without guile,"[73] her erotic glances at Merton, including an intriguing kiss scene where she keeps her eyes open, are undisguised and unapologetic, in marked contrast, for example, to Catherine Sloper's gaze at Morris Townsend. Merton looks at neither of the two women in this particular way, maintaining his Jamesian persona of "looking vague without looking weak," or as another critic suggested, looking simply "blank."[74] However, Merton as the desired male object remains alone, even as his status as subject has been rescued from Kate's "conniving" through Milly's "belief" in him.[75] (see Figure 6.4).

More viewers identified with this conservative spin on Henry James than they did with either of the other two films, and one reason may be that the contemporaneity of the film is quite different from that of the other two. If *The Portrait of a Lady* and *Washington Square* engaged questions of contemporary gender identity critically, in *The Wings of the Dove*, the values promoted seem more in keeping with "cinematic" norms. One critic has argued that *The Portrait of a Lady* is best understood in terms of the values of the "college dorm" or an episode of *Friends* in that the ways in which the characters interact with one another break with the behavioral and social norms of the nineteenth century.[76] Yet if any film relies upon the values of the dorm, indeed the high school scene, it is *The Wings of the Dove*. Indeed, Milly's "teflon contemporaneity"[77] derives largely from her school girl crush mentality, focusing upon Merton's looks—aptly described by one reviewer: "at a party, Milly catches a glimpse of Merton and likes what she sees,"[78] rejecting other men as "not her type," and finding herself victimized by high school clique sorts of vicious behavior, such as when Kate and Merton run off to have sex, pretending to have lost their friend. In contrast to *The Portrait of a Lady* and *Washington Square*, *The Wings of the Dove* relies upon a familiar formula of romantic rivalries as they are portrayed in series such as *Beverly Hills 90210* or, as Louis Menand thoughtfully noted, in movies like *The English Patient*, which apparently served as a model for the producers of *The Wings of the Dove*: "The formula is, if you like formula movies, a great movie formula. You need a historical period close enough to make the characters seem modern but distant enough to make a high style of living—with champagne, fancy dress, servants, and plenty of leisure for love—plausible. Add actors who need no better excuse for falling all over one another passionately in the hallway or the elevator than the fact that they are fabulously good-looking, and, finally, an exotic locale, and a story of love and death, preferably with a moral surprise."[79]

However, while this formula may have been more popular than the other two films—more successful at the box office—the internet reception of *The Wings of the Dove* suggests an increasing awareness on the part of audiences of such formulaic devices and a decreasing willingness to see style and emotional

Figure 6.4. Publicity poster for *The Wings of the Dove* with Allison Elliot (Milly Theale), Linus Roache (Merton Densher), and Helena Bonham Carter (Kate Croy). Note here another male character in a "reclining" posture. (Compare Figure 6.2) (Courtesy: Photofest)

intensity as interchangeable: "*Wings of the Dove* certainly looks good. The pitch for costume design Oscar is fairly obvious (how often does costume design make it into the opening credits?) and it even seems that Bonham Carter's elaborate dresses and hats become shabbier as her spirits sink."[80] Another reviewer, sounding somewhat like a character in *Fast Times at Ridgemont High*, puts forth: "I felt a rock in my throat for these characters, but I also did for Chad and Howard in *In the Company of Men*. These characters are disgusting yet amazing, since they hide themselves in clothes and attitude at parties, but have deep emotion and rock hard attitude when they are alone."[81] Comparing *In the Company of Men*, a withering black comedy about two men's scheme to seduce and dump a deaf female colleague with *The Wings of the Dove* suggests that the "sexy" elements of the film did not wholly succeed in overwhelming the moral implications of the characters' behavior.

* * *

In an internet review one critic praised *Washington Square* as "a moving and satisfying portrait of one woman's struggle for independence in a society where everything is defined by love, money, or both."[82] This intriguing formulation, positing independence as in opposition to "love, money or both," suggests that the realities that define contemporary consumer culture—love as sexual objectification and money as the means of accessing objects, i.e., "both"—cannot and do not encompass independence. Indeed, they must be called into question in order to achieve it. This tension between individual desire and sexual objectification is addressed, in more or less progressive forms, in all three James adaptations. However, where *The Portrait of a Lady* and *Washington Square* offered female subjectivity as a point of mediation between these two poles by way of a critique of male objectification, *The Wings of the Dove* rendered the male object the center around which questions of female independence and dependence revolved.

Why adapt James's fiction to explore such cultural issues? In an effort to historicize the development of James's "late style," Jean-Christoph Agnew has argued that what distinguished James's development as a writer of fiction was his increasing reliance upon a "proprietary vision," an "acquisitive cognition" that aesthetically prefigured a "phenomenology" of twentieth-century consumer culture. Insofar as significant shifts occur in this particular "way of seeing"—as opposed to "way of being,"—such as in the relationship between gender and sexual objectification, James's fiction offers a framework from which to proceed.[83] And it certainly helps to explain the interest filmmakers have always taken in James.

Ultimately, what can be gained by close attention to film adaptations of James, Austen, and others is a distinctive history of contemporary cultural issues. However, in order to "see" this history, it is necessary to distance the adaptations from the ahistorical generic categories within which such writers have been understood, both to undermine the hierarchical opposition between film and literature as well as to make possible a more historically informed understanding of the adaptation process: "Certainly, genres exist in cinema as they do in written production. Documentaries, musical comedies, and montage films are distinct from each other and each involves a different kind of cinematographic work. But for purposes of social and cultural analysis, they are all documentary objects ... One needs only to know how to read them."[84]

Notes

1. *The Portrait of a Lady.* Dir. Jane Campion. Writ. Laura Jones. Perf. Nicole Kidman, Barbara Hershey, and John Malkovich. PolyGram, 1996; *Washington Square.* Dir. Agnieszka Holland. Writ. Carol Doyle. Perf. Jennifer Jason Leigh, Ben Chaplin, and Albert Finney. Hollywood Pictures/Caravan Pictures, 1997; *The Wings of the Dove.* Dir. Iain Softley. Writ. Hossein Amini. Perf. Helena Bonham Carter, Linus Roache, and Alison Elliot. Miramax, 1997.

2. See, for example, Richard Schickel, "Misplaced Affections," *Time,* Vol. 150/No. 16 (20 October 1997): http: www.pathfinder.com/time/magazine/1997/; Evan Williams, Review of *Portrait of a Lady.* International Movie Database (hereafter, imdb.com) External Review, *Portrait of a Lady*: http://entertainment.news.com.au/film/70208c.htm. All of the following internet film reviews are accessible via the International Movie Data Base, listed either as "External Review,"—most of which have also appeared as published text, or as "Newsgroup Review." They do not contain page numbers.

3. According to *boxofficemojo.com, Portrait of a Lady* grossed $3,692,836 at the domestic box office, *Washington Square,* $1,851,761, and *The Wings of the Dove,* $13,692,848. The latter film was thus the most lucrative of the James adaptations, for reasons I will discuss later in this chapter.

4. It is the New Criticism's version of Modernism that continues to dominate the *reception* of the James adaptations, in contrast both to recent scholarship on James and, significantly, to the adaptations themselves.

5. See, for example, Richard Salmon, "Henry James, Popular Culture, and Cultural Theory," *The Henry James Review* 19.3(1998): 211–218.

6. Neil Sinyard, *Filming Literature: The Art of Screen Adaptation.* (London, 1986), 26.

7. Sinyard, *Filming Literature,* 25–43; Jean-Christophe Agnew, "The Consuming Vision of Henry James," in Richard Wightman Fox and T.J. Jackson Lears, eds., *The Culture of Consumption: Critical Essays in American History,* 1880-1980, (New York, 1983), 65–100; J. Sarah Koch, "A Henry James Filmography," *The Henry James Review,* 19.3(1998): 296–306; Alan Nadel, "Ambassadors from an Imaginary "Elsewhere": Cinematic Convention and the Jamesian Sensibility," *The Henry James Review,* 19.3(1998): 279–285.

8. See Ch. 4 of this volume.

9. James Naremore, "Introduction: Film and the Reign of Adaptation," in James Naremore, ed. *Film Adaptation* (New Brunswick, New Jersey, 2000), 1–16.

10. Stanley Kauffmann, "The Portrait Retouched," *The New Republic* (23 December 1996): 28.

11. Kathleen Murphy, "Jane Campion's Shining: Portrait of a Director," *Film Comment* (November/December 1996): 29.

12. Howard Feinstein, "Heroine Chic," *Vanity Fair* (December 1996): 210; Pia Horlacher, "Kein Platz an der Sonne," *NZZ(Neue Zürchner Zeitung) Online: Feuilleton* (22 May 1998): http://www.nzz.ch/online/01_nzz_aktuel...film9805/fi980522washington_square.htm.

13. Evan Williams, Rev. of *Portrait of a Lady*.

14. Ibid.

15. Kauffmann, 28.

16. Pia Horlacher, "Der Flügelschlag des Chaos," *NZZ (Neue Zürchner Zeitung) Online: Feuilleton* (24 July 1998): http://www.nzz.ch/online/ 01_nzz_aktuel...9807/fi980724 (-) the_wings_of_the_dove.htm.

17. Louis Menand, "Not Getting the Lesson of the Master," *New York Review of Books* (4 December 1997): http://www.nybooks.com/nyrev/WWWarchdisplay.cgi?19971204019R.

18. See for example, James Berardinelli, Rev. of *Washington Square*, http://movie-reviews.collossus.net/movies/w/washington.html; Roger Ebert, Review of *Washington Square*, http://www.suntimes.com/ebert/ebert_reviews/1997/11/111405.html.

19. Feinstein, 212.

20. Kauffmann, 28. See also Schickel, "Misplaced Affections," note 2 above.

21. Roger Ebert, Review of *The Wings of the Dove*, http://www.suntimes.com/ebert/ ebert_reviews/1997/11/111405.html.

22. Devin D. O'Leary, Interview with Iain Softley, http://weeklywire.com/filmvault/alibi/w/wingsof the dove1.html.

23. Robert Horton, "Henry and Jane," Rev. of *Portrait of a Lady*, http://www.film.com/film-review/1996/9261/18/default-review.html.

24. Edward Guthmann, "Arty Portrait Loaded with Heavy Symbolism," *San Francisco Chronicle* (17 January 1997) www.sfgate.com/cgi-bin/article.cgi?file=//chronicle/archive/1997/01/17/DD63103.DTL.

25. See, for example, Roger Ebert, Review of *Portrait of a Lady, Chicago Sun-Times*, http://www.suntimes.com/ebert/ebert_review/1997/01/011704.html; Richard Schickel, "Blurred Vision," *Time* (30 December 1996; 6 January 1997):[no pg. no] Anthony Lane, "Immaterial Girls," *The New Yorker* (6 January 1997): 75.

26. Ibid

27. *The Notebooks of Henry James*, eds. F.O. Matthiessen and Kenneth B. Murdock (New York, 1947), in Henry James, *The Portrait of a Lady* (Harmondsworth, 1986), 638.

28. Nina Baym, "Revision and Thematic Change in *The Portrait of a Lady*," reprinted in Alan Shelston, ed., *Washington Square and The Portrait of a Lady: A Selection of Critical Essays* (London, 1984), 184–202.

29. Guthmann, "Arty Portrait Loaded with Heavy Symbolism."

30. Ruth Sidel, *On Her Own: Growing Up in the Shadow of the American Dream* (New York, 1990).

31. Baym, 185; 194–95.

32. The character of Henrietta reinforces Alan Nadel's reading of *The Portrait of a Lady* as informed by twentieth-century behavioral norms. Yet on the whole, her role is so much more "minor" in the film than in the novel that this dimension does not dominate the film to the extent that it does, as I'll argue later, in *The Wings of the Dove*. See Alan Nadel, "The Search for Cinematic Identity and a Good Man: Jane Campion's Appropriation of James's *Portrait*," *The Henry James Review* 18.2(1997):182.

33. Dianne F. Sadoff, "Intimate Disarray": The Henry James Movies," *The Henry James Review* 19.3(1998): 293.

34. Henry James, *The Portrait of a Lady* (1881, 1908), ed. Geoffrey Moore, (Harmondsworth, 1986), 534–538.

35. Interestingly, though this connection was a point of criticism for a number of commentators, scholars have made connections between James's novel and Laclos's novel, *Les Liaisons Dangereuses*. (1782) See the notes by Patricia Crick in *The Portrait of a Lady* (Harmondsworth, 1986), 645.

36. Murphy, 31.

37. Stuart Ewen, *All Consuming Images: The Politics of Style in Contemporary Culture* (New York, 1988).

38. Barbara Ehrenreich, *The Hearts of Men: American Dreams and the Flight From Commitment* (New York, 1983); Steven Cohan, *Masked Men: Masculinity and the Movies in the Fifties* (Bloomington, 1997); *Harper* (1966) Dir. Jack Smight, Perf., Paul Newman, Lauren Bacall, Arthur Hill.

39. Roger Ebert, Review of *The Portrait of a Lady*.

40. Leon Edel, ed., *Henry James: Letters, Vol. 2, 1875–1883* (Cambridge, Massachusetts, 1980), 316.

41. F.O. Matthiessen and Kenneth B. Murdock, eds. *The Notebooks of Henry James*, 12–13.

42. John Carlos Rowe, *The Theoretical Dimensions of Henry James* (Madison, 1984), 91.

43. Ibid.

44. To her credit, though in a rather deterministic tone, Campion is very much aware of different types of "female psychologies": "I love [Isabel] … When I meet young women like that, I love and feel for them and know what they've got to go through. The more sensible girls, I like them too, but you know they're not going to learn the hard way." (Feinstein 212) Interesting to note here is that while Campion's "imaginative principle" seems to be "Jamesian," her "reality principle" appears to be "Austenian." (i.e. "sense" vs. "sensibility")

45. Menand, "Not Getting the Lesson of the Master."

46. "Tale of a String," lyrics by Marilyn and Alan Bergman, music by Jan A.P. Kaczmarck.

47. Menand, "Not Getting the Lesson of the Master."

48. Feinstein, 212.

49. Roger Ebert, Review of *Washington Square*.

50. John Berger, *Ways of Seeing*, (London, 1972).

51. Murphy, 29, 30.

52. Menand, "Not Getting the Lesson of the Master."

53. Henry James, *Washington Square/The Europeans*, intro. R.P. Blackmur, (New York, 1959), 190.

54. William P. Coleman, Review of *Washington Square*, http://www.wpcmath.com/films/washsquare/ washsquare2.html.

55. Dianne F. Sadoff, "Intimate Disarray": The Henry James Movies," *The Henry James Review* 19.3(1998): 286–295; Alan Nadel, "The Search for Cinematic Identity and a Good Man: Jane Campion's Appropriation of James's *Portrait*," *The Henry James Review* 18.2(1997): 180–183.

56. See the extended discussion of this point in Ch. 4.

57. Murphy, 31.

58. Edward Guthmann, "Arty Portrait Loaded with Heavy Symbolism," *San Francisco Chronicle* (17 January 1997) http://www.sfgate.com/cgi-bin/article.cgi?file=//chronicle/archive/1997/01/17/ DD63103.DTL

59. John Hartl, "Portrait is Difficult to Resist," http://www.film.com/film-review/1996/9261/109/default-review.html.

60. Donna Bowman, Rev. of *Washington Square* http://weeklywire.com/filmvault/nash/w/ws/html.

61. Mike Clark, "*Washington Square* can't replace *Heiress*," http://www.usatoday.com/life/enter/movies/lef927.htm.

62. Bowman, Rev. of *Washington Square*.

63. Susan Bordo, *Unbearable Weight: Feminism, Western Culture, and the Body* (Berkeley, 1993), 24–25.

64. Devin D. O'Leary, Interview with Iain Softley, http://weeklywire.com/filmvault/alibi/w/wingsof the dove1.html; Menand, "Not Getting the Lesson of the Master."

65. *The Wings of the Dove* far outstripped *Washington Square* and *The Portrait of a Lady* at the box office. See note 3 for exact figures.

66. Menand, "Not Getting the Lesson of the Master."

67. Richard Corliss, "All Hail to Helena!" *Time, Vol. 150, No. 20* (10 November 1997): http://www.pathfinder.com/time/magazin...71110/the_arts_cine.all_hail_to_h.html; Pia Horlacher, "Der Flügelschlag des Chaos," see note 12; Menand, "Not Getting the Lesson of the Master."

68. Menand, "Not Getting the Lesson of the Master."

69. Corliss, "All Hail to Helena!"

70. Henry James, *The Wings of the Dove* (1902), with an Introduction by John Bayley, (Harmondsworth, 1986), 261,351,502.

71. Jeffrey Gantz, Rev. of *The Wings of the Dove* and Interview with Helena Bonham Carter, *Boston Phoenix*, (17 November 1997), http://weeklywire.com/filmvault/boston/w/wingsofthe dovethe1.html.

72. Corliss, "All Hail to Helena!".

73. Ibid.

74. Menand, "Not Getting the Lesson of the Master"; Duncan Stevens, Review of *The Wings of the Dove*, http://us.imdb.com/Reviews/101/10153.

75. Nadel, "Ambassadors from an Imaginary "Elsewhere," 285.

76. Nadel, "The Search for Cinematic Identity...," 182.

77. Menand, "Not Getting the Lesson of the Master".

78. Marty Mapes, Review of *The Wings of the Dove*, http://us.imdb.com/Reviews/105/10580.

79. Menand, "Not Getting the Lesson of the Master".

80. Duncan Stevens, Review of *The Wings of the Dove*, http://us.imdb.com/Reviews/101/10153.

81. Jason Whyte, The Big Screen Cinema Guide, http://www.bigscreen.com/cgi/ShowRevi ew?WingsoftheDove.

82. James Berardinelli, Rev. of *Washington Square*, http://movie-reviews.colossus.net/movies/w/washington.html.

83. Agnew, "The Consuming Vision of Henry James," in Fox and Lears, ed. *The Culture of Consumption*, 65–100.

84. Marc Ferro, *Cinema and History*. (transl. by Naomi Greene). (Detroit, 1988), 83.

A Case for the Case Study

The Future of Adaptation Studies as a Branch of Transnational Film History

When Orson Welles, discussing his adaptation of Kafka's *The Trial* in an interview with Hollywood director Peter Bogdanovich, told him "to read the book sometime, it's short," he may have been playing with the pretentions of high culture in order to scold Bogdanovich for his lack of preparation, but he was not advocating the fidelity model of film adaptation. Likewise, when Emma Thompson was asked in an interview what she would ask Jane Austen today (1996) and she replied, jokingly, "what percentage she wants of the gross" of *Sense and Sensibility,* she was invoking Austen as a best-selling and successful author, collaborator, and filmic resource; not, however, as a superior blueprint. Both Thompson and Welles in their reliance upon fictional texts testify to the multifaceted relationship between the two media and that the significance of individual adaptations has never been solely dependent upon a hierarchical understanding of literature in relation to film.[1]

However, recent scholarly work on adaptation seems intent on eliminating the case study—the specific focus upon a film adaptation in relationship to its literary source—as a methodological tool in the study of film and literature. Classified primarily as a loyal servant of the fidelity school of adaptation, the case study has come to be understood as the main obstacle to a more sophisticated, more theoretical approach to adaptation study, one that would prefer to subsume specific cases under the rubric of "intertextuality," "intermediality," or "the adaptation industry." Unsurprisingly, most of these calls to eliminate the specific case stem from scholars in the areas of media studies, communication studies, and the more theory-focused branches of literary studies, fields generally less interested in historical analysis of media and culture.[2]

For film and cultural historians, the case study is the pivotal means into a broader exploration of the relationship between film, literature, and society. First, the analysis of an adaptation vis-à-vis a source text provides a chronological framework that effectively lends itself to historical analysis. Second, the case study can call attention to the transnational character of film adaptation and explain how transnational cultural processes affect the relationship between literature and film. Finally, cases of specific adaptations highlight aesthetic developments in film history and show how filmmakers continue to rely upon the adaptation of literary works to create new types of cinematic forms. Therefore, questions of time, place, and medium become central to an analysis of film adaptation as an historical phenomenon.

Case studies of specific adaptations foreground the crucial role of literature in the history of film and popular culture, as well as the ways the relationship between literature and film can be conceptualized for purposes of historical analysis. As Dudley Andrew has argued: "the explicit, foregrounded relation of a cinematic text to a well constructed original text from which it derives and in some sense it strives to reconstruct provides the analyst with a clear and useful "laboratory" condition that should not be neglected."[3] Implicit in the inherently chronological model of the relation of "cinematic text to well constructed original text" is an historical framework for evaluating the relationship between film and society. When filmmakers such as Ang Lee, Emma Thompson, or Orson Welles adapt "classic" works, they are inevitably faced with "reconstructing" those works within very different social, economic, and political contexts. Traditionally, that process of reconstruction has been linked to the creative license of individual filmmakers—"*la camera-stylo*," the camera as a pen, in Alexandre Astruc's terms, for example—without paying attention to the ways those filmmakers were and are products of their time and place.[4] Emma Thompson's interest in questions of contemporary gender identity and the ways women today negotiate the realms of economics and personal relationships is closely related to the ways she modified the dynamic between the two sisters, Elinor and Marianne, to include the third sister, Margaret, in her adaptation of *Sense and Sensibility*. Jane Austen could not have known what was in store for the youngest sister in her novel; Thompson's projection of independence onto the character of Margaret is a product of hindsight and so fundamentally historical in its implications.

The case of Welles's adaptation of Franz Kafka's *The Trial* can be analyzed similarly. Like Thompson's interest in issues of gender and contemporary culture, Welles wanted to link Kafka's pre-World War II text to the postwar world of the Cold War and state authoritarianisms. However, as a flamboyant U.S. filmmaker with transnational "auteur" status in the early 1960s, Welles and his filmic efforts would be linked by commentators to creative legerdemain rather than to his long time interest in the relationship between politics and culture.

The point is not that contemporary filmmakers inject aspects of the present moment into their "historical adaptations" but rather to show how their adaptations manifest—both consciously and unconsciously—change over time in the relationship between culture, narrative, and film. To remain with the Austen theme, adaptations of Jane Austen's works, in particular, are highly suggestive in this regard. Today, Thompson and Lee's adaptation of *Sense and Sensibility* can itself be situated within a context that demonstrates how differently Austen adaptations can function as cultural and historical markers. Let me illustrate by comparing the Austen boom of the 1990s with more recent trends in Austen adaptations.

The early twenty-first-century Jane Austen "boom" includes biographical renditions of Austen's life entitled *Becoming Jane* and *Miss Austen Regrets,* Bollywood and Hollywood versions of *Pride and Prejudice,* and an adaptation of a novel about reading Austen novels entitled *The Jane Austen Book Club,* among many others.[5] This new wave of Austen-oriented films is best understood in contrast and comparison to the Austen boom of the 1990s and should be looked at more closely. Patricia Rozema's 2000 adaptation of *Mansfield Park* might mark a rough transition of sorts between the emphasis upon the translation and performance of the original novels in the 1990s and the shift to a focus upon Austen as a female author and on reading Austen, in particular. In *Mansfield Park,* Rozema transforms Austen's morally upright, rigid heroine, Fanny Price, into a free-spirited authoress figure, who is supposed to be a stand in for Jane Austen herself. This well-made, very self-conscious production anticipated the trend toward the themes of both reading Austen and Austen as a writer, even as its main thrust was to present a politicized, "postcolonial" tale emphasizing subtextual references to slavery in the novel *Mansfield Park.*[6]

However, as several commentators have noted, the function of Austen's works in more recent productions such as *The Jane Austen Book Club* is largely privatized and personal.[7] Interestingly, if the more "conventional" adaptations of the 1990s, such as *Sense and Sensibility,* called attention to contemporary cultural struggles involving gender roles and gender identity, these newer productions seem to offer reading Austen's texts as a therapeutic solution to these cultural dilemmas.[8] As one enthusiastic viewer of *The Jane Austen Book Club* put it: "the conceit of this movie and the book it is based upon is that a shared love and appreciation of the works of Jane Austen can provide the currency through the exchange of which modern women (and a few selected men) can confront, share, and come to better understand their personal challenges and in the process, form bonds of friendship or even romance. The strength of this movie is that even if you have a tough time with that conceit, you will still enjoy the humor of it, and the strong performances."[9] A less enthusiastic commentator wrote: "there's a difference between connecting to a writer's work and reading too much of yourself in it, and the banal film version of Fowler's book crosses the line six too many times ... There's no subtext to *The Jane Aus-*

ten Book Club, just a skim across the books' surface that winds up re-shelving a great author in the self-help section."[10] This "privatizing" of Jane Austen, which also includes a subtheme of "missed romantic opportunities"[11]—definitely not a theme of the 1990s adaptations—is reminiscent of what Susan Faludi referred to years ago as "backlash": the media promoted notion that women had exchanged family, love, and relationships for an unsatisfying autonomy and empty independence and that the culprit was feminism.[12] If many of the films of the 1990s enlisted Austen for her public aspects, what is striking about this latest trend is the ways the films actively seek to re-privatize the writer and her themes. Rather than reading Austen as a sociohistorically relevant writer, which the best of the 1990s adaptations certainly tried to do (see, esp. *Sense and Sensibility* and *Persuasion*), this early twenty-first-century Austen boom actively seeks to "re-domesticate" her in the tradition of the nineteenth-century "cult of Jane Austen" that Henry James so disdained at the turn of the twentieth century.[13]

* * *

Closely related to their historical significance, specific cases of literature to film transformations can be effectively enlisted in the transnational reception study of adaptation. Hollywood film adaptations, ranging from Carol Reed's and David O. Selznick's production of Graham Greene's *The Third Man* (1949) and David Lean's adaptation of Pierre Boulle's *The Bridge on the River Kwai* (1957) to Ang Lee's production of Jane Austen's *Sense and Sensibility* (1995) and Jane Campion's production of Henry James's *The Portrait of a Lady* (1996) tend to share a "transnational" structure. This structure is composed of three parts: the transnational composition and interaction of the film production teams and the literary works upon which they rely, the transnational audiences for which these films were produced, and, more self-reflexively, the contemporary transnational scholarly contexts that influence the selection of films to analyze. Because the commercial goals of the Hollywood film industry sought to downplay the diversity and conflict of its transnational aspects in favor of a universalized notion of "popular entertainment," those aspects were often officially downplayed to accommodate standardized production structures. However, when these films are situated in specific national contexts, Hollywood's reliance on literary narratives and artists from around the world often destabilized its standardization goals, revealed in specific cases of filmic adaptation and the ways modifications between literary works and filmic works took place and were actively commented upon.

A recent example of such a process is illustrated in the reception of the American fashion designer Tom Ford's adaptation of the British writer Christopher Isherwood's 1964 novel *A Single Man.* The novel depicts a day in the life of an enraged and bereaved bohemian, homosexual man coming to terms with the death of his lover; Ford's adaptation (2009) transforms the angry and misogynistic protagonist into an elegant, well-mannered, and superbly dressed suicidal depressive played by the British actor Colin Firth. After Firth's Oscar nomination for the role, the British *Sunday Times* published an article focusing upon the "gay commentators and literary scholars in the U.S.," who accused the filmmaker of distorting Isherwood's novel by downplaying the gay theme and "discount[ing] the importance of gay identity." U.S. critics focused not upon what the *Times* defined as Tom Ford's "impressive debut" film; instead, they generated "a debate on gay politics and the pitfalls of adapting seminal works."[14] Thus, under the rather defensive guise of "fidelity criticism" (*A Single Man* is an adequate adaptation), the *Times* critic calls attention to important transnational dynamics related to contemporary filmic adaptations and what such adaptations might suggest about shifts in the history of gay literature, politics, and so-called "global" popular culture.

Historically, *The Third Man* (1949) can serve as a model of the ways transnational dynamics influenced the adaptation process and why these dynamics are significant. With its international acting and production team, its bi- and even trilingual script, and its theme of the four power occupation of Vienna in the early postwar period, terms such as "cosmopolitan" and "internationality" were readily invoked to discuss and market the film at the time of its release. However, within the early Cold War context, that "internationalism" could provide a cover for struggles over creative control and cultural authority between the U.S. and British film industries, while simultaneously raising important questions within the German context of the ideological function of the "international" in a country divided between capitalism and communism—even as it courted German audiences with German language dialogue over their disappointment and disillusion with the postwar occupation. In turn, the film's creative use of a team of international authors—both credited and uncredited—and actors encouraged a positive reconstruction of European cultural identity in the face of expanding Soviet state communism and U.S. cultural and economic imperialism.

The case of the two films *The Bridge on the River Kwai* and *Die Brücke* in the context of the West German debate over "pro-war vs. anti-war" films revealed cross-cultural and transnational dynamics at work in the heretofore exclusively German discussion of the politics of cultural memory in West Germany. Whereas *Kwai* was heralded as an "anti-war" epic in the U.S. producer's, Columbia Pictures, publicity campaign for the film in West Germany, critics and commentators questioned this version even prior to the film's German release. Instead, they made *Kwai* the center of a critical discussion about the ways ostensibly anti-war, U.S. productions were ambiguously pro-war in the

West German context, focusing attention upon the ways the film's music, its characterization of male identity in the context of military life, and the way the film altered key dimensions of the French novel upon which it was based ultimately encouraged a glorification of militarism as German commentators understood it based upon their own past experiences.

In contrast, Bernhard Wicki's *Die Brücke* (The Bridge), which was nominated for an Academy Award in 1960 and won that year's Golden Globe Award as "Best Foreign Film," offered a filmic "response" of sorts to *Kwai's* ultimately "Cold War Anti-War" formula. In Wicki's film, a different approach to the function of the bridge in the film's plot, different music, and very different male characters offered an implicit visual contrast and critique of the bridge, men, and music in *Kwai*. Thus could the definition of a "war film" be very much influenced not only by the national contexts in which such films were produced but also by the national, historical, and cultural contexts in which they were to be released.

* * *

Finally, case studies of specific adaptations are indispensible for gauging cultural and artistic development in the relationship between literature and film. If filmmakers in the "classic" Hollywood era tended to focus on "translating" literary texts into visual terms and filmmakers from the mid-century into the 1970s were more interested in using literary sources as a jumping off point for their own artistic "performances," then today, the economic pressures associated with the marketing of large scale productions both combine and compete with newer trends of independent multi-media filmmaking—everything from very small scale theatre releases to uploaded videos on YouTube.[15] Thus, adaptations of literary works today—understood as vehicles for negotiating cultural change over time—need to be evaluated in terms of both translation and performance, and how these two historical adaptation imperatives shape the ways literary works are transformed into film and received by audiences—in multiplex theatres, marginalized art houses, on television, and on the internet—worldwide.[16]

Within this context, one of the most significant developments on the adaptation scene today is the increased number of female "auteurs," women involved in the production of literary adaptations in the capacity of directors, producers, and screen-writers, as well as actors. How does the increasing involvement of women as filmmakers affect the ways literature is today transformed into cinema in terms of both translation and performance? In what ways do they enlist the process of film adaptation to achieve different goals? Figures such as Jane Campion, Agnieszka Holland, and Emma Thompson almost always tend—even if they themselves prefer to downplay it—to bring feminist themes foregrounding questions of female agency to bear upon their interpretations of literary works. If we compare a classic male auteur, for example, Orson Welles, with a figure such as Emma Thompson, we can note several interesting points of comparison. Like Welles, Thompson combines the roles of internationally respected film actress and screenwriter, though unlike Welles she has not yet ventured into the area of film direction. Also like Welles, she is very interested in adapting works of classic and non-classic literature for the screen. While Welles in such adaptations as *The Trial* sought to link Kafka to his own interest in the relationship between the male individual and the state in the Cold War world, Thompson is more interested in the fortunes of female individuals, or as she once put it in an interview, "demonstrating heroism by way of character rather than actions."[17] Her adaptations of female characters, such as Elinor Dashwood in *Sense and Sensibility* or the governess figure of Nanny McPhee in the film of the same name, exemplify a desire to situate female characters as active agents—heroes, in more conventional terminology—defined not primarily by their physical attractiveness, sexual attributes, or familial status but rather by the way they respond to social and personal crises.[18] In contrast, Welles's auteur status was based largely on his depictions of male figures as pawns of institutional power arrangements. The traditions of the male auteur as literary adaptor, which Welles's angle certainly represents, thus posits a very different framework for defining oneself as a "cinematic author." It remains to be explored in what ways female film adaptors are re-thinking the classic auteur pattern in their own efforts to negotiate a space between literature—both classic and popular—and commercial film.[19]

*   *   *

Thus, case studies of adaptation as historical, transnational, and cultural/aesthetic phenomena continue to be highly significant and should be given a central place within the history of film in the twentieth—and into the twenty-first—century. The film industry's reliance upon recognizable narratives is one of the key bases of its historical and material significance. If scholars insist on collapsing the specifics of adaptation as a historical phenomenon within an ahistorical conception of "intermediality" or "intertextuality," they will overlook what may perhaps be the most important aspects of the relationship. Moreover, "film adaptation" as such was always more than the subject of a subbranch of literary studies; it was the foundation of the mass-marketing of cinema through a reliance upon well-known narrative texts from the nineteenth century. As film scholars such as Timothy Corrigan and Joachim Paech have argued, film became a popular phenomenon when filmmakers began to rely on narrative and "stories" as the basis for films rather than other criteria such as scientific documentary investigation or avant-garde image experimentation.[20]

Overall, contemporary interest in questions of "intertextuality," particularly in the field of cultural studies, is all too eager to skip over the history of twentieth-century film and its specific relationship to literature in its desire to evaluate newer internet-based media phenomena. However, it will not be possible to grasp these contemporary developments without an understanding of how media such as film and literature have been combined in the past. Film adaptation study removed from its cultural pedestal and instead enlisted in a larger project of linking media and society can offer new ways of conceptualizing the relationship between film, literature, and history. As Marc Ferro has argued: "each film has a value as a document, whatever its seeming nature … By the way it affects people's imaginary universe, and by the very imaginary universe that it conveys, every film posits a relation between its author, its subject matter, and the viewer. Besides, if it is true that the not-said and the imaginary have as much historical value as History, then the cinema, especially the fictional film, open a royal way to psycho-socio-historical zones never reached by the analysis of 'documents.'"[21] Insofar as we wish to make history a central component of cultural studies, the concept of adaptation, along with the case study, will continue to be relevant.

Notes

1. Orson Welles and Peter Bogdanovich. *This is Orson Welles*, Jonathan Rosenbaum, ed. (New York, 1993), 285–86; Jan Stuart, "Emma Thompson, Sensibly," *Los Angeles Times Calendar* (10 December 1995): 85.

2. Thomas Leitch, "Adaptation Studies at a Crossroads," *Adaptation* Vol. 1.1(2008), 65; *Film Adaptation and Its Discontents: From "Gone with the Wind" to "The Passion of Christ."* (Baltimore, Md., 2007); Simone Murray, "Materializing Adaptation Theory: The Adaptation Industry." *Literature/Film Quarterly* 36.1(2008): 4–20; "Phantom Adaptations: *Eucalyptus*, the adaptation industry and the film that never was." *Adaptation*, Vol. 1, No. 1(2008): 5–23.

3. Dudley Andrew, "Film Adaptation," in James Naremore, ed., *Film Adaptation* (New Brunswick, New Jersey, 2000), 29.

4. Alexandre Astruc. "The Birth of the New Avant-Garde: La Camera-Stylo." In *The New Wave*. Ed. Peter Graham. (New York: Doubleday, 1968).

5. See Nancy Franklin, "Everybody Loves Jane," *The New Yorker* (21 January 2008): 82–83.

6. *Mansfield Park*, written and directed by Patricia Rozema, Miramax/BBC, 2000.

7. Karen Joy Fowler. *The Jane Austen Book Club*. (London, 2004).

8. This also seems to be the gist of a recent television series entitled "Lost in Austen". See Alice Ridout, "Lost in Austen: Adaptation and the Feminist Politics of Nostalgia." *Adaptation* 4.1(March 2011): 14–27.

9. Karen (surreyhill), IMDb user comments for *The Jane Austen Book Club*, http://www.imdb.com/title/tt0866437/

10. Tobias, Scott. Review of *The Jane Austen Book Club*, The A.V. Club. http://www.avclub.com/content/node/66867/print/

11. Franklin, "Everybody Loves Jane," 82–83.

12. Susan Faludi, *Backlash: The Undeclared War Against American Women.* (New York, 1991).

13. Henry James, "The Lesson of Balzac," *Atlantic Monthly* Vol. 96(1905): 166–180.

While some might interpret this phenomenon of a cultural pendulum favoring a "public" Austen here, a "private" Austen there, as an example of postmodern intermedial legerdemain, there may be a more historically and artistically compelling way out of this circle: attempting dramatizations of Austen works that have been ignored. One such work which could offer contemporary relevance is the short epistolary novel *Lady Susan*, a fascinating Austenian experiment away from her classic pattern: a scheming older woman seeking to find a spouse at the eleventh hour, exploiting her personal connections, her charm and her "happy command of language" to negotiate an advantageous position for herself on a tight marriage market. Those readers and filmmakers still interested in an Austen with both public and private dimensions and definitely not interested in yet another half baked version of *Pride and Prejudice* might find in *Lady Susan* a suitable alternative. See Jane Austen. *Lady Susan.* In: John Davie (ed.). *Northanger Abbey.* (Oxford, 1980). [1793 or 1805]

14. Eric Gutierrez. "Tom Ford was right about Isherwood: Don Bacardy, the Single Man novelist's partner, explains why the designer's new film deserves its Oscar nomination." *The Times.* 05 Feb. 2010. Web. 30 May 2011. http://entertainment.timeonline.co.uk/tol/arts_and_entertainment/film/article7015418.ece.

15. I take the framework of understanding newer adaptations in terms of the models of both translation, (associated with "fidelity"), and performance, (associated with "auteurism") from James Naremore, ed., *Film Adaptation* (New Brunswick, New Jersey, 2000), 7–8. Additionally, the superb argument made by Timothy Corrigan, James Naremore, and most recently, Guerric DeBona, that European "auteur" cinema did not signal the rejection of literature as the basis for films (as the filmmakers themselves often polemically argued), but rather advocated the adaptation of popular or 'mass cultural' works—and indeed even modernist works such as, for example, Kafka's *The Trial*—instead of classic "realist" canonical works, is also especially relevant here. See Corrigan, *Film and Literature: An Introduction and Reader.* (Upper Saddle River, NJ, 1999), 39–53, James Naremore, ed., *Film Adaptation,* 6 and Guerric DeBona, *Film Adaptation in the Hollywood Studio Era.* (Urbana, 2010), 32.

16. Indeed, much of what today is evaluated in terms of "intertextuality" and "intermediality" would be better understood in terms of the ways the imperatives of translation and performance influence the ways filmmakers receive and appropriate literary works. Here especially adaptation on the internet would be an important new area of exploration.

17. "Verflucht harte Arbeit": Interview mit Emma Thompson. *Der Spiegel* 10(4 March 1996): 230–231.

18. Thompson has now written two screen adaptations of the children's works of the British crime writer and children's author Christianna Brand. Comparing Thompson with another female filmmaker, Jane Campion, who has focused upon directing films rather than screenwriting, the tendency is to concentrate upon women as sexual or desiring subjects, and to rewrite classic canonical texts, such as Henry James's *The Portrait of a Lady*, in terms of female (sexual) agency rather than renunciation.

19. Discussions in Germany during the Berlinale Film Festival 2011 focused upon the increased role of women on the international film scene. See for example, Elisabeth Raether and Annabel Wahba, "Wir sollen immer nett sein: Warum haben es Frauen in der Film Branche schwerer als Männer? Ein Gespräch zwischen den Regisseurinnen Maren Ade und Doris Dörrie." *Zeit Magazin,* Nr. 7 (10 February 2011): 27–30 and Ole Häntzschel (Infografik), "In der Nebenrolle: Frauen und ihr Anteil am Filmgeschäft." *Zeit Magazin,* Nr.7(10 February 2011):

34–35. Recent work on gender and adaptation includes Shelley Cobb, „Revaluing Adaptation: Gender, Authority and the Problem of Fidelity." PhD Dissertation, University of East Anglia, 2008.

20. Corrigan, *Film and Literature*; Joachim Paech. *Literatur und Film, Zweite Auflage.* (Stuttgart, 1997).

21. Marc Ferro, *Cinema and History,* trans. by Naomi Greene, (Detroit, 1988), 82–83.

Appendix 1

Mediating Apparent
and Latent Content

Table 1

	society & ideology		
------------------	------------------	------------------	------------------
	search for		
fiction	signs		
			zone of nonvisible
apparent		latent	
content		content	(social) reality
image of reality			
------------------	------------------	------------------	------------------
	society & ideology		

from: Marc Ferro, *Cinema and History*. Trans. by Naomi Greene (Detroit: Wayne State University Press, 1988), 36.

Table 2

Modified version of Table 1 taking into account how comparison of literary narrative, filmic narrative and reception can mediate apparent and latent content.

	society & ideology		
-------------------	-------------------	-------------------	-------------------
	compare (e.g.)		
fiction	• literary narrative with filmic narrative		
apparent	• reception of film adaptation	latent	zone of nonvisible
content		content	(social) reality
image of reality			
-------------------	-------------------	-------------------	-------------------

from: Marc Ferro, *Cinema and History*. Trans. by Naomi Greene (Detroit: Wayne State University Press, 1988), 36.

Model of Adaptation as
a Process of Reception

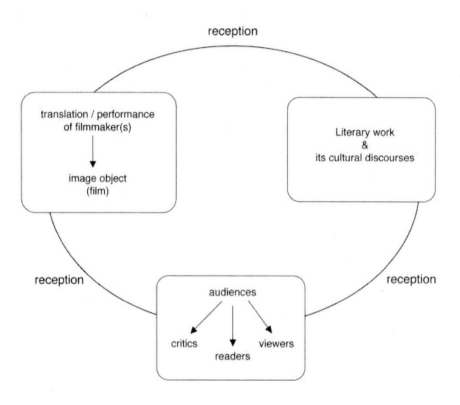

Filmography

Die Brücke. Dir. Bernhard Wicki. Screenwriter: Michael Mansfield, based on the novel by Manfred Gregor. With Volker Bohnet, Fritz Wepper, Michael Hinze, et al. Fono Films, 1959; Arthaus/Kinowelt Home Entertainment GmbH.

Harper. Dir. Jack Smight. Screenplay: William Goldman, based on the novel by Ross McDonald. Perf., Paul Newman, Lauren Bacall, Arthur Hill. Warner Brothers Pictures, 1966.

Mansfield Park. Dir. Patricia Rozema. Screenwriter: Patricia Rozema, based on the novel by Jane Austen as well as letters and early journals. With Embeth Davidtz, Jonny Lee Miller, and Frances O'Connor. Miramax/BBC Films, 2000.

Persuasion. Dir. Roger Michell. Screenwriter: Nick Dear, based upon the novel by Jane Austen. With Amanda Root and Ciàran Hinds. BBC, 1995.

Sense and Sensibility. Dir. Ang Lee. Screenwriter: Emma Thompson, based on the novel by Jane Austen. With Emma Thompson, Kate Winslet, and Hugh Grant. Columbia Tristar Home Video, 1995.

A Single Man. Dir. Tom Ford. Screenwriters: Tom Ford and David Scearce, based on the novel by Christopher Isherwood. With Colin Firth, Julianne Moore, and Matthew Goode. Senator Home Entertainment GmbH, 2010.

Thelma and Louise. Dir. Ridley Scott. Screenwriter: Callie Khouri. With Susan Sarandon and Geena Davis. MGM-Pathe Communications Co., 1991/ MGM/UA Home Video Inc., 1992.

The Bridge on the River Kwai (German title: *Die Brücke am Kwai*) Dir: David Lean, producer: Sam Spiegel. Screenwriters: Carl Foreman and Michael Wilson, based on the novel by Pierre Boulle. With Alec Guinness, William Holden, and Sessue Hayakawa. Columbia Pictures, 1957.

The Jane Austen Book Club. Dir. Robin Swicord. Screenwriter: Robin Swicord, based on the novel by Karen Joy Fowler. With Maria Bello, Emily Blunt, Kathy Baker, et al. Mockingbird Pictures, John Calley Productions, 2007. Sony Pictures Release.

The Portrait of a Lady. Dir. Jane Campion. Screenwriter: Laura Jones, based on the novel by Henry James. With Nicole Kidman, John Malkovich, and Barbara Hershey. Polygram Film Productions, 1996; Polygram Video, 1997.

The Third Man. Dir. Carol Reed. Screenwriter Graham Greene, based on the story by Graham Greene. With Joseph Cotten, Orson Welles, and Alida Valli. London Films, 1949.

"The Trial: A Film from Orson Welles," Dir. Orson Welles. Screenwriter: Orson Welles, based on the novel by Franz Kafka. Paris-Europa Productions, 1963; Video Release Fox-Lorber Associates, Inc., 1998.

The Wings of the Dove. Dir. Iain Softley. Screenwriter: Hossein Amini, based on the novel by Henry James. With Helena Bonham Carter, Linus Roache, and Alison Elliott. Miramax, 1997.

Washington Square. Dir. Agnieszka Holland. Screenwriter: Carol Doyle, based on the novel by Henry James. With Jennifer Jason Leigh, Albert Finney, and Ben Chaplin. Caravan Pictures/ Hollywood Pictures Home Video, 1997.

Bibliography

Archival Collections Consulted

Deutsches Filminstitut, Frankfurt am Main
Abteilung Dokumentation und Information
Der Dritte Mann (The Third Man)
Die Brücke am Kwai (The Bridge on the River Kwai)
Der Prozess (The Trial)

Filmmuseum Berlin, Bibliothek
Deutsche Kinemathek, Berlin
Der Dritte Mann
Die Brücke am Kwai
Die Brücke (The Bridge)
Der Prozess

Hochschule für Film und Fernsehen, Konrad Wolf, Potsdam-Babelsberg
Abteilung Pressedokumentation
Der Prozess

Magazine/Film Review Collections Consulted

John F. Kennedy Institut Library, Berlin
University of California, Irvine, Library

Primary Literary Works

Austen, Jane. *Lady Susan*. In: John Davie (ed.). *Northanger Abbey*. Oxford: Oxford University Press, 1980. [1793 or 1805]

Austen, Jane. *Persuasion*. (1817). Harmondsworth: Penguin, 1970.

Austen, Jane. *Sense and Sensibility* (1811). New York: Airmont, 1965.

Boulle, Pierre. *Die Brücke am Kwai*. Trans. Gottfried Beutel. Hamburg: Rowohlt-Taschenbuch-Verlag GmbH, [1958].

Greene, Graham. *The Third Man/The Fallen Idol*. Harmondsworth: Penguin, 1976. [1950]

Gregor, Manfred. *Die Brücke*. München: Deutsche Verlags-Anstalt, 2005.[1958]

James, Henry. "The Lesson of Balzac." *Atlantic Monthly* Vol. 96(1905): 166–180.

James, Henry. *The Notebooks of Henry James*, eds. F.O. Matthiessen and Kenneth B. Murdock. New York: Oxford University Press, 1947.

James, Henry. *The Portrait of a Lady* (1881, 1908), ed. Geoffrey Moore. Harmondsworth: Penguin, 1986.

James, Henry. *Washington Square/The Europeans*, [1881] intro. R.P. Blackmur. New York: Dell, 1959.

James, Henry. *The Wings of the Dove* (1902), with an Introduction by John Bayley, Harmondsworth: Penguin, 1986.

Kafka, Franz. *Briefe an Felice, und andere Korrespondenz aus der Verlobungszeit.* Hrg. Erich Heller und Jürgen Born. Frankfurt am Main: Fischer Taschenbuch Verlag, 1976.

Kafka, Franz. *Der Prozess* (1925). Frankfurt am Main: Suhrkamp Taschenbuch Verlag, 1998. Based upon the third edition: Franz Kafka, *Gesammelte Werke*, hrg. Max Brod. *Der Prozess. Roman.* S. Fischer Verlag. Lizenzausgabe von Schocken Books, New York, 1950.

Selected Secondary Works

Adamson, Judy, and Philip Stratford. "Looking for *The Third Man*: On the Trail in Texas, New York, Hollywood." *Encounter* Vol. L, No. 6 (June 1978): 39–46.

Agnew, Jean-Christophe. "The Consuming Vision of Henry James," in Richard Wightman Fox and T.J. Jackson Lears, eds., *The Culture of Consumption: Critical Essays in American History,* 1880–1980. New York: Pantheon, 1983: 65–100.

Aichinger, Ilse. *Film und Verhängnis: Blitzlichter auf ein Leben.* Frankfurt am Main: Fischer TV, 2003.

Allen, Brooke. "Jane Austen For the Nineties," *New Criterion* (Sept. 1995), quoted in Simon, 58– 59.

Allen, Robert C., and Douglas Gomery. *Film History: Theory and Practice.* New York: Alfred A. Knopf, 1985.

Altman, Rick. "General Introduction: Cinema as Event." In Rick Altman, ed. *Sound Theory, Sound Practice.* New York: Routledge, 1992. pp. 1–14.

Amis, Martin. "Jane's World," *New Yorker* (8 January 1996): 35.

Anderegg, Michael. *David Lean.* Boston: Twayne, 1984.

Andrew, Dudley. "Film Adaptation," in James Naremore, ed., *Film Adaptation.* New Brunswick, New Jersey: Rutgers University Press, 2000: 28–37.

[Anon]. Review of *Thelma and Louise*: http://xochi.tezcat.com/~annoir/thelou.htm.

Ansen, David, "In This Fine Romance, Virtue is Rewarded." *Newsweek* (9 October 1995):78.

Apel, Friedmar. "Der war ja gar nicht kafkaesk."*Frankfurter Allgemeine Zeitung,* 11 August 2008, Nr. 186/Seite 34, http://faz.net.

Apel, Friedmar. "Mythengestöber," *Frankfurter Allgemeine* Zeitung, 3 December 2008, Nr. 283/ Page 32, http://faz.net.

Armstrong, Nancy. *Desire and Domestic Fiction: A Political History of the Novel.* New York: Oxford University Press, 1987.

Astruc, Alexandre. "The Birth of the New Avant-Garde: La Camera-Stylo." In *The New Wave.* Peter Graham, ed. New York: Doubleday, 1968.

"Austen Anew," *New Yorker* (21 and 28 August 1995): 56.

Aycock, Wendell, and Michael Schoenecke, eds. *Film and Literature: A Comparative Approach to Adaptation.* Lubbock, Texas: Texas Tech University Press, 1988.

Bahners, Patrick. "Das Herz hat seine Gründe," *Frankfurter Allgemeine Zeitung* (3 December 1996).

Balestrini, Nassim Winnie, ed. *Adaptation and American Studies: Perspectives on Research and Teaching.* Heidelberg: Winter Verlag, 2011.

Baym, Nina. "Revision and Thematic Change in *Portrait of a Lady,*" reprinted in Alan Shelston, ed., *Washington Square and The Portrait of a Lady: A Selection of Critical Essays.* London: Macmillan Press, 1984: 184–202.

Bazin, Andre, Charles Bitsch, and Jean Domarch: "Gespräch mit Orson Welles," in *Cahiers du Cinema,* No. 87(September 1958); dt.Übersetzung in *Der Film: Manifeste, Gespräche, Dokumente.* Bd. 2 (Piper Verlag).

Becker, Wolfgang, and Norbert Schöll, *In Jenen Tagen...Wie der deutsche Nachkriegsfilm die Vergangenheit bewältigte.* Opladen: Leske and Budrich, 1995.

Behlmer, Rudy, ed. *Memo from David O. Selznick.* New York: Avon, 1973.

Beja, Morris. *Film & Literature.* New York: Longman, 1979.

Berardinelli, James. Rev. of *Washington Square,* http://movie-reviews.collossus.net/movies/w/washington.html.

Berger, John. *Ways of Seeing.* London: Penguin, 1972.

Bergfelder, Tim. *International Adventures: German Popular Cinema and European Co-Productions in the 1960s.* New York: Berghahn, 2005.

Beutin, Wolfgang, *et al. Deutsche Literaturgeschichte* (6th ed.) Stuttgart: J.B. Metzler Verlag, 2001.

Blank, Richard. *Jenseits der Brücke, Bernhard Wicki: Ein Leben für den Film.* München: Econ, 1999.

Bly, Robert. *Iron John: A Book About Men.* New York: Vintage Books, 1992.

Bock, Gisela. "Challenging Dichotomies in Women's History," in Mary Beth Norton and Ruth M. Alexander, eds. *Major Problems in American Women's History* (2nd ed.). Lexington, Massachusetts: D.C. Heath, 1996: 8–14.

Bordo, Susan. *Unbearable Weight: Feminism, Western Culture and the Body.* Berkeley: University of California Press, 1993.

Bordwell, David, Janet Staiger, and Kristen Thompson. *The Classical Hollywood Cinema: Film Style and Mode of Production.* New York: Columbia University Press, 1985.

Bourdieu, Pierre. *The Field of Cultural Production,* ed. Randal Johnson. New York: Columbia University Press, 1993.

Bowman, Donna. Rev. of *Washington Square* http://weeklywire.com/filmvault/nash/w/ ws/html.

Bowman, James. Review of *Persuasion, American Spectator* (December 1995): 69.

Bradley, John R., ed. *Henry James on Stage and Screen.* London: Basingstoke, 2002.

Brunsdon, Charlotte. "Post-Feminism and Shopping Films," in Joanne Hollows, Peter Hutchings, and Mark Jancovich, eds., *The Film Studies Reader.* London: Arnold; New York: Oxford University Press, Inc., 2000: 289–299.

Butler, Judith. *Gender Trouble: Feminism and the Subversion of Identity.* New York: Routledge, 1999.

Callenbach, Ernest. "The Trial," *Film Quarterly,* Vol. 16, No.4 (Summer 1963): 42.

Canetti, Elias. *Der Andere Prozeß: Kafka's Briefe an Felice.* Munich, Vienna: Carl Hanser Verlag, 1984.

Carlson, Margaret. "Is This What Feminism is All About?," *Time* (24 June 1991): 57.

Carpenter, Lynette. "I Never Knew the Old Vienna": Cold War Politics and *The Third Man. Film Criticism* 11(Fall-Winter 1987): 56–65.

Carr, E.H. *What is History?* New York: Vintage, 1961.

Carter, Erica. *How German Is She?: Postwar West German Reconstruction and the Consuming Woman.* Ann Arbor: The University of Michigan Press, 1997.

Cartmell, Deborah, I.Q. Hunter, Heidi Kaye, and Imelda Whelehan, eds. *Classics in Film and Fiction.* London and Sterling, Virginia: Pluto Press, 2000.

Clark, Mike. "*Washington Square* can't replace *Heiress,*" http://www.usatoday.com/life/enter/movies/lef927.htm.

Classen, Christoph. *Bilder der Vergangenheit: Die Zeit des Nationalsozialismus im Fernsehen der Bundesrepublik Deutschland, 1955–1965.* Cologne, Weimar, Vienna: Böhlau Verlag, 1999.

Cohan, Steven. *Masked Men: Masculinity and the Movies in the Fifties.* Bloomington and Indianapolis: Indiana University Press, 1997.

Coleman, William P. Review of *Washington Square,* http://www.wpcmath.com/films/washsquare/washsquare2.html.

Collins, James. "Jane Reaction," *Vogue* (January 1996): 70.

Corliss, Richard. "All Hail to Helena!" *Time,* Vol. 150, No. 20 (10 November 1997) http://www.pathfinder.com/time/magazin...71110/the_arts_cine.all_hail_to_h.html.

Corrigan, Timothy. *Film and Literature: An Introduction and Reader.* Upper Saddle River, New Jersey: Prentice-Hall, Inc., 1999.

Cotten, Patricia Medina. *Laid Back in Hollywood.* Los Angeles: Bell Publishing, 1998.

Crick, Patricia. "Notes" in Henry James, *The Portrait of a Lady.* Harmondsworth: Penguin, 1986: 642–650.

DeBona, Guerric. *Film Adaptation in the Hollywood Studio Era.* Urbana: University of Illinois Press, 2010.

Decker, Christof. "American Studies as Media and Visual Culture Studies: Observations on a Revitalized Research Tradition." *Amerikastudien/American Studies.* 57.1(2012): 115-128.

Del Río-Alvaro, Constanza & Luis Miguel García-Mainar, eds., *Memory, Imagination and Desire in Contemporary Anglo-American Literature and Film.* Heidelberg: Universitätsverlag Winter, 2004.

Denby, David. Review of *The Scarlet Letter* and *Persuasion, New York* (23 October 1995): 57–58.

Deutschman, Alan, and Jennifer Brown. "Men at Work," *Gentlemen's Quarterly* (January 1997): 101–107.

"Dialogue in Film: Carl Foreman," *American Film* Vol. IV, No. 6 (April 1979): 35–46.

Doran, Lindsay. "Introduction" in Emma Thompson, *The Sense and Sensibility Screenplay and Diaries.* New York: Newmarket Press, 1996: 7–16.

Drazin, Charles. *In Search of the Third Man.* New York: Limelight Editions (Proscenium), 2000.

Dubiel, Helmut. *Niemand ist frei von der Geschichte: Die nationalsozialistische Herrschaft in den Debatten des Deutschen Bundestages.* München: Carl Hanser Verlag, 1999.

Ebert, Roger. Review of *Portrait of a Lady, Chicago Sun-Times,* http://www.suntimes.com/ebert/ebert_review/1997/01/011704.html.

———. Review of *The Wings of the Dove,* http://www.suntimes.com/ebert/ebert_reviews/1997/11/111405.html.

———. Review of *Washington Square,* http://www.suntimes.com/ebert/ebert_reviews/1997/11/111405.html.

Edel, Leon, ed. *Henry James: Letters, Vol. 2, 1875–1883.* Cambridge, Massachusetts and London and Basingstoke, 1980.

Ehrenreich, Barbara. *The Hearts of Men: American Dreams and the Flight From Commitment.* New York: Anchor Books/Doubleday, 1983.

Elliott, Kamilla. "Novels, Films and the Word/Image Wars," in Robert Stam and Alessandra Raengo, eds., *A Companion to Literature and Film*. Massachusetts, Oxford, Victoria: Blackwell, 2004: 1–22.

"Emma Thompson, A Close Reading," *New Yorker* (15 November 1993): 47.

Ewen, Stuart. *All Consuming Images: The Politics of Style in Contemporary Culture*. New York: Basic Books, 1988.

External Review, *Portrait of a Lady*: http://entertainment.news.com.au/film/70208c.htm.

Faludi, Susan. *Backlash: The Undeclared War Against American Women*. New York: Doubleday, 1991.

Farnham, Christie."The Position of Women in the Slave Family," in Norton and Alexander, eds. *Major Problems in American Women's History*, (2nd ed.): 145–155.

Fehrenbach, Heide. *Cinema in Democratizing Germany: Reconstructing National Identity after Hitler*. Chapel Hill: University of North Carolina Press, 1995.

Fehrenbach, Heide, and Uta Poiger, eds. *Transactions, Transgressions, Transformations: American Culture in Western Europe and Japan*. New York: Berghahn Books, 2000.

Feinstein, Howard. "Heroine Chic," *Vanity Fair* (December 1996):210.

Ferro, Marc. *Cinema and History* (translated by Naomi Greene) Detroit: Wayne State University Press, 1988.

Fischer, Robert. *Bernhard Wicki: Regisseur und Schauspieler*. Munich: Heyne, 1994, und Autor.

Fowler, Karen Joy. *The Jane Austen Book Club*. London: Penguin, 2004.

Franklin, Nancy. "Everybody Loves Jane," *The New Yorker* (21 January 2008): 82–83.

Frei, Norbert. *1945 und Wir: Das Dritte Reich im Bewußtsein der Deutschen*. Munich: Verlag C.H. Beck, 2005.

Gans, Herbert J. *Popular Culture and High Culture*. New York: Basic Books, 1974.

Gantz, Jeffrey. Rev. of *The Wings of the Dove* and Interview with Helena Bonham Carter, *Boston Phoenix*, (17 November 1997), http://weeklywire.com/filmvault/boston/w/wingsofthedovethe1.html.

Garncarz, Joseph. "Hollywood in Germany: Die Rolle des amerikanischen Films in Deutschland, 1925-1990." In Uli Jung (Hg.). *Der Deutsche Film: Aspekte seiner Geschichte von den Anfängen bis zur Gegenwart*. Trier: Wissenschaftlicher Verlag, 1997: 167–213.

Gassert, Philipp, and Alan E. Steinweis, eds. *Coping with the Nazi Past: West German Debates on Nazism and the Generational Conflict, 1955–1975*. New York: Berghahn Books, 2006.

Geyer, Michael. "Cold War Angst: The Case of West German Opposition to Rearmament and Nuclear Weapons" in Hanna Schissler, ed. *The Miracle Years: A Cultural History of West Germany, 1949–1968*. Princeton University Press, 2001: 376–408.

Gienow-Hecht, Jessica C.E. *Transmission Impossible: American Journalism as Cultural Diplomacy in Postwar Germany, 1945–1955*. Baton Rouge: Louisiana State University Press, 1999.

Gillis, Stacy, Gillian Howie, and Rebecca Munford, eds. *Third Wave Feminism: A Critical Exploration*. New York: Palgrave-MacMillan, 2004.

Glaspell, Susan Keating. "A Jury of Her Peers," in *Lifted Masks and Other Stories*, edited by Eric S. Rabkin. Ann Arbor: University of Michigan Press, 1993: 279–306.

Glazener, Nancy. *Reading for Realism: The History of a U.S. Literary Institution*. Durham and London: Duke University Press, 1997.

Graf, Roland. "Anachronism or Sting in the Flesh: The Remarkable Success of Austria's Regional Communist Newspapers, 1948-2000." URL: http://users.ox.ac.uk/~oaces/conference/papers/Roland_Graf.pdf.

Grenier, Richard. "Killer Bimbos," *Commentary* (September 1991): 50–52.

Greven, David. "The Museum of Unnatural History: Male Freaks and *Sex and the City,*" in Kim Akass and Janet McCabe, eds., *Reading Sex and the City.* London and New York: I.B. Tauris, 2004: 33–47.

Greven, Michael Th., and Oliver von Wrochem (Hrg.) *Der Krieg in der Nachkriegszeit: Der Zweite Weltkrieg in Politik und Gesellschaft der Bundesrepublik.* Opladen: Leske und Budrich, 2000.

Griffin, Susan M. ed. *Henry James Goes to the Movies.* Louisville, KY: University of Kentucky Press, 2002.

Guthmann, Edward. "Arty Portrait Loaded with Heavy Symbolism," *San Francisco Chronicle* (17 January 1997) http://www.sfgate.com/cgi-bin/article.cgi?file=//chronicle/archive/1997/01/17/ DD63103.DTL.

———. "Repeat Performance: Welles' Rare Masterpiece Restored-Film Based on Kafka's *The Trial* opens at the Castro," *San Francisco Chronicle* (7 January 2000) http://www.sfgate.com/cgi-bin/article.cgi.../chronicle/archive/2000/01/07/DD15381:DTL.

Halsey, Katie. *Jane Austen and Her Readers, 1786-1945.* London: Anthem Press, 2012.

Häntzschel, Ole. (Infografik). "In der Nebenrolle: Frauen und ihr Anteil am Filmgeschäft." *Zeit Magazin,* Nr.7(10 February 2011): 34–35.

Hart, Lynda. *Fatal Women: Lesbian Sexuality and the Mark of Aggression.* Princeton, New Jersey: Princeton University Press, 1994.

Hartl, John. "Portrait is Difficult to Resist," http://www.film.com/film-review/1996/9261/109/default-review.html.

Herf, Jeffrey. *Divided Memory: The Nazi Past in the Two Germanys*: Cambridge, Massachusetts: Harvard University Press, 1997.

Hesse, Monica. "'Jane Eyre' movie rekindles Austen vs. Bronte, the battle of the bonnets." *The Washington Post* 17 March 2011: http://www.washingtonpost.com/lifestyle/style/jane-eyre-movie-rekindles.

Hickethier, Knut. "Der Zweite Weltkrieg und der Holocaust im Fernsehen der Bundesrepublik der fünfziger und frühen sechziger Jahre," in Greven/Wrochem, *Der Krieg in der Nachkriegszeit,* 93–112.

Higson, Andrew. "English Heritage, English Literature, English Cinema: Selling Jane Austen to Movie Audiences in the 1990's." in Eckart Voigts-Virchow, ed., *Janespotting and Beyond,* 35–50.

Höfele, Andreas. "The Rebirth of Tragedy or No Time for Shakespeare (Germany 1940)." *Renaissance Drama.* New Series 38(2010): 251–268.

Hollows, Joanne, *et al. The Film Studies Reader.* London: Arnold; New York: Oxford University Press, Inc., 2000.

Horlacher, Pia. "Der Flügelschlag des Chaos," *NZZ(Neue Zürchner Zeitung) Online: Feuilleton* (24 July 1998): http://www.nzz.ch/online/01_nzz_aktuel...9807/fi980724(-) the_wings_of_the_dove.htm.

———. "Kein Platz an der Sonne," *NZZ(Neue Zürchner Zeitung) Online: Feuilleton* (22 May 1998): http://www.nzz.ch/online/01_nzz_aktuel...film9805/fi980522washington_square.htm.

Horton, Robert. "Henry and Jane," Rev. of *The Portrait of a Lady,* http://www.film.com/film-review/1996/9261/18/default-review.html.

Hugo, Philipp von. "Kino und kollektives Gedächtnis? Überlegungen zum westdeutschen Kriegsfilm der fünfziger Jahre," in Bernhard Chiari, Matthias Rogg und Wolfgang Schmidt, ed. *Krieg und Militär im Film des 20. Jahrhunderts.* Munich: Oldenbourg Wissenschaftsverlag, 2003: 453–477.

Hutcheon, Linda. *A Theory of Adaptation.* New York and London: Routledge, 2006.

Huyssen, Andreas. *After the Great Divide: Modernism, Mass Culture, Postmodernism*. Bloomington and Indianapolis: Indiana University Press, 1986.

"Interview with Orson Welles." *Cahiers du Cinema*, No. 165 (April 1965); reprinted in *The Trial:
A Film by Orson Welles*, Modern Film Scripts; Eng. trans (of interview) by Nicholas Fry. New
York: Simon Schuster, 1970; London: Lommer Publishing Limited.

"Jane Addiction," *Show Sunday, Orange County Register* (14 January 1996): 1.

"Jane Eyre- do all good things come in threes? Fukunaga believes in thirties!" Weblog article,
storybird70.wordpress.com (placed online 23 January 2011).

Jarausch, Konrad H. "Critical Memory and Civil Society: The Impact of the 1960s on German
Debates about the Past." in Philipp Gassert and Alan E. Steinweis, eds. *Coping with the Nazi
Past: West German Debates on Nazism and Generational Conflict, 1955-1975*. New York: Berg-
hahn Books, 2006: 11–30.

Järv, Harry. *Die Kafka-Literatur: eine Bibliographie* (first edition). Malmö [*et al*]: Cavefors, 1961.

Johnson, Claudia, L. "Austen Cults and Cultures," in Edward Copeland and Juliet McMaster,
eds. *The Cambridge Companion to Jane Austen*. Cambridge, England: Cambridge University
Press, 1997: 211–226.

———. *Equivocal Beings: Politics, Gender and Sentimentality in the 1790's, Wollstonecraft, Radcliffe,
Burney, Austen*. Chicago: University of Chicago Press, 1995.

———. *Jane Austen: Women, Politics, and the Novel*. Chicago: University of Chicago Press, 1988.

———. "*Sense and Sensibility*: Opinions Too Common and Too Dangerous." in *Jane Austen:
Women, Politics and the Novel*. Chicago: University of Chicago Press, 1988: 49–72.

Jones, Ward E. and Samantha Vice, eds. *Ethics at the Cinema*. New York: Oxford University
Press, 2011.

Joos, Rudolf, et al. eds. *Mosaiksteine: Zum 65. Geburtstag von Dietmar Schmidt*. Frankfurt am
Main: Gemeinschaftswerk der Evangelischen Publizistik.[no date].

Jungeblodt, Werner. "Kriegsfilme-noch und noch," *Beiträge zur Begegnung von Kirche und Welt*,
Nr. 47, hrg. von der Akademie der Diözese Rottenburg, 1960.

Kallan, Richard A. "*The Bridge on the River Kwai*: The Collision of Duty and Pride," in Marilyn
J. Matelski and Nancy Lynch Street, *War and Film in America: Historical and Critical Essays*.
Jefferson, North Carolina, 2003: 13–24.

Kansteiner, Wulf. "Hayden White's Critique of the Writing of History," *History and Theory*, Vol.
32, No.3(October 1993): 273–295.

Kaplan, Deborah Kaplan, "Mass Marketing Jane Austen: Men, Women, and Courtship in
Two Film Adaptations," Linda Troost and Sayre Greenfield, eds. *Jane Austen in Hollywood*,
177–187.

Karen (surreyhill), IMDb user comments for *The Jane Austen Book Club*, URL: http://www.imdb
.com/title/tt0866437/User Comments.

Kauffmann, Stanley. "Joseph K. and Orson W," *The New Republic* (2 March 1963):34–35.

———. "The Portrait Retouched," *The New Republic* (23 December 1996): 28.

———. Review of *Emma*. *The New Republic* (19 and 26 August 1996): 38–39.

Kelley, Andrew. *All Quiet on the Western Front: the Story of a Film*. London: I.B. Tauris, 2002.

Klinger, Barbara. "Film history terminable and interminable: recovering the past in reception
studies," *Screen* 38.2(Summer 1997): 107–128.

Knoch, Habbo. *Die Tat als Bild: Fotografien des Holocaust in der deutschen Erinnerungskultur*. Hamburger Edition, 2001.

———. "The Return of the Images: Photographs of Nazi Crimes and the West German Public
in the 'Long 1960s.'" in Philipp Gassert and Alan E. Steinweis, eds. *Coping with the Nazi*

Past: West German Debates on Nazism and the Generational Conflict, 1955–1975. New York: Berghahn Books, 2006: 31–49.

Koch, Gertrude. "Das Riesenrad der Geschichte: *The Third Man* von Carol Reed," in R. Beckmann and C. Blueminger, eds. *Ohne Untertitel: Fragmente einer Geschichte des oesterreichischen Kinos.* Wien: Sonderzahl, 1996: 366–375.

Koch, J.Sarah. "A Henry James Filmography," *The Henry James Review,* 19.3(1998): 296–306.

Kracauer, Siegfried. *From Caligari to Hitler.* Princeton, New Jersey: Princeton University Press, 1947.

Kranz, Erhard. *Filmkunst in der Agonie* (Berlin: Henschelverlag, 1964).

Lane, Anthony. "Immaterial Girls," *The New Yorker* (6 January 1997): 75.

———. "Jane's World," *New Yorker* (25 September 1995):108.

Leitch, Thomas. "Adaptation Studies at a Crossroads," *Adaptation* Vol. 1.1(2008): 63–77.

———. *Film Adaptation and Its Discontents: From* Gone with the Wind *to* The Passion of Christ. (Baltimore, Maryland: Johns Hopkins University Press, 2007)

Lenk, Kristin and Franziska Korthals, "Macht und Weiblichkeit in *Buffy the Vampire Slayer*: Ausseinandersetzung mit einer postfeministischen Ikone," Magisterarbeit, Universität Bremen, Germany, 2004.

Leo, John. "Toxic Feminism on the Big Screen," *U.S. News and World Report* (10 June 1991): 20.

Leonard, John. "Jane-Mania," *New York* (15 January 1996): 55.

Löffler, Sigrid. *Kritiken, Portraits, Glossen.* Wien: Franz Deuticke Verlagsgesellschaft mbH, 1995.

Loock, Kathleen and Constantine Verevis, eds. *Film Remakes, Adaptations and Fan Productions: Remake/Remodel.* New York: Palgrave Macmillan, 2012.

Looser, Devoney. "Feminist Implications of the Silver Screen Austen," in Linda Troost and Sayre Greenfield, eds. *Jane Austen in Hollywood,* 159–176.

Major, Patrick. "'Our Friend Rommel': The Wehrmacht as 'Worthy Enemy' in Postwar British Popular Culture." *German History* (Oxford Journals) 26.4(2008): 520-535.

Major, Patrick, and Rana Mitter, eds. *Across the Blocs: Cold War Cultural and Social History.* London: Frank Cass, 2004: 1–22.

Malone, Paul M. "Trial and Error: Combinatory Fidelity in Two Versions of Franz Kafka's *The Trial*" in Deborah Cartmell, I.Q. Hunter, Heidi Kaye, and Imelda Whelehan (eds.) *Classics in Film and Fiction.* London and Sterling, Virginia: Pluto Press, 2000: 176–193.

Man, Glenn K.S., "*The Third Man*: Pulp Fiction and Art Film," *Literature/Film Quarterly* 21:3(1993): 171–177.

———. "Gender, Genre, and Myth in *Thelma and Louise*," *Film Criticism* 18.1(Fall 1993): 36–53.

Manvell, R., and J. Huntley. *The Technique of Film Music.* London: Focal Press, 1975.

Mapes, Marty. Review of *The Wings of the Dove,* http://us.imdb.com/Reviews/105/10580.

Marcuse, Herbert. *Feindanalysen: Über die Deutschen.* Hrg. Peter-Erwin Jansen. Lüneburg: zu Klampen Verlag, 1998.

May, Lary. *The Big Tomorrow: Hollywood and the Politics of the American Way.* Chicago: University of Chicago Press, 2000.

McGrath, Charles. "Another Hike on the Moors for Jane Eyre." 4 March 2011: http://www.nytimes.com/2011/03/06/movies/06eyre.html.

Meinig, D.W., ed. *The Interpretation of Ordinary Landscapes.* New York: Oxford University Press, 1979.

Mekas, Jonas. "Movie Journal," *The Village Voice,* Vol.8 (21 February 1963):15.

Menand, Louis. "Not Getting the Lesson of the Master," *New York Review of Books* (4 December 1997): http://www.nybooks.com/nyrev/WWWarchdisplay.cgi?19971204019R.

——. "What Jane Austen doesn't tell us," *New York Review of Books* (1 February 1996): 15.

Miller, Toby. *Spyscreen: Espionage on Film and TV from the 1930s to the 1960s*. Oxford: Oxford University Press, 2003.

Modleski, Tania. *Feminism without Women: Culture and Criticism in a "Postfeminist" Age*. London: Routledge, 1991.

Moeller, Robert G. ""Geschichten aus der 'Stacheldraht-universität': Kriegsgefangene im Opferdiskurs der Bundesrepublik," *Werkstadtgeschichte* 26(2000): 23–46.

——. "'In a Thousand Years, Every German Will Speak of this Battle': Celluloid Memories of Stalingrad," in *Crimes of War: Guilt and Denial in the Twentieth Century*, ed. Omar Bartov, Atina Grossmann, Mary Nolan. New York: New Press, 2002: 161–190.

——. "Victims in Uniform: West German Combat Movies from the 1950s," in Bill Niven, ed. *Germans as Victims: Remembering the Nazi Past in Contemporary Germany*. Basingstoke: MacMillan, 2006: 43–61.

——. *War Stories: The Search for a Usable Past in the Federal Republic of Germany*. Berkeley: University of California Press, 2001.

——. "What Did You Do in the War, *Mutti*? Courageous Women, Compassionate Commanders, and Stories of the Second World War," *German History*. 22(2004): 563–594.

Moss, Robert F. *The Films of Carol Reed*. New York: Columbia University Press, 1987.

Mull, Martin, and Allen Rucker, *The History of White People in America*. New York: Perigee, 1985.

Murphy, Kathleen, "Jane Campion's Shining: Portrait of a Director," *Film Comment* (November/December 1996): 29.

Murray, Simone. "Materializing Adaptation Theory: The Adaptation Industry." *Literature/Film Quarterly* 36.1(2008):4–20.

——. "Phantom Adaptations: *Eucalyptus*, the Adaptation Industry and the Film that Never Was." *Adaptation*, Vol. 1, No.1(2008): 5–23.

Nadel, Alan. "Ambassadors from an Imaginary 'Elsewhere': Cinematic Convention and the Jamesian Sensibility," *The Henry James Review*, 19.3(1998): 279–285.

——. "The Search for Cinematic Identity and a Good Man: Jane Campion's Appropriation of James's *Portrait*," *The Henry James Review* 18.2(1997):182.

Naremore, James. "Introduction: Film and the Reign of Adaptation," in James Naremore, ed. *Film Adaptation*. New Brunswick, New Jersey: Rutgers University Press, 2000: 1–16.

——. ed. *Film Adaptation*. New Brunswick, New Jersey: Rutgers University Press, 2000.

Nessel, Sabine. *Kino und Ereignis: Das Kinematographische Zwischen Text und Körper*. Berlin: Vorwerk 8, 2008.

Niehoff, Karena. *Karena Niehoff: Feuilletonistin und Kritikerin*, with an essay by Jörg Becker, "Wer das Schreiben liebt, wird es auch fürchten." München: Verlag edition text + kritik in Richard Boorberg Verlag GmbH & Co, KG, 2006: 9–77.

North, Julian. "Conservative Austen, Radical Austen: *Sense and Sensibility from Text to Screen*" in Deborah Cartmell and Imelda Whelehan, eds. *Adaptations: From Text to Screen, Screen to Text*. London: Routledge, 1999: 38–50.

Novick, Peter. *That Noble Dream: The "Objectivity Question" and the American Historical Profession*. London and New York: Cambridge University Press, 1988.

O'Leary, Devin D. Interview with Iain Softley, http://weeklywire.com/filmvault/alibi/w/wingsofthedove1.html.

Orr, John. "*The Trial* of Orson Welles," in John Orr and Colin Nicholson, eds. *Cinema and Fiction: New Modes of Adapting, 1950–1990*. Edinburgh: Edinburgh University Press, 1992: 13–27.

Paech, Joachim. *Literatur und Film,* Zweite Auflage. Stuttgart und Weimar: Verlag J. B. Metzler, 1997.

Palmer, James and Michael M. Riley, "The Lone Rider in Vienna: Myth and Meaning in *The Third Man,*" *Literature/Film Quarterly* 8:1(1980):14–21.

Passek, Oliver. "Die Gruppe 47 im politischen Kontext," in Peter Gendolla und Rita Leinecke (Hrsg.) *Die Gruppe 47 und die Medien.* MUK, Massenmedien und Kommunikation, Nummer 114/115 (Siegen: FB 3 Sprach- und Literaturwissenschaft an der Universität-GH Siegen, 1997):102–114.

Patalas, Enno. "Die Brücke," *Filmkritik* 3(Dec. 1959): 315–317.

Pells, Richard F. *Not Like Us: How Europeans Loved, Hated and Transformed American Culture Since World War II.* New York: Basic Books, 1997.

Petchesky, Rosalind Pollack. "Antiabortion and Antifeminism," in Mary Beth Norton and Ruth M. Alexander, eds., *Major Problems in American Women's History* (Lexington, MA: D.C. Heath and Company, 1996): 502–515.

Poiger, Uta G. "Commentary: Beyond 'Modernization' and 'Colonization'". *Diplomatic History,* 23.1(Winter 1999): 45–56.

———. *Jazz, Rock and Rebels: Cold War Politics and American Culture in a Divided Germany.* Berkeley: University of California Press, 2000.

Poole, Adrian. "Select Bibliography." In Henry James. *Washington Square.*[1881] Intro. Adrian Poole. Oxford: Oxford University Press, 2010: xxxi–xxxiii.

Poster, Mark. *Foucault, Marxism and History: Mode of Production vs. Mode of Information.* Cambridge; New York: Polity Press, 1984.

Prewitt-Brown, Julia. "The Feminist Depreciation of Austen: A Polemical Reading," *Novel: A Forum on Fiction* 23(1990): 303–313.

Raether, Elisabeth, and Annabel Wahba, "Wir sollen immer nett sein: Warum haben es Frauen in der Film Branche schwerer als Männer? Ein Gespräch zwischen den Regisseurinnen Maren Ade und Doris Dörrie." *Zeit Magazin,* Nr. 7 (10 February 2011): 27–30.

Rafferty, Terrance. "Fidelity and Infidelity," *New Yorker* (18 December 1995): 124.

Rapping, Elaine. "The Jane Austen Thing," *Progressive* (July 1996): 37–38.

Raw, Laurence. *Adapting Henry James to the Screen: Gender, Fiction and Film.* Scarecrow Press, 2006.

Ray, Robert B. "The Field of Literature and Film," in James Naremore, ed., *Film Adaptation.* New Brunswick, New Jersey: Rutgers University Press, 2000: 38–53.

Reich, R., and B. Bondy, eds. *Homme de lettres.* (Rudolf Köser). Freundesgabe, Zürich 1985.

Reichel, Peter. *Erfundene Erinnerung: Weltkrieg und Judenmord in Film und Theater.* Munich, Vienna: Carl Hanser Verlag, 2004.

Review of *Sense and Sensibility, Los Angeles Times Magazine* (January 1996): 108.

Ridout, Alice. "Lost in Austen: Adaptation and the Feminist Politics of Nostalgia." *Adaptation* 4.1(March 2011): 14–27.

Rowe, John Carlos. *The Theoretical Dimensions of Henry James.* Madison: University of Wisconsin Press, 1984.

Rubin, Steven Jay. *Combat Films–American Realism: 1945–1970.* Jefferson, North Carolina, 1981.

Rüsen, Jörn. "Historical Narration: Foundation, Types, Reason." *History and Theory.* Beiheft 26, No. 4(1987): 87–97.

Sadoff, Dianne F. "'Intimate Disarray': The Henry James Movies," *The Henry James Review* 19.3(1998): 293.

Salmon, Richard. "Henry James, Popular Culture, and Cultural Theory," *The Henry James Review* 19.3(1998): 211–218.

Samuelian, Kristin Flieger. "'Piracy is Our Only Option': Postfeminist Intervention in *Sense and Sensibility*," in Troost and Greenfield, eds. *Jane Austen in Hollywood*, 148–158.

Sarris, Andrew. "Carol Reed in the Context of His Time," *Film Culture* Vol. 3, No. 1(1957): 12,13.

Schickel, Richard. "Blurred Vision," *Time* (30 December 1996–6 January 1997): http://www.time.com/time/magazine/article/0,9171,985779,00.html.

———. "Kissing Cousins," *Time* (18 December 1995): 73.

———. "Misplaced Affections," *Time*, Vol. 150/No. 16 (20 October 1997): http://www.pathfinder.com/time/magazine/1997/.

Schissler, Hanna, ed. *The Miracle Years: A Cultural History of West Germany, 1949–1968.* Princeton University Press, 2001.

———. "Writing about 1950s West Germany," in Hanna Schissler, ed. *The Miracle Years*, 3–15.

Schmidt, Dietmar. "Heilsame Unruhe," *Kirche und Film*, Nr. 6/ Jg.6 (Juni 1963): 2–3.

Schmieding, Walther. *Kunst oder Kasse: Der Ärger mit dem deutschen Film.* Hamburg: Rütten und Loening, 1961).

Scholz, Anne-Marie. "Adaptation as Reception: How a Transnational Analysis of Hollywood Films can Renew the Literature to Film Debates." *Amerikastudien/American Studies* 54.4 (2009): 657–682.

———. *An Orgy of Propriety: Jane Austen, and the Emergence and Legacy of the Female Author in America, 1826–1926.* Trier: Wissenschaftlicher Verlag, 1999.

———. "'Eine Revolution des Films': *The Third Man*, the Cold War, and Alternatives to Nationalism and Coca-Colonization in Europe." *Film and History: An Interdisciplinary Journal of Film and Television Studies* Vol. 31.1(2001): 44–53.

———. "From Fidelity to History: Film Adaptations as Cultural Events in the Twentieth Century" Habilitationsschrift (Unpublished Postdoctoral Dissertation) University of Bremen, Germany, 2006.

———. "Jane-Mania: The Jane Austen Film Boom in the Nineties," in Peter C. Rollins, John E. O'Connor, and Deborah Carmichael, eds. 1999 *Film and History CD-ROM Annual* (Stillwater, Oklahoma: Film and History Press, 1999).

———. "'Josef K von 1963…': Orson Welles' 'Americanized' Version of *The Trial* and the changing functions of the Kafkaesque in Postwar West Germany," *European Journal of American Studies*, EJAS 2009-1, [Online], article 5, put online June 17, 2009. URL: http://ejas.revues.org/document7608.html

———. Review of Reinhold Wagnleitner, *Coca-colonization and the Cold War. Amerikastudien.* 42.1(1997):126–129.

———. "The *Bridge on the River Kwai* Revisited: Combat Cinema, American Culture and the German Past." *German History* (Oxford Journals) 26.2(2008): 219–250.

———. "Thelma and Louise and Sense and Sensibility: New Approaches to Challenging Dichotomies in Women's History Through Literature and Film." *Journal of South Texas English Studies* 1(2009): n.pag. Web. 10 December 2009. URL: http://southtexasenglish.blogspot.com

"Schorcht-Film stockte auf," *Hamburger Abendblatt* No. 162 (14.07.1962): 14.

Schwab, Lothar. "Der Identifikationsprozess im Kino-Film: Analyse des Films *Der dritte Mann*," in K.Hickethier and J. Paech, eds. *Didaktik der Massenkommunikation 4: Modelle der Film und Fernsehanalyse.* Stuttgart: J.B. Metzler, 1979: 24–62.

Shandley, Robert. *Rubble Films: German Cinema in the Shadow of the Third Reich.* Philadelphia: Temple University Press, 2001.

Shelden, Michael. *Graham Greene: Eine Biographie.* Translated by Joachim Kolka. Göttingen: Steidl Verlag, 1995.

Sidel, Ruth. *On Her Own: Growing Up in the Shadow of the American Dream.* New York: Viking Penguin, 1990.

Sigl, Klaus et al. *Jede Menge Kohle: Kunst und Kommerz auf dem deutschen Filmmarkt der Nachkriegszeit, Filmpreise und Kassenerfolge, 1949-1985.* Munich: Filmland Presse, 1986.

Simon, John. "Movie of the Moment," *National Review* (8 July 1991): 48–52.

———. "Novel Distractions," *National Review* (23 October 1995): 58.

Sinyard, Neil. *Filming Literature: The Art of Screen Adaptation.* London: Croon Helm, 1986.

Staiger, Janet. *Interpreting Films: Studies in the Historical Reception of American Cinema.* Princeton, New Jersey: Princeton University Press, 1992.

Stam, Robert. "Beyond Fidelity: the Dialogics of Adaptation," in James Naremore, ed. *Film Adaptation.* New Brunswick, New Jersey: Rutgers University Press, 2000: 54–76.

———. "Introduction: the Theory and Practice of Adaptation" in Robert Stam and Alessandra Raengo, eds. *Literature and Film: A Guide to the Theory and Practice of Film Adaptation.* Massachusetts, Oxford, Victoria: Blackwell, 2005: 1–52.

Stein, Benjamin. "Citizen Kane and Hedda Hopper," *New York Times* (13 Sept. 1987):7:1:47.

Stern, Frank. "Film in the 1950s: Passing Images of Guilt and Responsibility," in Hanna Schissler, ed., 266–280.

———. "Gegenerinnerungen seit 1945: Filmbilder, die Millionen sahen," in Greven/Wrochem, (Hrg.), 79–91.

Stevens, Duncan. Review of *The Wings of the Dove,* http://us.imdb.com/Reviews/101/10153.

Stölken-Fitschen, Ilona. *Atombombe und Geistesgeschichte.* Baden Baden: Nomos, 1995.

Stuart, Jan. "Emma Thompson, Sensibly," *Los Angeles Times Calendar* (10 December 1995): 85.

"Tale of a String," [song in the film *Washington Square*] lyrics by Marilyn and Alan Bergman, music by Jan A.P. Kaczmarek.

Tannen, Deborah. *You Just Don't Understand.* New York: Ballantine Books, 1990.

Tasker, Yvonne and Diane Negra, eds. *Interrogating Post-Feminism.* Durham, North Carolina: Duke University Press, 2007.

The New York Times Film Reviews, A One Volume Selection: 1913-1970. New York: Arno, 1971: 255–256.

Thiel, Reinold E.(til), "Der Prozess," *Film Kritik* (May 1963):244–248.

Thomas, Evan. "Hooray for Hypocrisy," *Newsweek* (29 January 1996): 61.

Thompson, Emma. *The Sense and Sensibility Screenplay and Diaries.* New York: Newmarket Press, 1996.

Timmermann, Brigitte und Frederick Baker. *Der Dritte Mann: Auf den Spuren eines Filmklassikers.* Wien: Czernin Verlag, 2002.

Tobias, Scott. Review of *The Jane Austen Book Club,* The A.V. Club. URL: http://www.avclub.com/content/node/66867/print/.

Trocha, Kirsten. "Das Lachen gefriert im Hals: The Reception of *Dr. Strangelove* (1964) as Cultural and Literary Document in Comparative Perspective: Germany and the United States," Magisterarbeit, Universität Bremen, Germany, 2003.

Troost, Linda and Sayre Greenfield, eds. *Jane Austen in Hollywood.* Lexington, Kentucky: University of Kentucky Press, 1998.[2001].

Turner, Graeme. *Film as Social Practice,* 2nd edition. London: Routledge, 1993.

URL: http://boxofficemojo.com/movies/?id=persuasion.htm.

URL: http://boxofficemojo.com/movies/?id=senseandsensibility.htm.

URL: http://boxofficemojo.com/movies/?id=thelmaandlouise.htm.

URL: http://en.wikipedia.org/wiki/The_Third_Man.

"Verflucht harte Arbeit": Interview mit Emma Thompson. *Der Spiegel* 10(4 March 1996): 230–231.

Voigts-Virchow, Eckart. "'Corset Wars': An Introduction to Syncretic Heritage Film Culture since the Mid-1990s," in Eckart Voigts-Virchow, ed., *Janespotting and Beyond: British Heritage Retrovisions since the mid-1990s.* Tübingen: Gunter Narr Verlag, 2004: 13–19.

———— ed. *Janespotting: British Heritage Retrovisions since the Mid-1990's.* Tübingen: Narr, 2004.

Voss, Ralph F. and Michael L. Keene. *The Heath Guide to College Writing: Annotated Teacher's Edition.* Lexington, Massachusetts: D.C. Heath and Company, 1992.

Wagnleitner, Reinhold. *Coca-Colonization and the Cold War: The Cultural Mission of the United States in Austria after the Second World War.* Chapel Hill and London: University of North Carolina Press, 1994.

Wagnleitner, Reinhold, and Elaine Tyler May, eds. *Here, There and Everywhere: The Foreign Politics of American Popular Culture.* Hanover, New Hampshire: University Press of New England, 2000.

Wasserstein, Wendy. "The *Premiere* Review: *Sense and Sensibility*" (February 1996): 17.

Weidermann, Volker. "Kafkas Welt in einem Kästchen. " *Frankfurter Allgemeine* Sonntagszeitung, 20 April 2008, Nr. 16/ Page 31, http://faz.net, http://www.faz.net/s/RubC17179.

Welles, Orson, and Peter Bogdanovich, *Hier Spricht Orson Welles.* Weinheim, Berlin: Quadriga Verlag, 1994.

————. *This is Orson Welles,* Jonathan Rosenbaum, ed. New York: HarperCollins Publishers, 1993.

White, Hayden. *Figural Realism: Studies in the Mimesis Effect.* Baltimore and London: The Johns Hopkins University Press, 1999.

————. "Historiography and Historiophoty," *AHR* Forum, *American Historical Review,* Vol. 93.4(1988): 1193–1199.

————. *Metahistory: The Historical Imagination in Nineteenth Century Europe.* Baltimore and London, 1973.

White, Rob. *The Third Man.* British Film Institute, 2003.

Whyte, Jason. The Big Screen Cinema Guide, http://www.bigscreen.com/cgi/ShowReview ?WingsoftheDove.

Wicke, Jennifer. "Celebrity Material: Materialist Feminism and the Culture of Celebrity." *South Atlantic Quarterley* 93.4(Fall 1994): 751–778.

Williams, Evan. Review of *Portrait of a Lady.* External Review, International Movie Database (http://imdb.com). URL: http://entertainment.news.com.au/film/70208c.htm.

Willis, Sharon. *High Contrast: Race and Gender in Contemporary Hollywood Film.* Durham, N.C.: Duke University Press, 1997.

Winecoff, Charles. *Split Image: The Life of Anthony Perkins.* Raleigh, North Carolina: Lightening Bug Press, 2001 [1996].

Wolfrum, Edgar (Hrsg.), *Die Deutschen im 20. Jahrhundert.* Darmstadt: Wissenschaftliche Buchgesellschaft, 2004.

Wulff, Hans J. „Bundesdeutsche Kriegs-und Militärfilme der 1950er Jahre: Eine Filmbibliographie." *Medienwissenschaft/Hamburg: Berichte und Papiere.* 132(2012): 1–13. http://www.rrz .uni-hamburg.de/Medien/berichte/arbeiten/0132_12.pdf.

Yong, Natasha. "Sexism and a Female Buddy Connection: Review of *Thelma and Louise,*" *Cyclone Films Movie Reviews:* http://www.swiftech.com.sg/~natvic/cr_telma.htm.

Zander, Peter. *Bernhard Wicki.* Berlin: Bertz, 1995. [1994] 2., überar. Aufl.

Index

Lightning Source UK Ltd.
Milton Keynes UK
UKOW01f0713181115

262976UK00010B/190/P